The Monkey's Bridge

The Monkey's Bridge

Mysteries of Evolution
in Central America

David Rains Wallace

Sierra Club Books · San Francisco

Copyright © 1997 by David Rains Wallace

Library of Congress Cataloging-in-Publication Data
Wallace, David Rains, 1945–
    The monkey's bridge : mysteries of evolution in Central
America / by David Rains Wallace.
        p.   cm.
    Includes bibliographical references and index.
    ISBN 0-87156-586-2 (alk. paper)
    1. Evolution (Biology)—Central America. 2. Paleobiogeography
—Central America. 3. Natural history—Central America.
4. Fossils—Central America. 5. Central America—Discovery and
exploration. 6. Central America—Description and travel. I. Title.
QH366.2.W35   1997
576.8'09728—dc21   97-8046

Production by Janet Vail
Jacket and book design by Amy Evans
Composition by Wilsted & Taylor Publishing Services

Printed in the United States of America on acid-free paper containing 50% recovered waste paper, of which at least 10% of the fiber content is post-consumer waste.

10 9 8 7 6 5 4 3 2 1

To the naturalists and conservationists
of Central America

Contents

I often think, it is not the poetical imagination, but bare Science that every day more and more unrolls a greater epic than the Iliad; the history of the World, the infinitudes of Space and Time!   EDWARD FITZGERALD

Acknowledgments

This book would have been impossible without the help of many people in my travels to and in Central America. Rick Taylor and Carlos Gomez were genial guides on my first trip to Costa Rica. T. H. Watkins of the Wilderness Society assisted my second Costa Rica trip by giving me a magazine assignment, and Daniel Janzen helped me to visit the Guanacaste National Park Project. David Wake, Harry Greene, Pedro Léon, and Alvaro Ugalde helped me to get a Fulbright Fellowship to spend several months in Costa Rica studying the parks. Richard Bangs of Mountain Travel/Sobek made it possible for me to spend some time in the Andes and Amazon. Michael Kaye of Costa Rica Expeditions provided a Pacuare River rafting trip. My wife Elizabeth Kendall and my friend Steve Mueller were helpful companions on some trips. Paul Feyling was a friendly source of information and conversation about Central America.

I'm particularly grateful to Archie Carr III, Kathleen Jepson, and Jim Barborak of the Wildlife Conservation Society, and to David Carr of the Caribbean Conservation Corporation (CCC) for hiring me to write for the U.S. AID–funded Paseo Pantera Project, which enabled me to visit the other Central American countries and take advantage of the network of contacts which those excellent organizations maintain in the region. These include Vince Murphy and Pat Niemeyer, who provided generous hospitality and advice on a Honduras trip; Stanley Heckadon and Tony Coates, who gave good advice on a Panama trip; Peter Gore of U.S. AID and Joe Kyle of the Peace Corps, who provided much logistical help on an El Salvador visit; Ralph Conley of U.S. AID and Stern Robinson and Nelbert Taylor of the CCC, who provided guidance and much useful information on a Nicaragua trip; Barry Bowen, Tom and Josie Harding, and Jim and Marguerite Bevis, who provided generous hospitality in Belize, and Bruce and Carolyn Miller, who offered friendly guidance.

Many other Central American conservationists provided advice and guidance over the years. These include Karen Wessberg, Juan Carlos Crespo, Mario Boza, and José Maria Rodriguez in Costa Rica; Jorge Betancourt, Jorge Salaverri, and Edgardo Benitez in Honduras; Indra Candañedo, Luis Moh, and Eneida Palma of INRENARE in Panama; Carlos Hasbun of CENREN and Carlos Linares of Salvanatura in El Salvador; Carlos Espinosa, Jacinto Cedeño, and Balbo Mueller of MARENA in Nicaragua; Ernesto Saqui and Lydia Waight of the Belizean Audubon Society; and Dr. Pedro Guzmán Mérida of Proyecto Cuchumatanes in Guatemala.

A number of biologists and other scientists took the time to talk to me and/or read what I'd written about Central America, including David and Marvalee Wake, Daniel Janzen, Winnie Hallwachs, Pedro Léon, Harry Greene, David Webb, Bruce McFadden, Tony Coates, David Clark, Rodrigo Gamez, Steve Mulke, Tony Stocks, Frank Whitmore, Gordon Frankie, and Bruce and Carolyn Miller. Thanks also are due to those, too numerous to name here (but I hope all are present in my bibliography), whose published or unpublished work informed me. Others who provided good advice and information include Kevin Schafer, Charley Spence, Antonio Miranda, and the Nature Conservancy's Kathy Moser and Scott Wilbur. Of course, I take responsibility for the opinions, speculations, and other material in the book, and for any errors or misinterpretations.

Jon Beckmann and Jim Cohee provided indispensable editorial support and assistance. The University of California at Berkeley's excellent library system was essential in researching the book, particularly the Bancroft, Life Science, and Earth Science libraries.

Parts of this book appeared in different form in *Zyzzyva*; *Pacific Discovery*; *The Nature of Nature* (Harcourt Brace), and in *American Nature Writing: 1994* and *American Nature Writing: 1996* (Sierra Club Books).

Prologue

The Latest Show on Earth

Central America deserves that most abused of adjectives—*unique*. Unlike the other land on the planet, it is neither a continent nor an island. It connects two continents, but it is not a subsidiary of either, like a peninsula or a cape. Geographers have characterized it by this connecting of continents, and called it, somewhat vaguely, a land bridge. Strictly speaking, there is another land bridge in the world today, the Sinai between Africa and Eurasia, but the Sinai is desert, and more of an obstacle to most organisms than a passage. Central America is so crowded with life that it supports seven percent of the earth's species on less than one-half percent of its land, and those species are an extraordinary mixture of North American and South American forms that have surged back and forth across it for millions of years.

Central America is unusual even among other land bridges that have existed in past epochs. The present Bering Strait, for example, is a continental shelf that has been land so many times during the sixty-five-million-year "age of mammals" that there is relatively little difference between Eurasia's and North America's temperate ecosystems, and almost no difference between their arctic ones. Part of Central America, on the other hand, has never been land before, but has risen from the deep ocean floor within the past five million years. North and South America existed in isolation from one another for most of the age of mammals, and evolved very different life forms.

The flow of organisms across the land bridge since that isolation ended has been one of the great evolutionary spectacles, a classic textbook example of life's restlessness that paleontologists now call the Great American Biotic Interchange. Fossils show that, after the Isthmus of Panama arose, North American animals such as dogs, cats, and deer moved en masse into South America, and South American ones like armadillos, porcupines, and opossums migrated as far north as Canada. South American monkeys and sloths met North American squirrels and raccoons in the tropical forest canopy. The movement of early humans across the land bridge was so swift that their appearances in Alaska and in Tierra del Fuego are almost simultaneous in the fossil record.

Yet Central America's classic status has rather obscured its importance—not unusual with classics. Central America barely comes into textbook land bridge accounts, wherein it is simply a small, connecting point between vast continental biomes—tropical and temperate forests, prairies, and pampas. An active land bridge is harder to contemplate than an Amazon or Arctic. It is mixed, blurred, unfinished. Its boundaries are hard to define. Central America is usually identified with the seven nations from Guatemala south to Panama, but Mexico's Yucatán Peninsula and Chiapas highlands are not entirely part of North America, and Colombia's Chocó Basin is not entirely part of South America.

Although it may seem merely a detail of a hemispherewide evolutionary spectacle, Central America is a complicated detail, and its complexity reflects on big things. Geologist Anthony Coates has written that the land bridge may have been "the most important natural event to affect the surface of the earth in the last 60 million years." Its final formation three million years ago, when eastern Panama rose above the sea, may have changed global climate dramatically, and the canal that was dug across it a century ago is a balancing point of global civilization. The bridge is more than a point between continents: it is the newest major piece of land on the planet. If it is hard to identify, it's harder still to dismiss, and those who have dismissed it have sometimes tripped over it.

I tripped and stumbled over Central America for months before I began to pay much attention to its land bridge identity. I'd known since elementary school that it is a land bridge, but I wasn't thinking about it when I took my first trip south in 1971. I'd decided to see the tropics, of which I had a vaguely idyllic notion—not a dream exactly, a day-dream. There would be lush evergreen forest, warm, but somehow also cool, with colorful birds and flowers. There might be mysterious white ruins among the trees. I couldn't afford to fly anywhere, so I looked around for the nearest lush evergreen forest with colorful birds and flowers.

"Go to Chiapas," someone said. "They have monkeys and parrots there." I looked at a map. Chiapas was Mexico's southernmost state, located just below the Isthmus of Tehuantepec, where North America dwindles to a point, and the land swells again toward Guatemala, El Salvador, Honduras. I had heard of them, and they'd sounded danger-ous. I hadn't heard of Chiapas, except I'd seen some pictures of Indians in smocks. I hitchhiked to Mexicali, got on a southbound bus, and rode for days across the Mexican Plateau, which looked like New Mexico to me. I stopped in Mexico City long enough to get an upper respiratory infection, and in Oaxaca long enough to get over it. Another bus ride led down a long canyon studded with maguey plants to a place on the Pacific called Salina Cruz. This was the Isthmus of Tehuantepec, but it seemed unpromising, a windswept brushland with dry mountains to the east.

I went into the nearby town of Tehuantepec to get a bus to San Cristobal de las Casas in Chiapas. While I waited, I stepped into a bar for a beer. Two men sat beside me and asked if I liked drugs. "*Flores, flores*," said one of the men, wriggling his fingers before his eyes in mock ecstasy. He reminded me of Oliver Hardy. I said I didn't, and when the men were convinced, they showed me their *Policia Judicial* badges and chummily escorted me to the bus station. The bus ran after dark, so I only caught moonlit glimpses of the steep road. Brush gave way to trees and pale, heavily grazed pastures, and when the bus reached San Cristobal, which is at about 2,000 meters, the dawn air was chill. The landscape around town was like northern California—a hilly woodland of pine and evergreen oak. Since I'd come from northern California, this was an anticlimax.

I walked into the woods the next day, following a rutted red dirt road. There were no parrots or monkeys, but great numbers of Chamula Indians in smocks, so many that I felt uncomfortable as I walked past men cutting pines, and women spinning wool from fluffy black-and-

white sheep. It was like sightseeing in backyards. I felt even more uncomfortable when, wandering off the road to the foot of a cliff, I came
upon a hole full of human skulls and bones. They looked old, but there
was a Phillips screwdriver with a yellow plastic handle lying on them.
When I asked other travelers about this, they said it might be connected
to sorcery. San Cristobal is hundreds of kilometers south of the Tropic of
Cancer, but I felt I'd wandered into a New World version of seventeenth-
century Spain.

So began a roller-coaster search for my tropical daydream as I went
up and down the Chiapas hills in search of lush evergreen forest, monkeys, and parrots. I heard about the Lacandon rain forest in the lowlands
to the southeast, so I took a bus in that direction, to where the dirt
road ended in a little foothill town. Although big treetops occupied the
eastern horizon, around town it was all pasture and cornfield. No road
led toward the forest, and all I had in the way of equipment was a
rucksack with a change of clothes. The only bird I recall seeing was a
roadside hawk.

I returned to San Cristobal and tried again. Someone said some missionaries were preserving a lush evergreen forest in the mountains to
the northwest. To get there, I had to return to the lowlands and stay
overnight in a dusty town called Chiapa de Corzo, where I finally saw
parrots, flying over the town square as I sat in a cafe. They made a
thrilling racket, and the sunset they flew against was yellow and green,
with purple rays fanning above the horizon. I was encouraged. Next
day I rode to a muddy settlement straddling a ridgetop, and found that
the missionaries had preserved some lush forest, parts of which were
satisfactorily exotic—orchids, tree ferns, and a hummingbird nest in a
liana. But again I encountered surprising familiarity. The trees weren't
like California's, but they resembled Florida's—sweet gum, sycamore,
bald cypress. Even the missionaries seemed dissatisfied with their subtropical surroundings, and spoke longingly of naked Indians in Darién.

I went back to San Cristobal, and heard there was a tropical park
with some lakes near the Guatemalan border, Los Lagos de Montebello.
I hitchhiked there with some hippies. On the way, we stopped at a
Maya ruin inhabited by a South Carolinian in a trailer who poached
orchids and artifacts. He offered us hashish cookies, complaining of
how weak they were. He was lying, and all that I can recall of Los

Lagos de Montebello is that the lakes were circular and various shades of blue, and that they were surrounded with pine forest, a warmer, wispier one than the San Cristobal forest, but a pine forest, without evident monkeys or parrots.

I decided I'd seen enough of Chiapas, and that Guatemala would be worth a try despite its turbulent reputation. I hitchhiked south, and found Guatemala a pleasant surprise, friendlier than Mexico. Women bathing near the customs post smiled and waved at me, and some highway workers in a truck gave me a ride immediately after I crossed the border, hiding me in the back when we passed an army checkpoint. The road ran through a steep gorge, then emerged on a rolling plateau dotted with towns full of colorfully dressed Mayas. A man who gave me a ride the next day said it was like the Peruvian altiplano. Still, it was settled farming country with pines, oaks, and eucalyptuses, not unlike California's farm valleys. I kept on to Guatemala City, where I got into conversation with an English-speaking black man in a market. I may have asked him about parrots and monkeys.

"You should go to the Petén," he said. "You can take a bus through the jungle to the coast. It will be a nice adventure for you." I looked at the map. The Petén was a huge province to the north, but it appeared low-lying and empty. A single road ran to a place with the promising name of Villaflores—and then to something called Parque Nacional Tikal, also enticing.

Another bus wound east out of the highlands into a steep gorge that contained not lush forest, but cardon cactus and prickly pear. This was the Motagua Valley, which runs from near Guatemala City to the Caribbean. I began to think I'd made another mistake, but as the bus continued, the valley turned bright green, with palm-covered hills alongside. After a night at the seaside town of Puerto Barrios, I got on another bus for the ride north, and this time the dirt road didn't run through pastures bordered by distant forest, but through forest broken only by occasional huts. Whenever the bus stopped, the forest drifted in, in the form of bugs and butterflies or strange fruits handed about by loitering children and embarking passengers. There were purple spheres with red pulp and milky juice, and rough pear shapes with custardy white flesh. They came from roadside trees, none of which I recognized. The only settlement we passed was an army post on a pine-wooded hillock.

Villaflores, reached at sunset, was a little stone city across a causeway in an azure lake. It looked as though conquistadors had left it to sleep in the forest long ago. I fell in with some traveling salesmen, men in their twenties like me. We sat in bars and walked the cobbled, unlit streets, stumbling over giant toads. They were enthusiastic about the Petén the way North Americans used to be enthusiastic about the West. Were there parrots and monkeys? Of course! I would hear howler monkeys in the hills if I listened. There were guerrillas in the hills as well; the Petén was famous for its guerrillas, the best in the country. At Tikal, I would see everything. A crocodile had eaten a child there the week before.

Next morning, the salesmen were quiet, and eyed me uneasily, perhaps regretting their expansive words. There were counterinsurgency agents around. But I'd absorbed their enthusiasm, and hurried off toward Tikal. The road ran beside the lake, Petén Itzá, which looked so inviting that I stopped to rent a dugout from a woman at a hut. I paddled out, watched turtles and colorful fishes against the white sand bottom, and swam in the perfectly cool and clear water. After I returned the boat, the woman offered me a *refresco,* a fruit drink, and pointed to another woman who was poling past on the lake.

"She's a witch," the woman said offhandedly.

As I walked on, a slender green lizard started up from the path. Accelerating away, it suddenly got up on its hind legs, like a little dinosaur. When it came to a large puddle, it kept running *on* the water, without sinking or even splashing. Then it disappeared so abruptly that I thought it might have been conjured up by the witch on the lake.

I reached Tikal at noon, and found the famous Maya ruins almost deserted. I had a little campground and picnic area to myself, and slept in a hammock I'd rented from a workman. The park was what the salesmen had promised, and it seemed my daydream had come true. Trees with buttress roots, spiky epiphytes and bright flowers engulfed the white-walled ruins—real tropical trees. In the mornings, I'd climb the temples and watch spider monkeys swing through the canopy, hanging by their tails to feed on cherry-sized orange fruits. In the evenings, parrots roosted in the campground trees, and toucans, black birds with huge, rainbow-colored bills, prowled among them, grunting and croaking. This annoyed the parrots, which screamed their heads off.

After dark, parauques, tropical whippoorwills, quavered in the grass around the moonlit ruins, and something whistled with exquisite plaintiveness in the forest, like Rima the bird girl in W. H. Hudson's neotropical fantasy, *Green Mansions*.

I had come to a marvelous place, yet there were undertones of puzzlement in my satisfaction. The forest wasn't warm yet somehow cool: it was blazing in the daytime, and so chilly at night that I had trouble sleeping. It was evergreen, but not lush. The ground seemed baked by the dry season, and although I was glad no rain fell, the air had a dusty, scratchy feel. No limpid streams ran nearby; in fact the only water was a muddy pond inhabited by a small crocodilian, perhaps the salesmen's supposed child-eater. Even most of the trees weren't my daydreams' liana-laced giants, but rather the size of the second-growth trees in the U.S. Every evening after the noise of the parrots and monkeys had subsided, a gray fox emerged from the forest and daintily patrolled the campground. I felt that this forest, which I'd traveled many weeks to reach, might have produced something more exotic than a species I'd often seen in California. After the fox, a creature that resembled a cross between a groundhog and a midget deer emerged to patrol in its turn. The creature was so strange that I had no idea what it was, and so found it nearly as unsatisfactory as the too-familiar fox. Exoticism must be identifiable to be appreciated.

One morning, the forest was full of a sound like basketballs bouncing on bass drums, and I found that tom turkeys were making this sound as they displayed before hens. They were a striking, irridescent blue, unlike North American turkeys, but I still felt slightly baffled at their familiarity. One afternoon, a flash of scarlet in the underbrush turned out to be a cardinal identical to the ones I'd grown up with in the eastern U.S. I wondered why the forest needed cardinals and turkeys, when it had parrots and toucans. Rather than a daydream forest, it wasn't so different from an Ohio woodland in August, with heat and cicadas in the afternoon, and chill and katydids at night.

I left Tikal after a few days, more because I couldn't cash traveler's checks than because of punctured daydreams. I got a ride to the then British Colony of Belize (of which I'd never heard) with two Guatemalan high school students on their way to scuba dive. As we neared the coast, the forest dwindled to a scattering of spindly pines and palmettos, which excited the students. "Savanna!" they exclaimed. "That's where the jaguars live!" To me, it looked like the red clay country of the Georgia piedmont. We drove into Belize City at sunset, and I confronted the Caribbean, which was gray and choppy, bordered by peeling frame houses and weedy canals. A large dorsal fin protruded from the waves, and skinny, big-eyed fish hung in the shallows. I had crossed Central America, one section of it. Belize City is about as far from Tehuantepec as San Francisco is from Los Angeles. Yet the cultural and natural diversity I'd encountered made me feel as though I'd crossed a continent, and this made my tropical daydream seem as trite as it was.

I didn't think much about it at the time. I checked into a hotel where the entertainment consisted of a 45-rpm record of Chubby Checker's "Let's Do the Twist." The first other guest I met introduced himself as a member of the American Nazi Party. He and an exotic pet dealer from Florida held a Mad Hatter court in the bar, attended by whoever wandered in. The bartender-bellhop did the twist occasionally, but everybody else just drank rum-and-Cokes, egged on by the nazi, who owned Miami parking lots. The next morning I heard something running down the hall, and when I opened my bedroom door, one of the green, water-walking lizards I'd seen at Tikal flashed past. The pet dealer told me it was called a basilisk, or *Jesucristo* lizard. He had other animals in his room, and as he drank in the bar that afternoon he kept one that resembled the groundhog-deer–like creature I'd seen at Tikal on the stool beside him. This animal was spotted, unlike the one at Tikal, and the dealer said it was called a paca. The one at Tikal had been an agouti, he told me. "A common South American rodent."

After many rum-and-Cokes, the pet dealer had a loud argument with a civil servant and a retired navy officer about the length of Belizean boa constrictors, which he insisted never exceeded twenty feet, to their scorn. Then he lurched into the unlit streets shouting abuse about a local celebrity and rival of his, a game guide or "bushman." The Belizeans said the bushman came back from the forest with jaguars unmarked by bullets, and that he sometimes came back without the gringos he was guiding. "At midnight," said a Belizean, "a white horse comes and takes him away." Such stories enraged the pet dealer, who shouted that the Belizeans were superstitious and the bushman was full of shit. After a night or two of this, I decided I'd better leave Belize

City, although the dealer warned me not to hitchhike at Eastertime because the Belizean country people practiced cannibalism for their Holy Week celebration. "They *say* they eat iguana," the Nazi added. "*Hah.*"

I started back toward California, and, with life's usual irony, encountered something very like my tropical daydream. After traversing Yucatán's dry brushland, I stopped at Palenque in the foothills a few dozen kilometers east of San Cristobal de las Casas. Palenque had truly lush forest, with huge trees and limpid streams. It had parrots, monkeys, and no wild turkeys to complicate things. With their elegant bas reliefs, even the Maya ruins there had a grace that seemed closer to my fantasy than Tikal's steep pyramids. Palenque came too late for daydreams, however. My ignorant journey had started a change in my thinking. I'd come south unconsciously regarding life as something to be adapted to desire. I disliked the usual way civilization reshapes nature by turning landscapes into suburbs or theme parks, yet my tropical daydream was also an attempt, psychological rather than technological, to make the landscape a desirable artifice. Central America's roller coaster of diversity had showed me how unimaginative that attempt was.

Central America aroused my curiosity after twenty years of an education that had seemed largely to dull it. I had been a mediocre student, partly because I was lazy, but also because my enthusiasms seldom followed the curriculum. Curiosity was encouraged in theory, but students were supposed to be curious about what the authorities wanted to teach. In Central America, there were no authorities, or none that I was supposed to consult. Trees had no labels or park rangers to identify them, and I suddenly wanted to know what they were. There was a sneaking satisfaction under my puzzlement with Tikal's gray foxes and turkeys, *because* they had not been in books about the jungle. In the books, the jungle was a remote and didactic, if romantic, category. In Central America, the jungle was much more provocative, part of a continuum that began with familiar foxes and merged unexpectedly into the unknown. Mixed, blurred, unfinished Central America seemed to say something about life that had not been said before.

That "something" seems connected to the land bridge and its unique evolutionary story, so perhaps I can get at it by telling the story, although it's not a simple one to tell. Like all evolutionary stories, it is really two—of how the land bridge evolved, and of how people discovered it. Evolution occurs in geological time but is perceived in historical time, so the story is end-first, starting with the land bridge's discovery and then turning back and starting again with what we know of its evolution, which still isn't very much. I can't even start with the land bridge's *evolutionary* discovery, because that depended on Western civilization's geographical discovery of Central America. (Of course, Native Americans discovered Central America, but it wasn't written down so it is part of evolution rather than history.) In a way, the four-hundred-year-long, stumbling discovery was not unlike my three-month-long one. It also began with ignorant daydreams, although of a more forceful sort. It also led to confusion and disillusionment, and to awakenings.

The Monkey's Bridge

EXPLORATION

Reasonably could Cristobal Colón *believe and expect,*
if such a great island as Plato's Atlantis had been
sunken and lost, that others might exist, or at least
tierra firme, and that by seeking he might find them.

Bartolomé de Las Casas, *History of the Indies*

Adventurers

A LAND BRIDGE WAS the last thing Western civilization wanted when it stumbled onto Central America. Christopher Columbus was looking for the opposite—a sea passage to India—as he coasted from Honduras to Panama during his fourth voyage in 1502. He wasn't the first European to see the isthmus: a notary public named Rodrigo de Bastidas reached Panama a few months earlier. Yet Columbus's encounter with what he called "the land of Veragua" set a pattern. He wanted an easy way to wealth, but also something harder to define. Perhaps one could call it a life adapted to his desires. What he found was the unexpected, and a good deal of trouble. Central America was so unexpected that Columbus died convinced it was a southern province of China.

Tales of Marco Polo's China travels had excited Columbus's greed, and he promised Ferdinand and Isabella "as much gold as they want . . . besides spices and cottons, as much as their highnesses shall command," if they funded his voyages. Yet he also had an almost childlike sense of wonder, and imagined during his third voyage that the Orinoco Delta might be the "terrestrial paradise." On his first voyage, he thought he'd found cinnamon, gum mastic, and other Asian plants along the Cuban coast instead of slightly similar American ones, and he was still misreading the clues a decade later when he decided Panamanian chile peppers indicated proximity to Indonesia's spice islands. Columbus's imagination was working harder than ever on his fourth voyage, because he was desperate. Rivals had grabbed his early discoveries in the

Antilles and had fanned out to the north and south, despite his complaints to the increasingly bored Spanish monarchs. Nobody had sailed straight west through the Caribbean, however, and this fourth voyage seemed his last chance.

The sovereigns finally lent him four leaky ships, and he reached the mainland in the summer of 1502, but found nothing more precious than tall pine trees at his first landfall, Honduras's island of Guanaja. When he showed the local Paya people pearls and gold, they were so ignorant of the pretty things that they offered to buy them from him. Prospects seemed better as the ships neared the Honduran coast, which even Columbus called vaguely "*tierra firme*" despite his conviction it was Asia. He encountered a giant canoe with a cargo of dyed cotton, flint-edged swords, and copper hatchets, and on shore hundreds of Indians eagerly traded "fowles of the country, which are better than ours, roasted fish, red and white beans" for hawk bells and glass beads. The land was "verdant and beautiful, although low," Columbus wrote in a letter to Ferdinand and Isabella, "and there are many pines, oaks, seven kinds of palms, and myrobalans like those in Hispaniola called hobi." Columbus also mentioned animals—"*leones, ciervos, corzos, otro tanta*"—which translators have rendered variously as "lions, stags, and fallow deer"; or "pumas, deer, and gazelles." He probably didn't care particularly what they were as long as they implied that he was in Asia.

The weather brought the expedition to a standstill for a month along Honduras's Mosquito Coast. "It was continual rain, thunder, and lightning," Columbus wrote. "The ships lay exposed to the weather . . . the people so exhausted and so down at the mouth that they were all the time making vows to be good." When the land finally turned south and west, the directions Columbus hoped to go, he named it Cabo Gracias à Dios, Thank God Cape. They proceeded to a place called Cariari near present-day Puerto Limón in Costa Rica, where many people called Talamancas gathered on shore wearing pendants of guanin, a low-grade gold-copper alloy. The Spaniards were impressed, Columbus's brother Ferdinand wrote, by the abundance of wild animals compared to the Antilles, and by "a great palace of wood . . . and within some tombs, and over each tomb was a tablet carved with figures and beasts, and on some the effigy of the dead person, adorned with beads and guanin." The Talamancas were eager to trade, and frustrated when

Columbus hesitated to exchange his beads for their low-grade pendants. As an inducement, and probably to see if he was human, they offered him two teenage girls, whom Columbus piously sent home, to the girls' relief.

The fleet continued to Panama's Almirante Bay, where Guaymi people wearing pure gold told Columbus their land was called "Quiriquetana." This was close enough to "Ciamba," Marco Polo's name for Cochin China, to excite him. The Guaymis said a great body of water lay at the other side of a strait, and Columbus hurried there, but found himself in a large lagoon, Chiriqui Lagoon, instead of an ocean. Yet Indians there said another great sea did lie nine days' walk away, and on it a kingdom called Ciguare where people dressed in gold and coral. Columbus decided Ciguare must be Ciamba, since he'd read that the Ciambans used coral for money. Back in Spain, his imagination would transform Ciguare into a place whose inhabitants not only dressed in gold, but used cannons and cavalry. Yet he didn't try to walk across the isthmus, a wise decision considering the fates of many later attempts.

They sailed east toward Darién and encountered bad weather again. "Eyes never beheld the sea so high, angry, and covered with foam," Columbus wrote. "Never did the sky look so terrible; for one whole day and night it blazed like a furnace." He turned back and decided to put in at Belen Harbor near today's Canal Zone until the rainy season ended, but rain never really ends along southern Central America's Caribbean. It fell through January 1503, hindering gold-prospecting trips up the Belen River. The men eventually found a deposit that they could pick off the ground with their knives, and Columbus decided to start a colony, leaving Ferdinand in charge while he returned to Spain for supplies. As he prepared to sail, however, the rains stopped and the river fell so that his ships couldn't cross the bar at its mouth.

The Indians had become hostile—not surprisingly, since Columbus had kidnapped their *cacique* and his family as hostages. Afraid the greedy strangers meant to stay, the Indians attacked the colony and killed several Spaniards. Ten days later, Columbus abandoned one of his ships inside the bar and fled, his fleet so decrepit that he barely reached Jamaica, and spent a year marooned there. A quarter of his men were dead. Yet all this weighed little against the glowing stories he told before his death in 1506. "I saw in the land of Veragua greater evidence of gold in the first two days than in all Hispaniola in four years," he proclaimed.

A rush of adventurers toward this "rich coast" followed. Like Columbus, they sought wealth with a seasoning of wonder, and this motive had such allure that it lingered long after Central America had been ransacked. As late as 1870, the English naturalist Thomas Belt wrote of "most fabulous stories . . . about the Rio Frio [in Costa Rica] and its inhabitants: stories of great cities, golden ornaments and light-haired people . . . a race of Indians who have never been subjugated, and about whom little is known." Even in 1971, lost-city stories still circulated in the Petén. I heard of a traveler who stumbled on a lake surrounded by Mayan ruins, one of which contained a gold statue so large he couldn't lift it.

Most of the adventurers were less intelligent and humane than Columbus, and they found more death than wealth, or even wonder. In 1509, a 700-man expedition led by Diego de Nicuesa dwindled to sixty, then disappeared. Rain and hunger were the main enemies in what would-be colonist Girolamo Benzoni called "the intensely sterile province of Veragua." It rained so much that the Indians built their houses in trees, and, unlike their Mexican counterparts, couldn't grow enough food to support conquistadors. The next Veragua expedition, led in 1513 by a legendary villain named Pedrarias, planned to strain gold from Panamanian rivers with nets of wool fleece. Dominican priest Bartolomé de Las Casas described their fate in his *History of the Indies*. "Nothing of the kind had ever been seen before, people richly dressed in silk and brocade worth a tidy sum of money falling down dead of pure hunger, others grazing in fields like cattle on the most tender grass and roots. . . . Everyone saw quite clearly then how gold came up by the netful!"

Pedrarias's governorship would have been as abortive as Nicuesa's if not for his captain, Vasco Núñez de Balboa, who got around the Indians by playing one *cacique* against another and feeding the hostile ones to his dogs. This diplomacy's reward was a successful crossing to the Pacific, then known as "the South Sea." Balboa took three weeks to walk across the Darién isthmus in September 1513, with about 200 Spanish soldiers and 1,000 Indians. After viewing the mud flats of the Gulf of San Miguel and claiming the land, he returned to the Caribbean with gold, slaves, and rumors of a *truly* rich civilization across the water to the south. That was the Inca empire, but Balboa never got a chance to employ his skills there, because a jealous Pedrarias had him beheaded in 1519.

Attempts to get rich from Veragua went downhill after that. Another Belen expedition, led by Felipe Gutierrez in 1534, showed a more practical response to starvation than Pedrarias's. Denied a share of the commander's food, the men ate Indians and each other. In 1541, Felipe's brother Diego led an archetypically disastrous expedition to present-day Costa Rica. Most of his force deserted to Peru before he even reached Central America. He organized another band and began extorting gold from the Indians along the Reventazon River, but they fled into the mountains. Afraid his soldiers would desert, Diego Gutierrez led them in pursuit. Somewhere in the cordillera, a large force in red and black battle regalia fell on the conquistadors and killed most of them, including Gutierrez, in December 1543.

Girolamo Benzoni was a young soldier on the expedition, and happened to survive the ambush because he put on the helmet of his companion "who had overlooked it from some leaves having fallen on it." After the fight, the helmet looked "as if a smith had hammered it all over." Benzoni returned to his native Italy in 1555, where he wrote, "It seems impossible that a human body could have undergone so much."

On the Plátano

It's still not hard to have a Veraguan-style adventure on Central America's Caribbean coast, depending on how adventurous one wants to be. In 1992, I took a trip partway up one of the rivers Columbus passed as he struggled along the Honduran littoral east of Cabo Gracias. This was the Plátano, still inhabited by descendants of the people Columbus met, who now call themselves Miskitos. I'd heard that the rain forest on the upper Plátano was pristine, and that it contained ruined cities which may have been inhabited when Columbus sailed past. In 1544, the archbishop of Honduras reported seeing "very great populations" from a peak near the colony of Trujillo east of the Plátano. Indians told him those "populations" ate from gold plates. Nothing further was heard of them, but expeditions up the Plátano in the mid-1980s found hundreds of stone structures, some of which were fifteen meters high and one hundred meters long.

After a day of flying, boating, and backpacking, I'd arrived at the Miskito village of Barra del Plátano with the name of a guide. His family told me, however, that the propeller had just fallen off his *pipante* and he would need at least a week to get another. He was still away at Brus Laguna with his broken boat, so I had to look for another guide. A cluster of unpainted board shacks on the floodplain beside the beach, the village lacked even the *hospedaje* of most small Central American towns. I spent the night as the not-very-welcome guest of the general storekeeper, a ladino married to a Miskito. I asked to sleep on his porch, but he insisted I sleep in his living room. When I asked why, he waved at the night and said: "*Es mal.*"

I'd brought a mosquito net instead of a sleeping bag, which was a mistake. I encountered almost no mosquitoes, but the nights were too cold for the sheet I'd brought. I wouldn't have slept much in the ladino's house anyway. His daughter was ill, semiparalyzed, and cried all night. Still, I was glad to be under a roof. It rained in the small hours, one of the tropical downpours that start in complete stillness, pound the earth a while, then stop as abruptly as they started.

I spent the next morning hanging around, watching boats arrive through the surf with giant plastic bags of secondhand clothes and depart loaded with green chains of live iguanas tied together by their long claws. The townspeople, tall and handsome, clustered along the riverbank, bathing, washing clothes, doing errands. Indeterminate pieces of meat hung from lines, and vultures sat hopefully around tubs of newly caught fish. One of the fishermen came over to chat with me, but vultures covered his tub in seconds, so he had to hurry back to chase them away. Then the police, a young man in vaguely military dress, questioned me. After I'd explained my hopes, he shook his head and said, cryptically, "*Nada.*"

Finally, the village ferryman, a dark-skinned individual with a large machete scar on his neck, helped me find another guide. The ferryman was a nice man, and an important one, because although his assets consisted of a skiff and a pole, his ferry was the only way to cross the river to the village. The new guide was a stout, brusque Miskito who traded up and down the river in a Boston Whaler with a large Yamaha outboard. He was expensive, and his affluent outfit was disquieting in a place where most boatmen used dugouts with engines like sewing machines, but he seemed the only option.

As soon as we'd set off, around 2 p.m., he and his scrawny, one-eyed assistant produced two bottles of *guaro*, sugar cane alcohol. They drank one during the next two hours, although the river was so full of snags that the assistant had to sit on the bow and fend them off with his feet. They didn't talk much, and the assistant seemed to speak only Miskito. When we passed a sungrebe, a little tropical water bird, I asked what they called it, hoping to learn its Miskito name. The guide said it was a *patito de agua*—"little water duck."

Pristine rain forest did not prevail on the lower Plátano. Willows bordered the river, the farthest south I'd seen them. Most of the trees were second-growth species like cecropia and balsa. Farther upstream, the forest was less disturbed, with big ceibas above the canopy, and flocks of parrots and keel-billed toucans. It was getting dark by then, and the guide had stopped to pick up two young women, who helped to drink the *guaro*. As the stars emerged, we came to a house where we were to stay overnight before going on to our destination, the Pech Indian village of Las Marías. There the guides, the women, and some older men drank more *guaro* while I reclined in a hammock in a little detached house which I thought might be a guest house. Rifles and machetes leaned against the wall. Birds called in the forest, but I barely could hear them above the flood of Miskito that came from the other part of the house. The guide was doing most of the talking.

I dozed a while and awoke to realize that it was not a guest house. The guide, the women, and the older men trooped in, hung up some coffin-shaped cotton mosquito nets above the floor, undressed, and climbed under them together, except for one old man who kept wandering naked about the room as though he'd forgotten something. From his cotton coffin, the guide kept talking, his tone suggesting a long-standing grievance. He talked and talked, although nobody answered. Another downpour came and went. I dozed again, and he was still talking when I awoke. The hammock was giving me a backache. I heard a noise in the wall, and asked the guide what it was.

"It's a mouse who likes to eat rice," he replied. "Don't be afraid, English." Not wanting to seem so, I asked him what a "bu-bu-bu-bu-

bu" noise in the forest was. "It's a frog who likes to sing," he said, in a tone that invited me to make something of it. I didn't answer, and he said that it was a frog who liked to sing several more times, until the general lack of response finally seemed to weary him, and he stopped talking.

The Miskitos were in surprisingly good shape the next morning, better than me. The guide seemed to have forgotten his predawn pique, and introduced me to an old man who he said spoke English, as though it were an ancient language. The man knew some English words, and said it had been more common when he was a boy, which must have been when the British Navy still plied the coast. I supposed that was why the guide had called me "English."

I had big shot of *guaro* in a cup of coffee before we pushed off, and the trip to Las Marías was a blur of river mist and foliage. The river was shallow and clear enough to see the bottom, but we went faster because there were fewer snags. Steep mountains appeared in the distance, and the riverbank rose in red and white strata that might have been painted by Jackson Pollock. Except for the parrots and toucans, and some big slider turtles on the bank, there was little sign of animal life. I'd come to the Plátano with the idea of ascending the river above Las Marías, where there were said to be scarlet macaws and harpy eagles as well as lost cities. To do that, I needed a canoe and polers, which the guide whose propeller had broken would have been able to provide. Any lingering hope of getting them by myself evaporated when we reached Las Marías, which consisted of a few thatch huts and was deserted except for an old man, a little girl, and sleeping pigs.

I hadn't eaten since leaving Barra del Plátano. The Miskitos evidently didn't need food during their weekend celebration. If I wanted to follow further in the footsteps of Nicuesa and Gutierrez, this was my chance. I returned downriver with the guide, twice as fast as we'd come up, except when he stopped to sell ammunition and other merchandise to people who hailed him from the bank.

Back at Barra del Plátano, I started walking north along the beach to where I could get a boat to the airport at Palacios. A flint-billed woodpecker flew past, a big bird, the same genus as the extinct ivory-billed woodpecker in North America. It looked strange in the tropical scrub along the beach. A lot of people were strolling up and down, many of them nattily dressed. This beach promenade apparently was part of regular Sunday activities. A tall young Miskito approached me, who turned out to be the guide whose propeller had fallen off. He seemed intelligent and sympathetic, and asked me how my trip had gone. I shrugged.

"I wish I'd been able to take you," he said.

"Bad luck."

The Conquest

Spain never conquered most of Central America's Caribbean, where groups such as the Miskito, Tawahka, Bri-Bri, Guaymi, and Kuna retain considerable autonomy to this day. The conquistadors might not have conquered any part of it if all Central America had been as hostile, but a determined leader named Gil González Dávila discovered otherwise in 1519 when he set out from Panama to explore "a thousand leagues westward along the South Sea." He had planned to use ships built by recently executed Balboa, but Pedrarias wouldn't let him, so he built his own, which promptly sank. He built some more, which floated, but not well enough, so Dávila walked up the Pacific coast with 300 men.

The Panamanian and southern Costa Rican part of this trek was like a Caribbean expedition. Rain fell so hard, and they had to cross so many rivers, that Dávila's legs failed. He stopped to rest with a local cacique, but the Rio Grande de Terraba overflowed its banks and flooded the house chest-deep. Then it fell down with Dávila inside, and his men had to extract him with axes. They spent the next few days in trees. Yet they kept going, a tribute to Dávila's determination, and to his unusually humane treatment of his men and the natives.

Things changed when they got to the Gulf of Nicoya midway up Costa Rica's coast. They entered a sunny country of maize fields, orchards, and plaster towns which must have seemed fabulous enough after the months of rain forest. Dávila had found a climate characterized by a yearly dry season that allowed intensive farming, and a culture different from the Caribbean's. The Nicoyans were urbanites related to the Aztecs, and like them were inclined by religious prophecies to accept Christianity. When the Spaniards entered the town of Nicoya, the cacique not only gave Dávila gold worth 14,000 castellanos, but allowed himself and 6,000 subjects to be baptized. The Nicoyans told of an even richer town beside a great lake to the north, but warned Dávila about its *cacique*, named Nicarao. Dávila pushed on to Lake Nicaragua anyway, and the feared Nicarao gave the Spaniards 15,000 castellanos' worth of gold and allowed himself and 9,000 subjects to be baptized. Dávila gave him a silk cape, a red cap, and some costume jewelry in return, which may have caused Nicarao second thoughts. He began asking awkward questions, such as why the almighty and benevolent Christian God had made darkness and cold when warmth and light were so much nicer.

Another *cacique* named Diriangen then appeared, leading a procession including ten men with banners, seventeen women covered with gold disks, five trumpeters, and 500 subjects carrying turkeys. Diriangen made an appointment to be baptized, but missed it, instead attacking the Spaniards with a force of 3,000. Dávila repelled him, but decided on a retreat, during which the backsliding Nicarao also attacked. Nevertheless, Dávila got back to Panama with gold worth 112,525 castellanos. "The country of Nicaragua is not very large, but fertile and delightful," Benzoni would write. "From the great abundance that reigned in the province when the Spaniards first subjugated it, they called it Mahomet's Paradise." As promising as Nicaragua's wealth were its huge lakes, Managua and Nicaragua, which Dávila thought might be the South Sea passage that Columbus had failed to find. Indians told him one could travel by water from the Pacific's Bay of Fonseca to the lakes, and then to the Caribbean.

Like Columbus, however, Dávila was too sanguine in his geography and not sanguinary enough in his politics. Bloodthirstier rivals had him carted back to Spain in chains, where he died in 1526. By then, much bigger land sharks cruised the isthmus. After subduing the Aztecs, red-bearded Hernan Cortés had led a fruitless expedition through the Petén forest, then had sent another red-bearded scourge named Pedro de Alvarado to conquer another fabled realm, highland Guatemala. Alvarado invaded Tehuantepec in 1524 under the pretext of helping a local *cacique* against enemies, then kept going across Chiapas's mountains until he reached what nineteenth-century historian Hubert Howe Bancroft described as "a vast tableland, with an Italian climate, made bright with meandering streams, studded with verdure fringed lakes." As they proceeded south, his vanguard kept hurrying back to the main column swearing that they'd found yet *another* city as big as Mexico. Bancroft described the Quiché Maya capital of Utatlán as "one of the most magnificent structures of Central America. It was built of hewn stone of various colors, mosaic in appearance, and its colossal dimensions and elegant and stately architectural form excited mingled awe and admiration."

Unlike the Nicaraguans, the highland Maya had no religious predilection to accept the Spaniards, and immediately resisted them. Unlike the Caribbean peoples, however, they lacked vast rain forests in which to hide. Alvarado played Balboa's game, siding with the Caxchiquel tribe against the Quichés, then turning on the Caxchiquels, and had extended his power to El Salvador and Honduras within the year. It took Francisco Montejo longer to subdue the Maya cities of Yucatán, but by the mid-1530s, half a lifetime from Columbus's arrival, native sovereignty had collapsed.

No sooner had this wealth fallen into Spanish hands, however, than it dwindled in an almost chimerical way. Alvarado had wrung Guatemala so dry by 1534 that he had to move on to Peru. The reason for this sudden impoverishment is no mystery. The people who had produced the wealth were dead. As Las Casas wrote, adventurers starved in *tierra firme* "because the Spaniards had depopulated it by killing its inhabitants or engaging in slave trade." Old World diseases conquered the land bridge even more quickly than Spanish troops. Most of the Caxchiquels already were dead of smallpox when Alvarado reached Guatemala. Benzoni saw desolation everywhere in what he still called India in the 1540s. In Panama he "found only the remains of the abandoned huts of the Indian villages"; on the Costa Rican coast, only "woods and swamps and mountains that were astonishing to the eye"; in Honduras, "not eight thousand left" of an original "four hundred thousand Indians."

Yet if the causes of collapse are obvious, the effects still seem strange. Central America's conquest is like one of the legends of elfin kingdoms which appear to knights in the forest, then vanish overnight, leaving the intruder with rusted armor in the morning dew. In Mexico and Peru, the walls of Tenochtitlan and Cuzco lie at the base of the modern cities. Of the Nicaraguan towns that Dávila encountered, nothing remains, and the resplendent Utatlán Bancroft described is now mossy mounds in the countryside. Even the name Utatlán is a form of erasure: *Utatlán* means "the conquered city" in the Nahuatl language of Alvarado's Mexican mercenaries.

This spectral quality is nowhere stronger than in the story of Tayasal. Founded on Lake Petén Itzá by an ousted Yucatán dynasty around 1300, Tayasal was the last Maya city, persisting like a dream in the forest for two centuries after the conquest. Its dynastic ruler, the Can Ek, greeted Cortés on his Petén expedition. Cortés left behind a horse, and the Itzá first tried to feed the strange creature on meat and flowers, then made an idol of its skeleton. In 1618, another Can Ek met an expedition led by two priests, but rejected Christianity and sent them away. Less fortunate intruders became sacrifices to the Itzá gods. In 1695, yet another Can Ek met an expedition led by Padre Andre de Avenado. As the Spaniards stood on the lakeshore, flower-decked canoes approached bearing a tall man in a gold crown and crest, his ears covered with gold disks. He conducted Avenado to an island of temples and statues, and showed him Cortés's horse before politely telling him to go away. When the Spaniards sent an armed force to subdue the city in 1697, the Itzá disappeared into the forest. It took a hundred men a single day to destroy the city's idols and temples.

John Lloyd Stephens, the North American entrepreneur and travel writer who became famous for exploring Copan and other Maya ruins in the 1840s, was half convinced Tayasal still existed. A priest in the Guatemalan town of Santa Cruz del Quiché near Utatlán told him that, in his youth, he had looked from a peak "over an immense plain extending to Yucatán and the Gulf of Mexico and saw at a great distance a large city spread over a great space, and with turrets of white glistening in the sun. The traditionary account of the Indians of Chajul is that no white man has ever reached this city; that the inhabitants speak the Maya language, are aware that a race of strangers has conquered the whole country around, and murder any white man who attempts to enter their territory."

"The interest awakened in us was the most thrilling I ever experienced," Stephens wrote. "One look at that city was worth ten years of every-day life. . . . We had a craving desire to reach that mysterious city."

2

The Bumpy Bridge

I N A WAY, IT'S not surprising that Spain conquered half of Central America in a few decades. From Tehuantepec to Darién, it is not much bigger than Texas. Yet two-dimensional size can be misleading. Central America is diverse as well as small, and in many ways is more like a continent than a state. It has continental features—two very long and involved coastlines, wide lowlands, and a continental divide. The weather has a continental scale and complexity, with a very wet, hot Caribbean coast, a comparatively dry and hot Pacific one, and inland climates ranging from semi-arid to temperate to semi-alpine.

On "real" continents, such features cover huge areas, simplifying the describer's task. But Central America has the exacting intricacy of miniaturization. "I regret that I cannot communicate to the reader," wrote John Lloyd Stephens, "the highest pleasure of my journey in Central America, that derived from the extraordinary beauty of scenery, constantly changing."

John Lloyd Stephens didn't even see it all, traveling overland by horseback, and such a trip from Tehuantepec to Darién would not be easy today. The term "land bridge" implies smoothness and simplicity, qualities that rarely confront the Central American traveler. To the conquistadors, the terrain must have seemed a fortress moated with reefs and swamps, walled with mountains, even defended with artillery of a sort as earthquakes shook their houses and volcanoes rained fire and brimstone on their heads. Perhaps that is why they called *it* the mainland, *tierra firme*, as much as the bigger but flatter continental coasts to the north and south.

Columbus was lucky that he bumped into Central America where he did, in the Gulf of Honduras, for it is one of the less tortuous stretches on the Caribbean coast. If he'd hit farther north, at Belize, he'd have run into a maze of mangrove-covered coral reefs from which he might never have emerged if bad weather had caught him. Hurricanes roar out of the central Caribbean with the climatic equivalent of earthquakes. They leveled Belize City so often that in 1961 the government moved the capital fifty kilometers inland to Belmopan. Winter "northeasters" can be almost as violent. Such a storm on the Honduran Bay Island of Utila once woke me with a start when it hit at midnight, and detained me on the island a couple of days. An old resident said islanders almost starved when northeasters lasted weeks, because no boats could reach them.

There are coral reefs along the Caribbean south of Belize, but they are more scattered and farther offshore. Much of the coast Columbus explored consists of long barrier beaches fronting lagoons that can have a lakelike placidity, although the Caribbean's shallow waters also resemble lakes in the speed with which bad weather can arouse them. I experienced this during a sudden thunderstorm while crossing Ibans Lagoon on the way to my Plátano River trip. It was in one of the motorized dugouts called "tuk-tuks," and the waves were higher than the boat within minutes. As we bounced along, the bottom felt palpably close, but not close enough to be of much use if the boat swamped.

Columbus also may have been lucky he *didn't* find a strait into the Pacific, which is much deeper and rougher than the Caribbean, as Dávila learned when he tried to launch his homemade ships. Columbus's leaky tubs might have fared as badly. Along the southern Pacific coast, at least, he would have found shelter. Large peninsulas such as the Azuero and Nicoya form over a dozen bays and gulfs, some of them sizable, like the Golfo Dulce inside Costa Rica's Osa Peninsula, which biologist William Beebe compared to the lower Amazon. On the other hand, the Pacific north of Costa Rica has few bays and only one large one, the Gulf of Fonseca. Most of the Guatemalan, Salvadoran, and Nicaraguan west coasts are straight beaches backed by coastal plains or volcanic uplands, and interrupted only by swampy estuaries. The long Pacific swells hit them hard.

"Guatemala's coast seemed too smooth and even, on the chart, to suggest good shelter," wrote William Beebe, on a marine collecting expedition from Mexico to Panama in the 1930s. He sailed past it without landing, as had many earlier mariners. Even pirates had trouble on windblown Pacific strands. One of them, William Dampier, sailed along the whole coast north from Nicaragua without a single chance to be piratical. Off El Salvador and Guatemala, his fleet "met with very bad weather as we sailed along this coast: seldom a day past but we had one or two violent tornadoes, and with them very frightful flashes of lightning and claps of thunder." Off Tehuantepec, "the waves all along this coast run high, and beat against the shore very boisterously, making the land wholly unapproachable against boats and canoas." When a party tried to go ashore to attack the town, their canoes overturned in the surf, and they got lost in mangrove swamps.

Lowlands and Rivers

If adventurers found Central America's coasts forbidding, they found its coastal plains more so. The biggest is the plain of rolling limestone that covers Yucatán and much of Belize as well as northern Guatemala's Petén. I had never encountered anything like it when I looped across in 1971. At first a pleasant change from the lowering highlands, its flatness became oppressive as it continued day after day. The only change from the Caribbean at Puerto Barrios to the Gulf of Mexico at Merida was that the vegetation turned shorter and drier, from evergreen forest to brushland. I could walk for hours and never see a stream, because surface water quickly sinks into the porous limestone. Formed in shallow seas a hundred million years ago, then uplifted to its present few hundred meters above sea level, the limestone didn't seem quite "land" as I understood it. The elements were there—rocks, soil, plants— but arranged in too rudimentary a combination. Maya homesteads seemed more campsites than settlements.

The Petén does have large rivers like the Usumacinta on its north side, and a huge "everglades" of sawgrass and hammocks, the Laguna del Tigre. I don't understand why a region largely without streams should have a "river of grass" at one edge, but limestone terrain has its own mysterious ways. Arthur Morelet, a French explorer who in 1847 was one of the first non-Spanish Europeans to traverse the Petén, wrote: "Nothing can be more complicated than the hydrography of this little corner of the globe, where the capricious waters percolate slowly from lagoon to lagoon, and seem to run athwart of each other in their devious courses."

Northern Central America's other big lowland is the Mosquitia in southeast Honduras and northeast Nicaragua. Once a mountainous landmass, it sank beneath the Caribbean about thirty million years ago, then emerged as a low plain twenty million years later, and has accumulated some 4,500 meters of sediments since. Being an alluvial lowland instead of a limestone one, the Mosquitia is laced with rivers like the Plátano, and these make it a less bizarre landscape than the Petén. They haven't made it more amenable to human settlement, however; in fact, it is less so. The rivers spread out to form almost impenetrable wetlands which look from the air like vast algal blooms, and some are so impregnated with minerals from the ancient seabed that plants become coated with black calcium in a kind of a living petrification. Uplands are mainly sterile white sand.

Except for the Plátano's mysterious ruins, the Mosquitia seems never to have been occupied by more than shifting agriculture. Early adventurers hurried past, and it remained largely unknown in the 1850s when E. G. Squiers, the United States chargé d'affaires to Nicaragua, published accounts of his explorations there. They sound like my Plátano trip. "Throughout it wore the same flat, monotonous appearance," he wrote, "a narrow strip of sand in front of a low, impenetrable forest, in which the fierce northeaster had left no tree standing." In one book, Squiers described a failed German colony's relics—a graveyard, rusting farm gear, a few dazed survivors—and concluded, "The folly of attempting to plant an agricultural colony on a lone, murky tropical shore, is inconceivable."

Beside these huge plains, many depressions or "grabens" slice across northern Central America, formed by land subsidence along faults. The Motagua Valley where cactuses surprised me in 1971 is one, not so much a valley as a trough beneath the almost perpendicular Sierra de las Minas, which soars from near sea level to over 2,500 meters and cuts off damp Caribbean air. Fault depressions tend to be more habitable than coastal lowlands—fertile, healthful, and protected from hurricanes. John Lloyd Stephens was rhapsodic about Guatemala's Rio Dulce, part of the Motagua fault zone: "On each side, rising perpendicularly from three to four hundred feet was a wall of living green. . . . For nine miles the passage continued thus one scene of unvarying beauty, when suddenly the narrow river expanded into a large lake, encompassed by mountains and studded with islands, which the setting sun illuminated with gorgeous splendor." Lakes are typical of large grabens, as land subsidence turns floodplains into pools. Central America's biggest are in the Nicaraguan Depression, "Mahomet's Paradise," which runs 500 kilometers long and fifty kilometers wide from the Gulf of Fonseca to the Bay of San Juan. It is half-covered by water, mainly Lake Nicaragua, the greatest freshwater expanse between lakes Superior and Titicaca.

Yet the habitability of grabens has been a mixed blessing because of the earthquakes which have toppled Central American cities since they were first built. The biggest recent earthquake was a 1976 *terremoto* along the Motagua Fault which nearly razed Guatemala City and killed over 20,000 people. In the Nicaraguan Depression, quakes are particularly destructive because the floor is composed either of unstable lake sediments or of recent volcanic deposits, which Nicaraguan naturalist Jaime Incer has described as "layer upon layer of old volcanic mud flows, ash, cinders and pumice—which is really just hardened volcanic foam." Managua is a monument to this instability: its downtown was leveled in a 1972 quake and is still unrestored.

The Nicaraguan Depression demarcates northern Central America, which has been land since the dinosaur age, from southern, most of which has arisen from the ocean within the past fifty million years. There is less of this new land. Costa Rica's only really large lowland is its swampy northeast, which is really just the southeast end of the Nicaraguan Depression, although it is still impressive, particularly in the Tortuguero area where the forest remains uncut. I've never felt more strongly the sense of invincible wildness a tropical lowland can evoke as when I stood on the tiny volcanic cone of Cerro Tortuguero and looked northeast across an unbroken expanse of treetops to hazy mountains.

Costa Rica and western Panama have coastal plains and fault zone depressions, but they are smaller than northern Central America's. Even in the largest depressions, like Costa Rica's Valle Central, the mountains never seem far away, and calling a basin at 1,500 meters a lowland is stretching a point anyway. For every flat expanse in the Valle Central there seems to be a corresponding steep gorge—in one of which I almost got trapped during a rainy season afternoon. I'd climbed to the stream at the bottom to look at fish, and it was so narrow I'd easily jumped it. When the daily storm came, as though somebody had turned on celestial firehoses, I took shelter under a rock overhang. An hour later, I had to wade up to my waist to cross water roaring and red with silt from coffee plantations above.

Central American rivers in general have this unpredictable mixture of insignificance and intransigence. Even the biggest ones, like the San Juan, Coco, or Usumacinta, aren't on the scale of an Amazon or Orinoco. They simply don't drain enough territory. Yet the combination of gravity and rain can give them a force out of proportion to their size. When I rafted down Costa Rica's Pacuare River in April 1990 in the late dry season, the river's ponded stretches were swimmable in a few strokes, but rapids still had enough strength to bounce several rafters into the water. Where the river entered the coastal plain was an unforgettable display of its downcutting power. At a place called Dos Montañas it sliced through sheer cliffs of volcanic stone so high I barely could see the twilight between their tops.

Darién and the Chocó Basin, where Panama and Colombia ambiguously meet, do rival the northern Central American lowlands, and in a sense surpass them, since they are the newest substantial dry land on earth and never have been anything but lowlands. They are not an eroded mountain range like the Mosquitia or even a mildly elevated bit of shallow sea bottom like the Petén, but basaltic deep ocean floor thrust into the daylight. Flying over southern Darién, it's not always clear where the Gulf of Panama ends and the land begins. Richard Weyl, a German geologist who studied Central America from the 1950s to the 1980s, observed of central Darién: "The valley floor divide between the river systems of the Río Bayano and Río Chucunaque is so flat that it cannot be seen from the air, and the inhabitants of the country cross it in their boats."

Plateaus and Sierras

Central America's highlands are safer than its lowlands, free of hurricanes and malaria. Their subtropical climate is as close to perfect as anywhere on earth. Yet they are mostly too steep and rugged for more than marginal occupation. It took the conquistadors a long time to reach them, and they remained difficult of access. "For five long hours," John Lloyd Stephens wrote of his 1839 ascent from Caribbean coast to Guatemalan Plateau, "we were dragged through mudholes, squeezed in gullies, knocked against trees, and tumbled over roots; every step required care and great physical exertion." And that was just the beginning.

Modern transportation masks this ruggedness somewhat. The Chiapas plateau's limestone strata accumulated over 400 million years—most of the Paleozoic and Mesozoic eras—but the steepness of its slopes seemed unreal from a bus in 1971, and when I reached the relatively level top, I forgot how high I was. I retained no memory at all of Central America's highest plateau, the Altos Cuchumatanes, which I skirted after leaving Chiapas for Guatemala. When I returned in 1995, it seemed incredible that I could have forgotten that rock wall looming overhead. It is a cliché to liken mountains to walls, but the Cuchumatanes really do look like walls. Their escarpment is straight, almost perpendicular, with jagged peaks on the tops like the broken bottles that line the walls of Huehuetenango, the city at their foot. "We must imagine the Cuchumatanes as a gigantic, uplifted block," wrote Richard Weyl, and it takes little effort to do so.

The Cuchumatanes' top is a huge tableland whose Mam Maya inhabitants are little more influenced from outside today than when an Englishman named Thomas Gage crossed in the 1600s, staying at villages and finding "the poor Indians willing to give me whatsoever I demanded." It seems as close to a lost world as exists today, and I had a craving to see it, like John Lloyd Stephens with his Maya city. Even in 1995 there were no towns on the plateau, however, and the only bus service was to the valleys on the other side. A theater of the 1980s guerrilla war, it still wasn't a good place to wander alone, but I was lucky. When I went to the office of a rural development organization, Proyecto Cuchumatanes, and expressed my interest, Director Pedro Guzmán Mérida invited me to join his next trip to the top.

Dr. Guzmán's four-wheel-drive took an hour to switchback up the dirt road from Huehuetenango's 1,700 meters to the plateau's 3,500. First we passed through a brush-covered belt of red and green serpentine rocks, the source of pre-Columbian jade as well as the gold and silver the Spanish coveted. Such riches are long gone, but little mines have been opened beside the road, dug to quarry gravel from limestone strata above the serpentine, the bed of a two-hundred-million-year-old sea. Guzmán, who had a veterinary degree from U. C. Davis but was interested in everything, said he'd found coral fossils in the greenish-white stone. The limestone is fertile, and the steep roadside was solidly planted with maize, although the air grew chill as we got higher. "The people here have varieties of maize for every microclimate, over a hundred of them," Guzmán said. "It grows right to the top of the plateau, then it stops. They can't grow anything on the top except crops like potatoes."

We crested the rim, and entered a grassy valley lined with gentle limestone hills. It did seem a lost world, the air and light somehow older, mellower than below. A dense scrub of agaves, junipers, and cypresses covered the hills, reminiscent of northwest Mexico a thousand kilometers away. We drove past tile-roofed cottages and potato patches, then entered a winding rocky defile where Mam Maya shepherdesses in black and red tended little black and white flocks or reclined on the greensward as in a Claude Lorraine alpine pastorale. An old man, also handsomely dressed in red and black, led two small and bony but pretty horses beside the road. He waved, and came to the window.

"Give me a quetzal, *Tat*," he said. (The quetzal is the Guatemalan currency unit.) I gave him the coins I had in my pocket, and he looked at them disapprovingly as Dr. Guzmán drove on.

"What does '*Tat*' mean?"

"It's a Mam term of respect. It means 'father' literally."

Above the defile we entered an even older world, where the lower valleys' tile roofs and plastic trash disappeared, and Mam homesteads were built of rough-hewn planks. Women sat outside some, weaving on hand looms. Others looked deserted, and Guzmán said the owners were away in the Pacific lowlands, doing seasonal work on export farms. "The people here may have lived a migratory life even before the Spanish came," he said, "going back and forth between the mountains and the coast." He showed me where the Guatemalan army had cut roadside woodland to stop guerrillas from ambushing convoys. The trees were growing back vigorously, forming a thick scrub. We passed a concrete foundation, all that remained of a North American missionary's house burned in the 1980s. Near it, an old Mam man appeared who might have been the brother of the one who'd asked for a quetzal. This man, who carried an axe and wore a tweed jacket over his red and black tribal costume, was friendlier than the first, and didn't ask for money. He shook hands ceremoniously, and questioned us diplomatically as to what we were doing there. He didn't call us "*Tat.*"

A jeep trail led to a craggy ridge which Guzmán said was the highest point in the Cuchumatanes, about 3,700 meters. From it, an endless tangle of blue mountains extended to the eastern and southern horizons. Kestrels and red-tailed hawks swooped past, but to see the black vultures that always seem overhead in Central America, I had to look far down into the Huchuetenango Valley.

Some of the mountains I saw from that vantage were jagged sawtooth ridgelines, bedrock thrust up endwise by fault line pressures instead of plateau walls. The Sierra de las Minas above the Motagua Valley is a classic example (sierra means "saw"). It is largely marble, limestone hardened by heat and pressure, and such metamorphic rocks predominate south of central Guatemala. With greater resistance to tropical rains than sedimentary ones, they can have extraordinary peaks. Honduras's north coast has some of the most spectacular summits I've seen, particularly where Pico Bonito rises to 2,435 meters. Forested to the top, it seldom has been climbed because the only trails on most of it are those made by tapirs. From the Bonito River below it, waterfalls many meters high appear as silver threads, and the landscape is an archetype of tropical splendor. The river boulders are the deep red color of which only metamorphic rocks seem capable, and they glow under the blue peak. When I was there, in February, the gallery forest was rose and gold with new growth, parakeet flocks flashed iridescent emerald in shafts of sunlight, and a rainbow hovered against bruise-colored clouds.

Similar ranges run southward through Honduras to the Sierra Isabellia of northern Nicaragua, where 1,990-meter Cerro Saslaya is that country's highest peak. Because of heavy forest cover and almost continuous guerrilla warfare since the Spanish chased the Matagalpa tribe into them after the Conquest, Nicaragua's cordilleras are probably the least explored in Central America. Nobody I talked to had set foot in their remoter parts when I was there in 1993. "I've flown over" was the refrain. They're not that high as mountains go, however, and they vanish into the Nicaraguan Depression.

One might expect southern Central America's mountains to be like Nicaragua's—impressive enough for their jungled wildness, but not as dizzying as Guatemala's continental massifs. A land under the ocean until recent geological times would logically have a certain inconsequence. Yet a wall as impressive as Guatemala's ancient plateaus rises at the south end Costa Rica's Valle Central—the Talamancas, a granitic mass which has attained its present elevation within the past three million years. A conquistador named Perferan de Rivera who crossed it in 1572 is said to have done so on the backs of Indian porters, too cold and exhausted to move. His expedition returned to civilization presenting what Benzoni called "a sad but curious spectacle . . . for their clothes had rotted on their bodies."

The Talamancas' highest peaks lie around 3,819-meter Cerro Chirripó east of the town of San Isidro El General. Rimmed by foothills, Chirripó lacks the overbearing immediacy of the Cuchumatanes or Pico Bonito, but its distant, rectangular summits seem mystically remote from San Isidro, like jungle fantasy mountains. It takes an afternoon on narrow dirt roads to drive to their base, and a day to climb to the alpine zone on a trail that ascends over 2,000 meters in fourteen kilometers. I heeded Rivera's plight when I was there in 1995, and hired a local man named Cristobal to carry my backpack as far as the National Park Service shelter at 3,500 feet. It seemed a good way to celebrate my fiftieth birthday. The men of San Gerardo de Rivas at the mountain's foot don't only work as porters, they race up for fun. Cristobal got me up at 4 a.m to start the climb, and gave me a glass of sweet tea at his house. The lower part of the trail is called *el gymnasio*, and although it was still dark, my glasses fogged so in the humid air that I might have been climbing in a shower room.

"*Es duro*," Cristobal said encouragingly. I stopped trying to keep up with him and his teenage son, and met them coming down when I was still approaching the shelter around eleven. A chill, driving rain was falling by then, and I was glad I'd been self-indulgent. A young couple equipped with new backpacks and Spandex clothes reached the shelter two hours later, when it was raining even harder. They crawled into their fiberfill sleeping bags, muttering about hypothermia, and the next morning turned around and climbed right back down.

Southern Central America's surprising heights dwindle as suddenly as they appear, however. Granite peaks continue along the Talamanca crest as far as the Panamanian border, but elevation drops to about 2,000 meters in the western Panama cordillera. Impressive heights remain visible west of Panama City, but east of the canal the sense of mountains piled on mountains that prevails in most of the land bridge ends. Darién has only narrow *serranias* along the Caribbean and the Gulf of Panama. On the Colombian border, the Tacarcuna and Pire highlands rise to around 1,000 meters, but on the other side the swampy Chocó Basin extends to the Andes' northern foothills.

Caves

The land bridge's complications aren't only aboveground. In one of the Altos Cuchumatanes' little valleys, Dr. Guzmán showed me an opening among some boulders at the roadside. It didn't look like much, a grassy pit, but when I dropped a stone we could hear it echoing down a long way. Caves open throughout "karst" landscapes like the Cuchumatanes, carved by groundwater dissolving the soft limestone. Subterranean rivers flow through them, rising to the surface in places, then descending again. As far as I know, the Cuchumatanes' caves are unexplored.

The largest known Central American caves are in Belize's Maya Mountains, which I first glimpsed in 1971, when a blue escarpment loomed south of the jaguar-haunted savanna that the Guatemalan students who gave me a ride from Tikal found so exciting.

This also had excited them. "The Maya Mountains!" they cried. "Nobody knows what lives up there!" A mass of granitic rock which has thrust 1,000 meters above southwestern Belize, the mountains may be a continuation of the highlands farther west, although their geology is not well understood. As they rose above the plain, they lifted limestone strata into which groundwater carved spectacular passages. The Chiqui-bul Plateau just west of the mountains conceals a vast underground system that includes the largest known cavern chamber in the western hemisphere, but cave formations are common almost everywhere around them.

Typical of these is a place called Blue Hole at the east edge of the Mayas, where a cave river rises in a cliff-ringed pool, runs aboveground for a few meters, then dives back into a low limestone portal. When I was there in 1994, cichlids swam in the sunny shallows, and big mountain mullet lurked in the depths. The fish struck at thrown fruit, but fled into the darkness when I approached the water. A park ranger told me the river surfaced again downstream in a much bigger hole frequented by tarpon and snappers that swim up from offshore springs where it flows into the Caribbean.

A half mile from Blue Hole, the same river is accessible by a cave which yawns on the side of a forested hill, Herman's Cave. Big tooth- and claw-shaped stalactites hang from its portal, and rough-winged swallows and large bats fluttered among these as I entered. Their twittering combined with the drone of cicadas in huge overhanging trees to sepulchral effect, as though I was at the mouth of Xibalba, the Maya underworld. In fact, the Classic Maya had cut steps down into its mouth. They led me past slippery boulders, then became a faint, sandy trail into utter darkness from which came the sound of running water. By the time I reached the river, the last faint light from the entrance had disappeared, and I could hear only water. Nothing moved as I shined my flashlight along the bank and in the water. When I turned it on the distant ceiling, I saw what looked like thousands of tiny eyes, but they were only reflecting water droplets. The cave seemed lifeless, and when I turned off the light, I began to wonder if *I* was alive.

Stories of bizarre cave fish, salamanders, and insects always have attracted me, and I was disappointed at the relative lifelessness inside Herman's Cave. Yet I did find a cave that crawled with life. Limestone caves aren't confined to northern plateaus—the scraped-up seafloor of southern Central America has them too, mainly in coastal lowlands and offshore islands. This cave, known simply as La Gruta, is a tunnel a few hundred meters long in the coral rock of Panama's Isla Colón, where a stream has cut through a hillock. A Panamanian I met there named

Appolonio told me it is a religious site for local people, who had planted flowers and placed statues of the Virgin Mary at the downstream entrance. When a first statue was erected, Appolonio said, the real Virgin had made an appearance, so a second one commemorated that event.

La Gruta's entrance yawns jaggedly like Herman's Cave's, but seems gentler. Ferns grow around it instead of giant tree roots, and the stalactites on the upper portal look more like elongated breasts than teeth and claws. Inside, translucent, ivory colored stalactites and stalagmites form vaulted chambers above the stream bed. Other Central American caves had grown quieter as I entered, but this one got noisier. Energetic "*treet, treet, treet*" calls filled the darkness, made by big, spindly beige crickets which occupied every square meter of the pockmarked ceiling. They waved their antennae and sang by rubbing tiny vestigial wings together. One was eating a moth. Scattered among them were whip scorpions, large arachnids that resemble a cross between a scorpion and a tarantula, and big, black millipedes. All this creeping and crawling might have been unnerving, but the crickets' song gave the cave an incongruous cheeriness, like a shady woods on a summer's day.

A muffled roar came from a dark corner, and I turned my flashlight to where the ceiling rose in a conical chimney. Dozens of bats flew around in this: the roar was the reverberation of their wingbeats from stalactites so thin they rang when struck. Most of the bats were so small that they looked mothlike in my flashlight beam, but a few were much larger—vampires, Appolonio said. Perturbed squeaking came from the circling throng, so I turned the light away, and they settled back into their roost. Farther in, the cave took a bend. As the light from the downstream entrance disappeared, a dim glow from the upstream one touched the walls. Small reddish brown bats with the long snouts and large eyes of nectar feeders seemed unbothered by my flashlight, peering down at me from the ceiling and occasionally yawning. The chamber turned again, and the upstream entrance came into sight. Another vampire colony fluttered and squeaked there, and the volume of cricket song, which had dwindled in the darkness of the interior, increased again.

It seemed strange that this little cave had so much more life than the big Belizean one. Even the entrance of Herman's Cave had fewer bats, and I'd seen no crickets or whip scorpions. Air currents moving between the two entrances of La Gruta probably carry a more reliable supply of cricket and whip scorpion food than at the larger cave's single entrance. Yet the crickets at La Gruta seemed specialized for cave life, pale and flightless, and I wondered how they'd colonized such a small, apparently isolated one. There may have been other caves nearby, but I didn't hear of any. Similarities between cave organisms in widely separated places have led biologists to suspect that cave networks may extend surprisingly far through limestone terrain. Perhaps the La Gruta crickets arrived through such an underground pathway.

Volcanoes

Volcanoes ultimately express the ambiguities that bless and curse the land bridge: rich coasts and hurricanes, sheltered valleys and earthquakes. Except for the earthquakes, they make its biggest surprises. Huge cinder cones accumulate in a few generations or blast into nothingness too quickly for flight, and ash deposits from such explosions blanket about 400,000 square kilometers, reaching far out into the Pacific. Fertile with erupted minerals, volcanic soils have supported rich civilizations for over three millennia, but cones provoke an endemic anxiety which seventeenth-century Englishman Thomas Gage expressed in describing two of them, Agua and Fuego: "That of water hanging on the south side, almost perpendicularly over the city; the other of fire standing lower. . . . That of water . . . yields a goodly prospect to the sight, being almost all the year green . . . but the other . . . is unpleasing and more dreadful to behold. . . . Thus is Guatemala seated in the midst of a paradise on one side and a hell on the other."

Central America's highest mountain, 4,220-meter Tajumulco volcano, looms directly east of the high Cuchumatanes, and the two awesome heights form a kind of demon portal for the Pan-American Highway. I passed through this obliviously in 1971, but encountered the active volcanic zone a little farther south, at Lake Atitlán, where an ancient cone has collapsed to form a caldera ringed with basalt cliffs and younger cones. One of my hitchhiking rides called it "the most beautiful place in the world," and it was certainly spectacular, but the thing that struck me about Atitlán was an apparent discrepancy of scale. To my unaccustomed eye, its cones looked more like the rear-projected backgrounds of movies than real mountains. They seemed too high to believe.

Volcanic disasters have been horribly real, however. One of Atitlán's cones exploded ten times in the nineteenth century, and "unpleasing" Volcán Fuego has erupted fifty times since 1524. Girolamo Benzoni described how a landslide and flood from Volcán Agua, the *less* threatening cone Thomas Gage mentioned, destroyed Guatemala's first capital in 1541. "Soon after midnight there began to arise from that mountain so great and so terrible a quantity of water, and with such an impetus and fury, as to precipitate rocks of incredible size, carrying along and destroying whatever it met with in its course; and there were heard in the air cries and lamentations and frightful noises." A dose of riding rickety, overcrowded buses around the highlands, and the sense of ever-impending disaster that conveyed, cured my initial incredulity about Guatemalan volcanoes. Perhaps because the country around them is so high and steep, they never seemed safely distant as they might have, however deceptively, on a lowland plain. It seemed they might slide downhill anytime, as they have in the past.

Guatemala's volcanoes are the highest in Central America because they stand on a twenty-million-year-old plateau accumulated as eruptions spewed lava and ash 2,000 meters deep over 10,000 square kilometers. The plateau also covers western Honduras and eastern El Salvador, and I got a sense of its massiveness where it looms above the breezy Salvadoran town of Metapán. Because it isn't near an active fault, Metapán gets fewer earthquakes than most Central American towns, so it has some of the oldest churches. This makes it seem anachronistic, which is typical of the volcanic plateau, a region that remains remote although the Spanish settled it in the early 1500s. With black vultures on its slaughterhouse roof and bats emerging from downtown eaves at dusk, Metapán probably was much the same in 1993 as in 1893.

The peak that marks the plateau's south edge, 2,418-meter Montecristo, has some of El Salvador's last virgin forest and was one of its two functioning national parks when I was there, but getting up it wasn't easy. First I had to walk five kilometers from town to the park entrance because there was no other transportation. Even walking wasn't encouraged, since it had been a guerrilla zone during the recent civil war. When I got to the entrance, I found another reason why walking *to* the park wasn't encouraged. My permit had a provision I'd overlooked: *"No se permiten caminatas dentro del parque"*—no walking *in* the park. I had to wait until a vehicle would pick me up. Luckily, some meteorologists soon came along on their way to examine a weather station abandoned since the war's beginning, and I got a spine-jarring ride in the back of their pickup with the ranger assigned to accompany them. He had worked in the park before the guerrillas took it over, then had returned, but wasn't happy about the situation. Poaching was common because the staff didn't have the equipment to stop it. The local police poached. When I asked why I couldn't walk in the park, he said it was because of the danger of assault.

As the truck banged up increasingly steep switchbacks of red and white volcanic dust and mud, I was glad I hadn't walked. I'd never have made it in a day. The trees at the top had seemed close from Metapán, but Metapán didn't look at all close from the plateau slopes, in fact, it soon disappeared. Above about 2,000 meters, we were climbing in the clouds. Four kilometers from the station the road got too muddy even for a four-wheel-drive, and we walked the rest of the way through huge, epiphyte-covered trees. Birds I'd never seen before flew among them: bushy-crested jays, dark blue like North American Steller's jays, but bigger, with yellow eyes. They made squeaky, murmuring sounds, stealthily feeding on grubs in the branches. The station was in a steep pasture, but the clouds obscured everything more than a few meters away, so I didn't see the plateau top at all on that trip.

In the rest of northern Central America, volcanoes rise above lower lands, like central El Salvador's Valle de las Hammacas. One cinder cone there, 1,870-meter Izalco, has grown from a cornfield in the last two centuries. A local clergyman told John Lloyd Stephens it had been "a small orifice . . . puffing out . . . pebbles," in 1798. By 1840, it was so high that the fire of its eruptions were visible from far out to sea, a growth that excited Stephens to a semierotic enthusiasm. "The sight was fearfully grand," he wrote. "The crater had three orifices . . . and after a report, deep in the huge throat of the third appeared a light blue vapor and then a mass of thick black smoke, whirling and struggling out in enormous wreaths, and rising in a dark, majestic column, lighted for a moment by a sheet of flame." Izalco kept this up almost continuously until 1957, when entrepreneurs who shared Stephens's enthusiasm built a hotel with bedrooms overlooking it. Then it stopped, although when I saw it in 1993 it remained bare of trees, a gargantuan slag heap above the fields.

Salvador's volcanic past has been even more active. Like Guatemala's Atitlán, its Lake Ilopango is an ancient caldera whose explosion about 1,800 years ago destroyed an area 3,000 kilometers square and expelled the region's population for centuries. Thick layers of pumice called "*tierra blanca*" cover ruins from that period. A later explosion created a miniature Pompeii at a place called Ceren, entombing a clay-walled farmstead which yielded traces of a flock of domestic ducks and a Maya book. Ilopango remains active, periodically extruding domes that could explode, and more Cerens undoubtedly lie in El Salvador's future. Surrounded by live volcanoes and built on volcanic calderas, its towns made me feel not just under volcanoes, as in Guatemala, but *in* them.

The active zone changes in Nicaragua. Volcanoes there rise from the Depression's level floor and thus seem preternaturally high. When I drove north from Managua one morning in 1993 with Jacinto Cedeño of the Nicaraguan National Park Service, I had to crane my neck to see their tops through his pickup's windshield. Each cone or cluster of cones stood isolated, gargantuan, like a receding file of Goya colossi. One would loom over the horizon, stand obdurately for awhile, then disappear, replaced by another.

Cedeño had invited me along while he did some park business near Cosigüina, the northernmost Nicaraguan volcano, which is also Nicaragua's first nature reserve, established by the Somoza government in the 1950s. Cosigüina is unimpressive now, low and tree-covered, only 870 meters high. In 1836, it stood at almost 3,000 meters when it exploded with the biggest bang in Central American history, which, John Lloyd Stephens wrote, "startled the people of Guatemala four hundred miles off." Just hearing about the explosion excited Stephens to an apocalyptic vision: "The cone of the volcano was gone . . . a mountain and field of lava ran down to the sea; a forest as old as creation had entirely disappeared, and two islands were formed in the sea; shoals were discovered in one of which a large tree was fixed upside down; one river was completely choked up, and another formed, running in an opposite direction . . . wild beasts, howling, left their caves in the mountains, and ounces, leopards, and snakes fled for shelter to the abodes of men."

The country around Cosigüina still looked disaster-stricken. The only modern homesteads were big export *fincas*, apparently abandoned, their fields overgrown with orange sunflowers. Everybody else seemed to live in palm-thatched huts dotted about the savanna. Cedeño, a portly, patient man, said it was "*tierra maliosa*." The people were withdrawn, distrustful. He'd come to dispute with a *finca* heir who'd returned from living in England during the Contra War, and wanted some forest land from the government. They argued a long time, standing outside a tumbledown worker's barracks, while orange-chinned parakeets and ladder-backed woodpeckers squabbled in the trees above them.

"*La lucha para la tierra*," Cedeño sighed, getting back in the truck. The struggle for the land. We drove south again to the beachfront resort of Jiquilillo. I was scouting locations for an ecotourism guidebook, but a *maremoto*, a tsunami, had swept through the resort the year before, and it looked like it. The wave had buried the asphalt beachfront road in a sandbar and stranded houses out in the surf. "This used to be a very popular place," Cedeño said. "Lots of people came out from Managua for the weekend." Smoke billowed from Volcán San Cristobal, the next peak south of Cosigüina, as we continued south toward Managua. A perfect 1,780-meter cone, Cristobal is Nicaragua's highest, and its cap had shone white as snow when we'd driven past it in the morning, but that had been only the mist and smoke that usually hangs there. It glowed red in the twilight. When we stopped for gas in León, the station attendant told us there had been an earthquake about an hour earlier, just about when we were driving along the devastated Jiquilillo beach. It had been a deep one out at sea, probably the kind that had caused the previous year's tsunami, but we hadn't felt a thing.

Perhaps the most awesome Nicaraguan volcano is the twin one of Concepción and Maderas in Lake Nicaragua. The lake can be as rough and dark as the sea, and the two cones, Maderas black with forest, Concepción gray with cinders, appear fantastically high from its surface. Their scale seems incongruous with the historical world of towns and ferryboats, as though the backdrop for a Jurassic diorama of plesiosaurs and ichthyosaurs has fallen over the horizon by mistake. All I saw in the way of dinosaur relatives while crossing to Omotepe was a flock of cormorants, but they looked antediluvian enough beneath the cones.

"The lake is too large to be called beautiful," wrote Thomas Belt, "and its large extent and the mere glimpses of its limits and cloud-capped peaks appeal to the imagination rather than to the eye."

Concepción and Maderas are visible from far to the south in Costa Rica, where their starkness looks even stranger. Southern Central America's volcanic zone, where new oceanic land replaces old continental land, is very different from the north's. Indeed, volcanoes change so quickly below the Costa Rican border that they seem to have a kind of national identity. Compared to Guatemala's lowering cones and Nicaragua's looming ones, Costa Rica's seem amorphous, almost understated, although there is one remarkable exception. The huge cone of Arenal in north central Costa Rica exploded so violently in 1968 that cannonading boulders covered twelve square kilometers with impact craters, and glowing clouds filled the sky. The eruption killed seventy-eight people, and lesser eruptions continued through the early 1970s. When I was in the adjacent Cordillera de Tilaran in the late 1980s, Arenal's occasional rumbles shook the ground like sonic booms.

More typically Costa Rican is Volcán Rincón de la Vieja northwest of Arenal. It looks impressively volcanic from the Guanacaste coastal plain, and has ejected jets of ash as recently as the 1950s and 1960s. When I camped at Rincón's foot in 1990, however, the cone seemed to fade into the dense forest that covered its lower slopes, and trees even obscured the fumaroles and other infernal devices that welled up at the base. Living gumbo limbos grew over mudpots that periodically flung boiling glop four meters in the air, and strangler figs enclosed fissures that steamed sulfur like a mineral bath.

The big volcanoes of Costa Rica's Cordillera Central—Poás, Irazu, Turrialba—seem even more cryptic, clumped together in cordilleras so massive that the active craters are obscured. It's not that they aren't dangerous. Volcán Poás near San José expelled an 8,000-meter smoke plume which blanketed most of the Valle Central with ash in 1910, and did similar things in 1952, 1974, and 1978. When I was there in 1990, the farms around it had been declared a disaster area because of poisonous fumes and acid rain. Poás has the potential to become as explosive as Cosigüina. Yet my first sight of its active crater was anticlimactic. One moment, I was walking through a gently sloping meadow of ragwort and blueberry bushes, the next I was standing before what might have been an open-pit sulfur mine dug out of the forested ridge. There were great heaps of yellow ash and steaming green lakes, but less sense that this was an opening to internal fires than in Nicaragua.

Inactive craters seem mere lakes buried in elfin forest, and their cones may be hard to recognize as volcanoes, they are so heavily covered with clouds and plants. At an extinct cone called Volcán Cacao in northwest Costa Rica, I embarrassed myself by referring to some "sandstone" outcrops when talking to a geologist. The brown, granular stone of the outcrops was volcanic ash, of course, not sedimentary sandstone, but in the damp forest it was hard to remember that the mountain had once been smoking and barren. Much of Cacao never has been mapped because continual cloud cover prevents aerial photographs.

I'm not the only one who has been fooled by Costa Rican vulcanism. Early geologist Miguel Obregon thought he'd found an active volcano at a hill called Barra Honda on the Pacific coast's Nicoya Peninsula because vertical holes on the top issued sulfurous fumes and rumblings. In 1937, ornithologist Alexander Skutch recognized the holes as "sinkholes, such as one finds in many calcareous formations, rather than volcanic vents," but also described inexplicable volcanolike features. "From this cavern issued a gas with an unpleasant odor, which was neither that of hydrogen sulphide nor that of sulphur dioxide. From the depths of the cavity came a continuous fine, shrill whistle, as of gas escaping under pressure from a narrow orifice." Skutch's guide told him that the gas came out of one vent "with sufficient volume and force to sway the boughs of trees." Skutch speculated that roosting bats in the limestone caves might be causing the noises and smells, but couldn't think of any reason why "so much gas issued from them." A cave explorer told me that the gases might in fact have come from thermal vents under the limestone, but when I visited Barra Honda in 1990, I found neither smells, noises, gas, or bats, only a juvenile mottled owl teetering on a branch above one cave's mouth.

The final surprise of Central America's active volcanoes is that they suddenly stop. No active volcanoes occur south of Volcán Irazu in central Costa Rica, and even inactive ones disappear from the Talamanca mountains. There are volcanoes in western Panama, but they are inactive. The southernmost, El Valle, last erupted about 40,000 years ago. The most impressive is Volcán Barú, a peak which, although quiescent, seems a kind of sum of Central American volcanoes. Like Guatemalan and Salvadoran volcanoes, Barú looms over a plateau broken by deep gorges—the gorge of the Río Caldera just east of it is one of the most dizzying I've seen. Like Nicaraguan volcanoes, Barú is isolated and brooding, its summit often capped by cloud. Like Costa Rican ones, it lacks a classic cone shape, and might seem nonvolcanic if it didn't have seven craters at its top and hot springs at its bottom.

Like all the others, Barú has attracted a large human population with its fertile ash. I met a Guaymi man in the Caldera Gorge who was staring up at the cliffs, which are fluted with basalt blocks so regularly shaped they might have been hand-carved. When asked what he was looking at, he said he was thinking how to grow vegetables up there.

3

Pirates and Engineers

CENTRAL AMERICA'S ruggedness and evanescent wealth did not dispel Western civilization's desire for a passage to India. If Central America was not India, it was still the narrowest land lying in the way. A disappointing destination, it became a fascinating obstacle, and Spaniards started talking about building a canal across it as soon as they realized there was no strait. A kinsman of Cortés raised the notion, and a priest, Francisco Lopez de Gomara, named likely locations: the Isthmus of Panama, the Nicaraguan Depression, and the Isthmus of Tehuantepec. "There are mountains," he wrote, "but there are also hands, and for the King of Castille, few things are impossible." Another priest was less sanguine. José de Acosta, a Jesuit who crossed the Panama isthmus in 1570, observed that the trip's eighteen leagues were "more painful and changeable than 2,300 by sea."

"I believe there is no human power able to break down those strong and impenetrable mountains which God placed between the seas," Acosta wrote. "And though it were possible for men, in my opinion they should fear punishment from heaven in seeking to correct the works which the Creator in his providence has ordained."

Later centuries showed that many things were impossible for the King of Castille, as competitors grabbed at Spain's locked-up colonies.

Prominent among them were enterprising seafarers who tried to use Central America as a passage to the Pacific, including admirals like Francis Drake and Horatio Nelson, as well as freebooters like Henry Morgan. Another Englishman, the William Dampier I mentioned earlier who got lost on the Tehuantepec coast, vividly described Central America from the buccaneer's viewpoint in the late 1600s. Dampier drifted into piracy while engaged in the logwood trade (a small tree used for making dye) in Mexico's Bay of Campeche. His crew deserted en masse in 1679 to raid Panama supposing," as he wrote, "that the South Sea shore is nothing but gold and silver." After some hesitation, Dampier joined them on an odyssey of rapine that he described with peculiar clarity.

The 400-man expedition first sacked Portobello on Panama's Caribbean, then crossed the isthmus in nine days, "carrying with us such provisions as were necessary, and toys wherewith to gratifie the Wild Indians," and did the same to Santa Maria on the Pacific. There they climbed into "such canoas and periagos as our Indian friends furnished us," and marauded their way down South America as far as Chile. Eventually, most were killed attacking a Peruvian town, and Dampier turned back and recrossed the isthmus in 1681. This was much harder than the first crossing because they had to go the long way around, through the Atrato River valley in the Chocó. "We gave out that if any man faltered in the journey over the Land he must expect to be shot to death, for we knew that the Spaniards would soon be after us, and one man falling into their hands might be the ruin of us all." The party of forty-four pirates, three Indians, and an unspecified number of slaves took twenty-three days to cross, "in which time by my account we traveled 110 miles, crossing some very high mountains, but our common march was in the Valleys among deep and dangerous rivers."

They forded one river thirty times in a day. "Not a man of us but wisht the journey at an end, our feet being blistered and our thighs stript from wading so many rivers." When a man carrying "300 Dollars" of loot drowned, the stragglers who found his body were too weak to take the money. The pirates lived on "macaw berries," stolen plantains, and peccary meat bought from the Indians. They were afraid to sleep at night, "otherwise our own slaves might have knockt us on the head." Dampier doubted they would have survived without the Indians' help, but even that was problematic, since some of the Darién Indians were "very dreadful. . . . They use trunks about eight foot long, out of which they blow poysoned darts, and are so silent in their attacks on their enemies, and retreat so nimbly again, that the Spaniards can never find them."

Dampier relearned the conquistadors' lesson: Stay out of the Caribbean lowlands. The next time he went pirating, he sailed around South America rather than walk across Panama again. Two centuries after him, the passage to India remained a dream, and it wasn't getting any easier to cross the isthmus without a canal. "For no consideration come this route," wrote a Massachusetts man in 1849. "I utter the united sentiment of every passenger who I have heard speak." Two years later, a California-bound detachment of U.S. infantry lost 150 men, women, and children to disease during the Panama crossing. "The horrors of this road in the rainy season are beyond description," wrote the officer in charge, Ulysses S. Grant.

One Panama expedition relived the miseries of sixteenth-century Veragua. In 1854, U.S. Navy Lieutenant Isaac Strain led twenty-seven men into the forest at the same point on the Caribbean where Balboa had begun his 1513 crossing. Edward Cullen, an Irish physician and geographer, claimed to have located a 150-foot-high pass through the Darién mountains, and Strain was ordered to investigate. Cullen said he'd crossed the isthmus in a few days, so Strain carried limited rations, but it took him six weeks to reach the Pacific, and when he did, he wore a Panama hat, one boot, and a blue flannel shirt, and weighed seventy-five pounds. Most of his men took over two months, and five died from starvation and exhaustion. The Americans didn't descend to cannibalism like their conquistador antecedents, but gave it serious thought.

The pass through the mountains was a lie: Strain couldn't even find Cullen's supposed path. Kuna Indians burned their houses and disappeared into the forest at the expedition's approach, and attempts to get their guidance failed. A later Navy expedition wrote of the Kuna, "They believe that God made the country as it is, and that he would be angry with them and kill them if they assisted in any work constructed by the white man." Strain was hopelessly lost in a week, and then made the fatal mistake of trying to follow a river to the Pacific. The river was the Chucunaque, which was only about thirty kilometers north of the Pacific where he encountered it, but which runs east *parallel* to the coast for most of its length. Strain and his men struggled along the river week after week, growing more and more exhausted. They built rafts, but they sank or were lost in rapids. They could find no food except birds and palm fruits that burned their stomachs and corroded their teeth. Toward the end, they were eating toads and vultures. Mosquitoes, black flies, and botflies tortured them.

Eventually, Strain had to leave most of his men behind while he went for help. When he returned with a rescue party, the men had given up and were trying to return to the Caribbean. Two more died on the way home, and Strain died three years later at age thirty-six. As David McCullough wrote in his Panama Canal history, *The Path Between the Seas*, the Strain expedition "left the Navy with a profound respect for the terrors of tropical wilderness." Contemporary historian Hubert Howe Bancroft described the isthmus as an outdoor mortuary: "The trees are concealed by the dense masses of vine which . . . in certain lights present plays of light comparable only to the richest velvet. . . . But like the plumes and velvet of the funeral pageant, they serve but to conceal and adorn corruption. Behind them stretches, far away, the pestiferous swamp."

Cerro Pirre

Crossing Darién along the Atrato or Chucunaque today could be as difficult and dangerous as in Dampier's or Strain's time. Its malignant historical reputation remains justified to some extent: it's the nearest thing left in Central America to the "green hell" that swallowed Strain and company. Even a short hike there brings a sense of envelopment, especially in what remains of the primary forest, under the sixty-meter canopy of hundreds of tree species so festooned with epiphytes and lianas as to be sometimes indistinguishable as separate organisms. The forest itself is not particularly dangerous to anyone who is adequately equipped and guided, but real malignancies lurk. Darién is the only Central American region where yellow fever and drug-resistant *falciparum* malaria occur; their carrier mosquitoes breed in water that accumulates everywhere in the rainy season. Colombian guerrillas control the hinterland, and have a reputation for murdering travelers and kidnapping local people for slave labor.

As I sat in a Panama City restaurant the night before a 1993 trip to Darién National Park, the TV news blared "*Secuestro!*" and showed long helicopter shots of treetops stretching to the horizon. Guerrillas had kidnapped three North American missionaries and disappeared into the forest with them. I was afraid my plane to the town of El Real near the park would be canceled. It wasn't, although it was the last to go to El Real for a while.

The flight east along the Gulf of Panama coast next morning passed over little forest at first, but not much sign of humanity either, just the opaque gulf with its drift lines and clots of pinkish foam, and great expanses of mangroves, mud flats, and wet savannas. Forest increased farther east, mostly second growth, but with big trees on hills. Low mountains appeared in the distance. The plane circled a brown estuary and came down over a few blocks of houses in scrubby pastures—the ancient town of El Real, founded by the Spanish in the sixteenth century. It crawled with helicopters and heavily armed police, but I left that behind after walking the eleven kilometers to Cerro Pirre Station in the park. Most of the wavering track ran through jungly second growth, but the primary forest sprang up as the land rose toward the Cerro Pirre Serrania. The canopy closed overhead, and fast-flowing streams laced the foothills.

The rain forest was so tall that it hardly seemed like a climb as I walked up the low escarpment. It was like being in a tunnel, where uphill can be indistinguishable from downhill. Although I caught glimpses of summits above and the plain below, there was little sense of elevation. The land's very lowness neutralized the hills, the opposite of the Guatemalan plateaus, where level tops masked height. It was rain forest in depth, literally. During the rainy season, the path to the station would have been flooded so deep I'd have had to take a boat.

Giant almendros, espavels, and scarlet-blossomed rosa de montes filtered the light, and their vaulting trunks and epiphyte-covered branches were like an intricately decorated Victorian palace, a place of opulence, and of a strange decorum. Even the weather was decorous: cool, misty mornings; hot, sunny noons; a patter of afternoon showers;

a quick twilight; and another day was gone. A few mosquitoes whined discreetly at sunset, but soon retired. Except for its lack of ruins, Cerro Pirre seemed even closer than Palenque to the rain forests as I'd imagined them before my first trip to Central America in 1971. The station was bucolic, a thatched compound staffed by two indigenous rangers, an Embera named Oliver Dogirama and a Wounnan named Dolicho Barrigon, who showed me around. They were particularly proud of the *cascada*, a place farther into the hills where water roared down a long rocky chute. At the station, they were friendly but reserved—there they turned into shouting daredevils, whizzing down the slippery rock to crash headfirst into the pool at the bottom. Aside from them—captive informants who patiently answered questions—I had the place to myself, except for a passing film crew, dislodged by the kidnapping from another station.

Still, there were reminders that I was suspended by a thread of petroleum over a fate like Isaac Strain's. Palaces and the better class of mortuaries have much in common. Tiny ticks dug under my fingernails and toenails, impossible to remove. The even tinier mites called chiggers did their work, their bites itching fiercely in the small hours, when the only sound beside my scratching was fog drip from the treetops. One day a malaria control officer arrived to distribute Mefloquine, which gives at least partial protection against the *falciparum* parasite. Oliver was used to it—he'd been living in Panama City. Dolicho came from the forest, and had never had such a substance—it made him see double. I also came to understand better why starvation was such a constant theme of Caribbean rain forest exploration. There was about as much to eat at Cerro Pirre as there would have been in Queen Victoria's palace between mealtimes. Visitors had to bring their own food, and I made do with pasta and soup mixes. Oliver and Dolicho let me sample their more substantial boiled plantains and manioc, but they weren't rolling in food either.

My Darién trip resembled more strenuous explorations in another way. Getting in was easier than getting out. My guide didn't show up on the day I was supposed to leave, and one of the rangers accompanied me to the first village outside the park, where we found him drinking beer. Much more talkative than during the walk in, the guide came the rest of the way to El Real with me. "The airport's closed," he said happily, "and the police have filled the hotel. You'll have to try to fly out of Yaviza." Yaviza is a town on the Chucunaque, at the end of the Pan-American Highway. Since the plane would leave at 7 a.m., I asked the guide if I should go there to spend the night. He grinned and drew his forefinger across his throat. *"Assesinos!"*

When we got in sight of the still-swarming police, the guide asked if I had any *armas,* because they would probably search me. They didn't, but they had indeed closed the airport and filled the hotel. I spent the night on the Park Service office floor and got up at 4 a.m. to hire a boat to make the Yaviza flight, which cost more than the plane fare. El Real was completely dark and silent as I walked to the river, which was equally dark. The darkness didn't deter the boatman from going full throttle. Dawn formed like a photo image on the emulsion as we zoomed through ranks of water hyacinths, and when we reached Yaviza the sun was blazing down full strength, drawing strong smells from the warren of mud and shacks on the bank.

I saw what the guide in El Real had meant. Yaviza seemed a town designed not simply for but *by* muggers. The unlit, unpaved main street was entirely occupied by bars, each of which was closed off from it by heavy wooden shutters. Walking on it at night would have been like being in an alley. The boatman stayed close by my side until we got to the grass airstrip, as though unsure whether his presence was protecting me, or vice versa. When I finally got on board, the tall trees around town seemed to clutch at the plane as it labored to rise. The police never found the missionaries, who emerged on their own months later.

Cutting Through

Columbus's next descendants in Central America were the nineteenth century's canal builders, who followed closely on the buccaneers and sometimes behaved like them, although they were better at getting what they wanted. Pirates never controlled more than stretches of Caribbean coast. Their attempts to penetrate farther were so ill-organized that ragtag colonial militias repulsed them promptly. Horatio Nelson's 1790 raid up the San Juan River began with 200 men and ended with twelve.

The canal builders, on the other hand, rearranged Central America's map almost as much as did the 1820 revolutions against Spain.

After 1820, when it became clear that nothing was possible for the King of Castille in Central America, the isthmus began drawing canal entrepreneurs like a magnet. Even savants who didn't go there had opinions. The German genius Alexander von Humboldt got no closer than Mexico, but wrote a long discourse advocating the Nicaraguan route under the impression that Darién's mountains were three times their actual height. Thomas Jefferson wanted to know all about it when Humboldt visited him in 1804. The implications for the expanding United States were obvious, and the 1849 California gold discovery made an isthmian passage inevitable. John Lloyd Stephens awoke from his dreams of Maya cities to become president of a trans-Panama railroad company, and Cornelius Vanderbilt steered a steamboat 119 miles up the San Juan River to open a ship and stage line across Nicaragua. William Walker and his filibusters, an evolutionary link between pirates and canal builders, grabbed the Nicaraguan route in 1856, and might have held it had the machinations of his rival Vanderbilt not driven Walker to the fatal mistakes of trying to reinstate slavery and annex Nicaragua to the southern United States.

Yet if walking across the isthmus cost lives, building things across cost more. John Lloyd Stephens's descent into a malarial coma in 1852 was one of at least six thousand deaths caused by construction of the seventy kilometer Panama Railroad from 1850 to 1855. Most of the dead were Chinese or West Indian laborers, and tropical diseases were the main killers, although many workers committed suicide. The railway company financed its hospital by shipping unclaimed corpses to medical schools in giant brine barrels. The company doctor accumulated a "museum of racial types" from their bones.

A railroad wasn't enough. Ferdinand de Lesseps's successful Suez Canal in 1870 made a canal across Panama irresistible, and de Lesseps made the first, disastrous attempt. A French diplomat with limited knowledge of technology and finances, de Lesseps was like Columbus in his gift for imposing his vision on others and his inability to distinguish vision from reality. Where Columbus had envisioned Cathay, de Lesseps saw a world saved, as David McCullough put it, "from poverty and war—through immense public improvements, networks of high-ways, railroads, and two great ship canals through the Isthmus of Suez and the Isthmus of Panama." De Lesseps proclaimed Panama "the most beautiful region in the world" when he inaugurated work in 1879, then returned to France as Jamaican laborers began clearing forest for the giant steam shovels that had dug through Suez.

The French spent a lot on health care, but workers quickly began dying of yellow fever. Apparently healthy men could die overnight, vomiting black blood, and the usual mortality rate was fifty percent. In de Lesseps's hospitals, the rate went up to seventy-five percent because the sick weren't protected from the mosquitoes which, unknown to the French doctors, carried the disease. Yellow fever survivors at least became immune. Malaria victims could suffer repeated attacks and die from ghastly complications. Cholera was another quick killer; dysentery another slow one. An average of 200 workers a month were dying by the summer of 1883. In 1885, workers were dying so fast that three or four trainloads of corpses a day ran to the cemetery.

Disease wasn't the only obstacle. An 1882 earthquake was the worst recorded in the area, and caused extensive damage. In 1885 a storm raised the Chagres River thirty feet in a few hours, collapsing part of the Panama Railway and driving thousands of tarantulas into trees protruding from the floodwater. Even normal rains caused continual mudslides on the canal walls. Isthmian geology is complex and unstable, with seventeen rock formations, six major faults, and five volcanic cores in the seventy kilometers from the Caribbean to the Pacific. At a place called the Culebra Cut, coal-bearing clay strata became as slick as soap when wet, and entire hillsides tumbled into the diggings, burying steam shovels.

In 1889, the Canal Company went bankrupt, devouring the investments of 800,000 French families. De Lesseps's failure cost 1,435,000 francs and an estimated 22,000 lives, but it didn't discourage the canal builders. One of his engineers, Phillipe Bunau-Varilla, formed a new company, and set out to sell the French ditch to the United States. He and his Washington allies edged out competition from Nicaragua canal boosters, detached Panama from its too-demanding mother country, Colombia, and set the U.S. canal in motion in 1904. It succeeded because health officer William C. Gorgas controlled the mosquito vectors of malaria and yellow fever, and because American engineers abandoned the French attempt to dig a sea-level canal as at Suez. Instead, they built a lock and dam system fed by damming the Chagres River.

Success didn't come easily. Digging the twelve-kilometer Culebra Cut took 6,000 workers six years, with hundreds pulverized by dynamite or smothered in landslides. The earth behaved strangely under pressure of the excavations. Cracks opened in the canal sides and bottom, and steam and boiling water poured out. The bottom might rise six feet in five minutes as the weight of the cut's sides pushed up soft underlying strata. A *Scientific American* article by Lieutenant David Gaillard described one landslide as "a tropical glacier—of mud instead of ice . . . stakes aligned in its moving surface and checked every twenty-four hours by triangulation showed a movement in every respect similar to stakes on moving glaciers in Alaska." Disease remained a major danger, particularly among black workers, whose housing wasn't screened. An estimated 4,500 black workers, 350 whites, and 795 others of unspecified race died building the American canal. The cost of the fifty-one-mile-long canal was $352 million, over four times the cost of building the Suez Canal, which is almost exactly twice as long.

For all their *realpolitik*, the United States canal builders still were Columbus's descendants. Their attitude toward costs was not unlike his toward the lost ships and men of his last voyage, and they also had a boundless faith in the wonders that awaited them beyond the isthmus. The only major difference was that the Americans proposed to build the wonders instead of merely discovering them. Panama Railroad official Tracy Robinson thought the canal demonstrated that the tropics had been "set apart for higher things. . . . The evolution of mankind toward a higher destiny is involved." His words echoed Hubert Howe Bancroft's of three decades earlier: "First things and first views of things set faster the beating of the heart. . . . It is the joy of development, the ecstacy of evolution." Bancroft was referring to Balboa's first view of the Pacific in 1513, but he might have been writing of the first ship to navigate the canal in 1913.

The canal certainly would have dazzled Columbus, Balboa, and the other adventurers. I can imagine their ghosts bobbing in the wake of that first 1913 ship, like the dwarved spectres of Hendrik Hudson's crew in *Rip Van Winkle*. To glide so easily out of the starving, stormy Caribbean and then, only hours later, into the gold and silver South Sea would have seemed an earthly paradise. Yet I can also imagine the spectral Columbus looking back at the Panama coast as the bow wave carried him toward China. If the dwindling strip of forested hills against which he'd dashed his hopes was not the Cathayan Province of Ciamba, then what was it?

4

Naturalists

B EFORE HIS EARLY death, John Lloyd Stephens was the most enthusiastic of canal boosters. "It will compose the distracted country
of Central America," he wrote of a Nicaraguan canal, "turn the sword,
which is now drenching it in blood, into a pruning hook; remove the
prejudices of the inhabitants by bringing them into closer connexion
with people of every nation; furnish them with a motive and a reward
for industry, and inspire them with a taste for making money, which
after all, opprobrious as it is sometimes considered, does more to civilize
and keep the world at peace than any other influence whatsoever."
When Stephens saw an actual proposed canal route, however, it shook
his faith in progress.

Trying to follow a survey line along the southwest Nicaraguan border
in 1840, he wrote: "Our whole road had been desolate enough, but
this far surpassed anything I had seen. . . . Flocks of sopilotes or turkey
buzzards, hardly disturbed by our approach, moved along at a slow
walk, or, with a lazy flap of their wings, rose to a low branch in the
nearest tree. In one place, a swarm of the ugly birds was feasting on
the carcass of an alligator. Wild turkeys were more numerous than we
had seen before, and so tame I shot one with a pistol. Deer looked at
us without alarm, and on each side of the valley large black apes walked
on the top of trees, or sat quietly in the branches looking at us. . . .
This was the proposed termination of the great canal to connect the
Atlantic and Pacific coasts. . . . I had been sanguine, almost enthusiastic,
in regard to this giant enterprise, but on the spot the scales fell from

my eyes. The harbor was perfectly desolate, for years not a vessel had entered it, primeval trees grew up around it, for miles there was not a habitation. . . . We heard the barking of wolves, the scream of the mountain cat, and other beasts of the forest."

Stephens had been traveling through Central America for almost a year when he encountered this "desolation," but evidently had learned little about fauna. The only animals he identified correctly at the site were white-tailed deer and turkey vultures, North American species he probably knew from home. All the rest, what he called wild turkeys, alligators, wolves, and apes, were other things. The "turkeys" were probably guans or curassows, the "alligators" crocodiles or caimans, the "wolves" coyotes, and the "apes" howler monkeys. Wild turkeys, alligators, wolves, and apes don't live in Nicaragua.

Stephens was like earlier Central American travelers when he awoke from visions of desire to find himself in an unknown place. The confusion of unfamiliar animals with familiar ones had begun with Columbus's mention of "*leones, ciervos, corzos, y otro tanto*" on the Cariari Coast, and chroniclers like Girolamo Benzoni bestowed Old World identities on *tierra firme*'s animals as freely as Stephens would bestow North American identities three centuries later. "A very great number of wild hogs were found in the province, and most fierce tygers" he wrote, "together with some lions . . . there are also peacocks, pheasants, partridges, and other sorts of birds." Benzoni seems to have been more observant than Stephens, because he added that the birds were "all different from ours."

Of course, Columbus and Benzoni weren't naturalists, but adventurers. Yet superior knowledge often compounded the confusion of the first naturalist who tried to identify the Central American flora and fauna, Captain Gonzalo Fernández de Oviedo y Valdés. Like his rival chronicler, Bartolomé de Las Casas, Oviedo spent the first half of the sixteenth century in Central America. Both started out as conquistadors, accumulating land and slaves, but Las Casas repented and devoted his life to ending slavery, while Oviedo stayed in business, with natural history as a sideline. Predictably, they despised each other. "What I think of Oviedo's writing and all his chatter is that he is correct whenever he describes the trees and plants of the region," Las Casas wrote. "He saw them, and so can anyone who wants to see them. . . . Whenever he writes about Indians, his *History* is nothing but blasphemy and annihilation . . . persuading the reader unjustly to hate all Indians."

Las Casas seems to have had more confidence in his rival's botanical abilities than Oviedo himself, who may have equivocated in disparaging Indians, but was frank about his real knowledge of plants. "Generally, the trees found here in the Indies is a subject that cannot be described of their great numbers," Oviedo wrote in his floundering style, "and many sections of the land are so full of them and they are so different and unlike each other both in size as well as in their trunk, branches, bark, leaf, and appearance and in their fruit and flower, that not even the native Indians can tell them apart nor can they name the greater part of them. . . . And what could be told in this regard is a *vast and hidden ocean*, for though it can be seen, most of it is unknown." He also threw up his hands before zoology's bushier branches. "There are innumerable lizards here," he wrote. "There are green lizards, there are brown, and others are almost black . . . and just as they vary in colors, so do they vary in size. . . . Let us leave this subject about the lizards, for it is a very ordinary and unimportant and almost *in infinito* subject."

With more substantial fauna, Oviedo managed to avoid some of the adventurers' errors, recognizing that he saw animals unknown in the Old World. "No mention is made by any of the ancient writers of many of the animals found here on *tierra firme*," he wrote, "inasmuch as they are in provinces of which they were ignorant." He corrected some errors. Pedro Marter, a chronicler who had never crossed the Atlantic, had written that iguanas were the same as Nile crocodiles. "Those who write about these things from hearsay are bound to make such evident mistakes," Oviedo scoffed. An even more prevalent confusion was that between the Old World lion and New World puma. (Stephens would be relieved when his guide told him that a lion they heard in Costa Rica was "a different animal from the roarer of African desert.") Oviedo distinguished between the two clearly, although still using the Old World term: "There are some real lions on the mainland, but they are smooth coated and look exactly like a big scotch grayhound except that they are very robust and have no mane. Neither are they as bold as the African lions, rather they are timid and run away."

Oviedo was more vague about the other confusions, like that between tigers and jaguars. He described the jaguar in detail, but waffled as to its identity. "I would not call them tigers, observing what is written about the speed of the tiger and what is observed of slowness of the ochis which we call tigers. . . . But how much more extreme the creatures are in one place than they are in another, depending on the diversity of the provinces and climates where they grow." Oviedo excused such vagueness by the enormity of his task, contrasting himself to the Roman naturalist Pliny, who wrote "what many others wrote and what he knew most, thus he had less trouble to accumulate facts," whereas, "what I am writing and relating comes from my pen and feeble efforts . . . because the country is new to us, and the greater part of it still unexplored."

Oviedo's excuse was only partly justified, since he had good informants in his victims. Most of his writing concerned flora and fauna already identified and used by the Indians, who had extensive natural history traditions. Three centuries later, French naturalist Arthur Morelet, who found 150 new mollusk species in northern Central America, noted that the Kekchi Maya of Coban had "a separate and distinct name for each kind of mollusc." Morelet thought this was because the mollusks were important food, and that useless animals would not be classified. When zoologist Ivan T. Sanderson collected among the Yucatec Maya in the 1930s, however, he found that they had descriptive names even for obscure creatures like rats and arachnids, "an accomplishment that European science did not perfect until the later nineteenth century, and then only after tremendous wrangling." Farmers in the village of Tekom could distinguish not only between different spiders, but between spiders and other arachnids such as solpugids. "No other native group that we have encountered, and no educated white man that I ever heard of who was not specifically a zoologist, could classify them," Sanderson wrote, "and yet these people must have perfected their opinions on the subject before Columbus discovered America."

Later naturalists brought more clarity to less ambitious accounts than Oviedo's. The seventeenth-century pirate William Dampier was one of the best observers, with an unexpectedly sharp mind for a dissolute profession. His portrait shows a thin-faced, bright-eyed man who looks more scholar than outlaw. Of his *Voyages*, sailor-poet John Maesfield wrote: "The supreme faithfulness and care of Dampier's chronicling can only be gauged by those who take the trouble to compare the work of even the best of the chroniclers who have succeeded him." Dampier described only what he'd seen himself, and his insights would satisfy a modern zoologist. Where Oviedo was content to distinguish crocodiles from iguanas, Dampier saw the difference between crocodiles and caimans. When "a learned friend" from Holland thought the tapir, or mountain cow, was actually a hippopotamus, Dampier wrote: "I am of the opinion that they must needs be of different species, for the mountain cow . . . is not above half so big, and has no long teeth."

Dampier even described the invertebrates that distinguish neotropical forests, the tarantulas, huge balas ants, acacia ants, and nest-building termites. A column of leafcutter ants was "a pretty sight, for the path looked perfectly green with them." He was matter-of-fact about army ants, unduly sensationalized in later accounts. "These would march in troops, as if they were busie in seeking somewhat. They were always in haste. . . . Sometimes a band of these ants would happen to march through our huts, over our beds, or into our pavilions, nay sometimes into our chests and there ransack every part. . . . We never disturbed them, but gave them free liberty to march where they pleased." The ants ate up the other bothersome insects.

Dampier still had some confusion about Old and New World animals. He wrote that the "tigre-cat" was "in all things (viz), its head, the color of its hair, and the manners of its preying much resembling the tigre," although the New World animal was smaller, "about the bigness of a bull-dog," and "less to be feared." But he more often saw clearly what set the hemispheres apart. The animals he described in most detail were the least familiar to Europe—sloths, armadillos, anteaters, kinkajous. In describing the howler monkeys Stephens would call apes, Dampier emphasized the prehensile tail that distinguishes New World primates from Old World ones. "The underside of their tails is all bare, with a black, hard skin. . . . The first time I met them there was a great company dancing from tree to tree. . . . At last one bigger than the rest, came to a small limb just over my head; and leaping directly at me, made me start back; but the monkey caught hold of a bough with the tip of his tail, and there continued swinging to and fro, and making mouths at me."

In 1722, shortly after Dampier's time, a Dominican priest named Francisco Ximénez wrote the most concise and systematic early Central

American natural history. Ximénez was a kind of amalgam of Oviedo and Las Casas, both a naturalist and an advocate of the Indians, whom he praised as "scientific about the animals of the forest." Drawing on indigenous lore, he described hundreds of organisms in a few hundred pages, some for the first time, and also wrote perceptively on geology and hydrology. Ximénez had a strong sense of the differences between Old and New World, noting that American cottontails don't live in tunnels like European rabbits, and that American monkeys differ from African ones in that all have tails. He knew some of his subjects from having kept them as pets (such as an agouti that liked to play with cats), and his descriptions have an unassuming familiarity unlike Oviedo's often overblown ones. Oviedo had described the "wolves" of Nicaragua as "very big, larger than a big mastiff. They have hair like a cow, teeth like a dog, and very strong fangs . . . and devour some Indians." Ximénez noted simply that coyotes were very common, damaging to livestock, and adept at outwitting domestic dogs.

Ximénez rivaled Dampier in the exactness of his observations of even small things like ants and termites. His description of the native stingless bees which Indians used for honey is still among the best. He was less well-traveled than Dampier, however, and in his desire to be comprehensive sometimes wrote from hearsay. Although his account of American monkeys began clearly by describing their differences from Old World monkeys, it grew vague as he tried to cover the different kinds he'd heard about. He described howler monkeys with Dampier's exactitude —"they give terrible cries when it rains, and swell their throats greatly when they call"—but some of his other monkeys don't sound like anything known. "There are others like big dogs, and extremely ugly, and of these some are black, and some brown," he wrote. "Still others, not so big, have faces like black peoples' . . ."

The Black Monkey

There is still plenty of vagueness and uncertainty about Central American flora and fauna, particularly when one is there. It's easier to look down on ancients like Oviedo and Ximénez in the library than when you're actually in the forest. I heard stories of scientifically unknown animals on the lightly explored Caribbean slope. In 1995, someone told me that a wild turkey smaller than the ocellated species, with little plumes on its head, lived in remote lowlands north of the Altos Cuchumatanes. A meter-long green lizard like a miniature komodo dragon was said to live there too. Another obscure area is southeast Nicaragua's vast Indio-Maíz Reserve along the San Juan River downstream from the town of El Castillo. Three monkey species —the golden mantled howler, the red spider, and the white-faced capuchin—and two deer species— the white-tailed and brocket—are supposed to live there. Yet when I asked an El Castillo resident, the ex-mayor in fact, about the reserve's wildlife, he told me unexpected things. He said it contained three deer species—a "little fat one" as well as white-tailed and brocket deer— and five monkey species, including a "titi monkey, active at night," and a "big black monkey with a short tail that lives in the mountains."

The former mayor also said the Indio-Maíz contained pre-Columbian ruins bigger than the Spanish fort for which El Castillo is named, and I was skeptical. I'd first met him lying in a hammock in what a local policeman had told me was the office of MARENA, the natural resources agency. The policeman had seemed suspicious when I'd asked him where the MARENA office was, and I later found out why. The police in town were Sandinistas, and the ex-mayor was a Contra who had just returned from a dozen years in exile, and more or less had appropriated the MARENA office, apparently unoccupied otherwise. He was a very determined man, the former mayor, indefatigably loquacious and resilient, as though made of rubber. I encountered him again that evening, and he started leading me around to the houses of the townspeople, introducing me as though I were some kind of celebrity. He evidently was trying to rebuild his power base.

We ran into a young Danish woman I'd met on the boat downriver from Lake Nicaragua, and the ex-mayor dragged her along too, maintaining a running political commentary as we trailed through the unlit backstreets. This included possibly slanderous remarks about the police, which made me nervous because we kept running into the officer I'd asked directions from, who would smile knowingly. It also included admiring stories about William Walker.

"But didn't Walker try to reinstate slavery and annex Nicaragua to the United States?" the redheaded Dane asked, a little weakly. She hadn't expected to hear praise for Yankee imperialists halfway down the San

Juan River. The ex-mayor denied this firmly. Walker was a Nicaraguan patriot to his dying day.

"Just before they shot Walker," he proclaimed, striking his chest, "He said: 'I am the president of Nicaragua. *Matame!*'"

Still, everything else the ex-mayor said about local wildlife seemed accurate. He mentioned five cat species, two macaw species, two peccary species, agoutis, pacas, and so forth. Another El Castillo man thought there were at least four monkey species. A robust old hunter who'd used monkey meat to bait jaguar traps, the man said the fourth species was bigger than the spider, or yellow, monkey, and had a black face and hands. I'd also come across mention of another deer species like the ex-mayor's "little fat" one in an early natural history account. Arthur Morelet, the Frenchman who explored the Petén in the 1840s, wrote of an animal called the "chacyuc," or "cabra del monte," that was smaller than whitetail and brocket deer, although he hadn't seen it.

Whatever his veracity, the ex-mayor was friendly and accommodating. He helped me hire two local boys to take me into the reserve on their *pipante* the next morning, and also invited the Dane along, although she didn't show up. He didn't come either, perhaps afraid that the police might contrive a permanent absence if he left town even for a day. They missed a nice trip. We ascended as far as the boat would go up the Río Bartola, a tributary that ran semitranslucent over big shelves of red rock. The forest on its banks seemed as undisturbed as Darién's. I've rarely felt such a sense of the infinite, quiet patience of forest evolution as I did in the blue-gray-green light there. It was early dry season, and the air spun with yellow ceiba and barrigon leaflets, which somehow emphasized the timelessness, leaves falling in a place where autumn never comes. A snowy cotinga sat with characteristic languor on a branch, its laundry white plumage incongruous with the endless shadings of green. A chickadee-sized bird with a tail longer than its body hawked insects from a snag in midstream, a long-tailed tyrant, a kind of flycatcher.

Where the Bartola joined the San Juan, I visited the ranger, an intelligent, amiable man, although formidably large, with one of the thickest, glossiest black beards I've seen. He gave me lunch, a green coconut from a tree near his house which he deftly processed with his machete to get first milk, then meat. Then we went for a walk on a steep little trail. He said jaguars and tapirs were abundant farther into the reserve, but "it took a lot" to see them. We crossed many deer and peccary tracks, winding lines of them worn so deep by the sharp hooves that the thin leaf litter was churned into mud. *"Que barbaridad!"* he exclaimed, which seemed incongruous considering how literally barbaric *he* looked.

When I asked how many deer species lived in the reserve, the ranger mentioned the expected two. When I asked about monkeys, he first said there were three species, then changed his mind and said there were four—howlers, capuchins, yellow monkeys, and black monkeys. The black monkeys were like the yellow, but smaller, with black faces and hands. When we got back near the station, we heard screeching from a barrigon tree. A very pregnant monkey sat there scolding us. It looked like a spider monkey, but with a black face and hands, and tan fur that seemed different from the reddish-furred spider monkeys I'd seen in Costa Rican Caribbean rain forests.

"That's a black monkey," the ranger said. I took his word for it. I'd seen spider monkeys ranging from pale tan to dark gray in other parts of Central America, and I wasn't prepared to make any judgments.

Buffon's Confusion

Early Central American naturalists didn't speculate in print as to why New and Old World organisms were different, or why they were sometimes remarkably similar given the distance between them. They may have wondered about such things, but they lacked the intellectual background to address them. In Oviedo's lifetime, geographical variation was little known, and even in Dampier's and Ximénez's time, the vastness of unexplored territory obscured it. Ximénez was almost a scientist. He performed experiments, as when he tried to verify spontaneous generation by putting horse hairs in water to see if they'd turn into snakes. (He kept an open mind when they didn't, speculating that conditions might not have been right, since he *had* seen living "serpents"—actually horsehair worms—in road puddles.) Yet 1722 science may have been more hindrance than help to thinking about geographical variation. Ximénez was an orthodox taxonomist in classifying worms as snakes, bats as birds, and manatees and turtles as fish. Anatomy confused him, as when he wrote that the tapir "doubtless is the elephant" because "it holds its trunk like the elephant, to guide it."

Before 1750, scripture remained the authority on geographical variation. A Jesuit, Athanasius Kircher, tried to prove mathematically that Noah's ark could have accommodated all the world's animal species. Another Jesuit, the same José de Acosta who had warned against a Panama Canal, used the similarity between New and Old World animals such as bears and foxes to support the ark doctrine, speculating sensibly that after the deluge the animals could have migrated from Old World to New "in some part by which these beasts might pass." Yet solely New World animals stumped Acosta. "If the llamas of Peru, and those they call alpacas and guanacos, aren't found in other parts of the world," he wrote, "who brought them to Peru? Or how did they get there? . . . If they didn't come from elsewhere, how were they formed and brought forth there? Perhaps God made a new creation of beasts." One of the most perceptive early naturalists, Acosta also was among the first of many who commented on New World animal distribution without becoming familiar with Central America. Aside from his Panama crossing, he spent his sixteen-year American sojourn in healthier, wealthier Peru and Mexico.

By the mid-eighteenth century, the vast increase of known organisms had made an ark seem unlikely. The Swedish taxonomist Linnaeus thought all organisms were Biblical flood survivors, but had survived on a high mountain instead of an ark. Linnaeus's mountain echoed Columbus's terrestrial paradise, but also made some biological sense. As observers like Acosta had remarked, mountains recapitulate the global range of climates, from warm low altitudes to cold high ones, so Linnaeus's ancestral mountain could have preserved a global range of organisms. Yet Linnaeus's mountain still didn't explain how organisms had dispersed throughout the world, or why many Old and New World organisms differ although they live in similar climates. It remained for his successor as leading biological authority, the Comte de Buffon, to address the questions in a new way.

The Comte de Buffon based his explanation of geographical differences on fossils. Animal bones resembling those of living African elephants and rhinos had been unearthed in Siberia and Scandinavia. Given the bones' antiquity, Buffon interpreted them as evidence that life had been created (or "born," as he put it) in northern latitudes when the rest of the newly formed planet had been too hot for it. As the planet cooled, organisms had migrated south, elephants and rhinos arriving in tropical Africa and Asia perhaps five thousand years before the present. Discovery of elephantlike fossils in North America supported Buffon's theory, since he could say that the elephants had migrated to North America when it was connected to Asia, then had become extinct from the growing cold like their Old World counterparts.

Buffon's theory encountered problems below North America, however. In effect, the Count tripped over the Central American land bridge, and might thus be considered its discoverer if his notion of its function hadn't been as the opposite of a bridge. Buffon wasn't aware that fossil elephant (actually mastodon) bones had been found in Peru in the sixteenth century. (Acosta had thought they were giant human bones.) He maintained that the apparent absence of fossil elephants from South America indicated a fundamental difference between that continent's fauna and the rest of the world's. "In effect," he wrote in his *Epochs of Nature* (1780), "If one considers the surface of the New World one sees that the tropical regions around the Isthmus of Panama are occupied by very high mountains: the elephants couldn't overcome these impassable barriers because of the excessive cold they experienced in the heights. They thus didn't get past the lands of the Isthmus, and didn't survive in temperate America because it wasn't warm enough for them to reproduce. It's the same for all the other animals of the tropical parts of the Old World, none is found in the tropics of the New."

Buffon's excessively cold heights would have surprised Acosta and Dampier as they sweltered over the 300-meter Panama divide. Yet errors of paleontology and geography led the Count to some interesting ideas. He was largely right about the great differences between not only Old and New World, but North and South American organisms. He thus drew a logical inference about South America: "That part of the world was thus not populated like the others or at the same time: It remained isolated from the rest of the earth by seas and high mountains." Although Buffon failed to recognize Central America as a land bridge, he saw the long isolation that preceded its formation.

Buffon's ideas about what happened during South America's isolation were muddled, however. He had two mutually exclusive sets of ideas. The more consistent theory was that South America had been a separate center of creation, an inferior one where "animated nature is weaker, less active, and more circumscribed in the variety of her productions." Buffon saw the present absence of huge mammals such as elephants and rhinos in the New World as proof of this inferiority. The less consistent theory contradicted his perception that South America had been isolated. In his *Natural History of the Quadrupeds*, Buffon wrote that New World animals had been born in the Old World, then had degenerated in the New because "the climate of America is so joined and situated that every circumstance concurs in diminishing the action of heat." He cited llamas, peccaries, and tapirs as New World species that had degenerated from camels, pigs, and elephants.

Such ideas raised many more questions than they answered. If tropical animals couldn't get from North to South America via Panama, but got there anyway, how did they manage it? If they became new species by degeneration, how did that work? Buffon left the questions adrift in a sea of writings even more voluminous, if less firsthand, than Oviedo's, and his successor as doyen of French biology, Baron Cuvier, made a point of dismissing his ideas about New World prehistory. In his 1817 *Essay on the Theory of the Earth*, Cuvier noted with satisfaction that Baron Alexander von Humboldt had discovered elephantlike fossils in South America, yet hastened to add that they did nothing to prove Buffon's theory that elephants had originated in northern Eurasia and migrated south. "No established fact authorizes the belief of changes so great as those which must be assumed for such a transformation. Nor is there any decisive proof of the temperature of northern climates having changed during this epoch."

Cuvier thought faunas could change through migration, but not in Buffon's evolutionary way, with new species developing because of changed conditions. Rising oceans might flood a continent's fauna out of existence, and "the same revolution" might "lay dry the numerous narrow straits" between the inundated continent and another. "Thus a road would be opened" for intercontinental migration. Yet Cuvier didn't apply faunal migration to South America. Instead, he stressed its uniqueness. "When the Spaniards penetrated into South America," he proclaimed, "they did not find it to contain a single quadruped exactly the same as those of Europe, Asia, and Africa. The puma, the jaguar, the capybara, the lama or glama, the vicugna, and the whole tribe of sapajous were to them entirely new animals."

Darwin's Astonishment

For all their differences, Cuvier and Buffon probably would have agreed that a link between North and South America wasn't particularly important to New World biology. It was yet another great naturalist who never visited Central America who seems to have been the first to get some idea of its role as a land bridge. Charles Darwin came no closer to Panama than the Galápagos Islands during his 1831–36 *Beagle* voyage, but when he found the bones of "nine great quadrupeds" eroding out of Argentinean cliffs, he saw sweeping implications for the entire hemisphere. The fossils included species—ground sloths, glyptodonts, mastodons, horses—that had been dug up in North America as well. Darwin realized that South America's isolation had been far from complete, and that its fauna actually had been *more* like North America's in the recent past than the present.

"It is impossible to reflect on the changed state of the American continent without the deepest astonishment," Darwin wrote in *The Journal of the Beagle*. "Formerly it must have swarmed with great monsters; now we find mere pygmies, compared with the antecedent, allied races. If Buffon had known of the gigantic sloth and armadillo-like animals, and of the lost pachydermata, he might have said with greater semblance of truth that the creative force in America had lost its power, rather than it had never possessed great vigor."

Yet Darwin got the significance of a North to South America land link backward in *The Journal of the Beagle*. He thought that "the recent elevation of the Mexican plateau" had caused the present differences between North and South American organisms by *preventing* migration except in a few cases. "Some few species alone have passed the barrier," he wrote, "and may be considered as wanderers from the south, such as the puma, opossum, kinkajou, and peccari." (He didn't give any evidence as to why he considered these animals originally South American. Only opossums are.) Darwin thought that ground sloths, glyptodonts, horses, and mastodons had crossed between the Americas not via Central America but by a now submerged Antillean route. "The South American character of the West Indian mammals seems to indicate that this archipelago was formerly united to the southern continent, and that it has subsequently been an area of subsidence."

Darwin evidently changed his mind later. He cited evidence for a Central American link in his chapter on migration in *The Origin of Species*. Some plants at 2,000-foot elevation in Panama were like those of Mexico, "with forms of the torrid zone harmoniously blended with those of the temperate." Fifty species of North American and European plants had been identified in Tierra del Fuego. Yet it was Alfred Russell Wallace, Darwin's codiscoverer of natural selection's evolutionary role, who first drew the relationship between North and South America more or less as we now see it. Wallace never got to Central America either, but his long familiarity with a kind of incipient land bridge, the Malay Archipelago between Asia and Australia, gave him particular insight.

In his *Geographical Distribution of Animals* (1876), Wallace maintained that recently discovered fossils of "South American types" of animals in North America were "unmistakable evidence of an extensive immigration from South into North America, not very long before the beginning of the Glacial epoch." He deduced that "the fact that no such migration had occurred for countless preceding ages proves that some great barrier to the entrance of terrestrial mammalia which had previously existed must for a time have been removed." Wallace thought a submerged Nicaragua instead of Panama had been the "great barrier" between the continents, and many of the animals he believed came from South America are actually North American. (He thought it "a great mystery" that "defenseless creatures" such as tapirs "could have made their way into a country abounding in large felines equal in size and destructiveness to the lion and tiger.") His picture of the relationship between the continents was essentially modern, however. He is the land bridge's official discoverer, although he didn't use the term.

A paleontological explosion that hit both North and South America in the late nineteenth century gave substance to Wallace's ideas. Enthusiastic young diggers ransacked prairies and pampas, unearthing an array of bones that would have astonished Darwin even more than in 1833. As fossils multiplied, it became evident that hundreds of species had thundered back and forth between the continents. One of the young diggers, George Gaylord Simpson, called Darwin's nine quadrupeds "a clue to a great event . . . The Great American Interchange."

Exploring sediments that dated back to the Dinosaur Age and thus included most of the Cenozoic era, or Age of Mammals, the diggers constructed a picture of two continents that had evolved apart until a few million years ago. Argentinian brothers, Florentino and Carlos Ameghino, unearthed a South American mammal fauna unlike anything in the world. Giant marsupials were its main predators. Ground sloths and glyptodonts (giant armadillolike edentates) shared the herbivore niche with even more bizarre creatures—three-meter-long toxodonts like clawed rhinos, horselike liptoterns with nostrils on the tops of their heads, typotheres like long-tailed rabbits, elephantlike pyrotheres. Although these mammals were placentals like those of other continents except Australia, most belonged to unique families unknown elsewhere. Other fossils showed that South America's isolation hadn't been total— a few familiar groups like rodents had arrived before the land bridge formed. Even they had evolved in peculiar ways afterward, however.

In North America, paleontologists like W. B. Scott and Henry Fairfield Osborn unearthed an entirely different Age of Mammals in which regular land bridge intermigration with the Old World had evolved a fauna more like Eurasia's and Africa's than South America's. The animals were strange in older fossil formations, but became more familiar in younger ones. By the end of the Miocene epoch, about five million years ago, most would have been recognizable to modern eyes. Many animal families were the same in Old and New worlds—bears, dogs, cats, deer, horses, bison, elephants, camels, and even tapirs. (Buffon, Cuvier, and Darwin had been mistaken about the origin of most living South American large mammals, as the mid-nineteenth-century discovery of a Southeast Asian tapir species demonstrated.) Even strictly North American families were related to Eurasian ones—raccoons to pandas, mountain goats to antelopes.

Fossils younger than the late Miocene began to show a very different fauna in both North and South America, however. South American ground sloths appeared in California and North American raccoon-bears in Argentina. By the Pleistocene, the Ice Age, South American fossil formations included dogs, bears, cats, horses, camels, deer, and elephantids, and North American fossil formations yielded not only ground sloths but armadillos, anteaters, toxodonts, and glyptodonts. In 1893, leading paleontologist Karl Alfred von Zittel called this "one of the most remarkable faunal migrations in the geological record." It was spectacular, as though paleontologists had discovered two separate oceans of fossils, then watched as geological time opened a valve between them, so that they rushed together into the zoological melange that had astonished Darwin.

5

Land Bridge Fossils

NORTH AND SOUTH America have abundant fossil records of the Age of Mammals because both have huge sedimentary deposits where, during much of the past sixty-five million years, streams spread silt over interior basins. The silt encased the bones of fallen animals, beginning the gradual formation of fossil beds. Conditions are perfect for paleontology where such basins are now located in semi-arid grasslands like the Great Plains and pampas. Sparse rainfall and vegetation make fossils accessible and durable, since they are easy to spot and decay slowly when exposed at the surface. Anybody who has visited the Dakota badlands knows how an entire landscape can be a boneyard.

Yet, although paleontologists found enough South and North American fossils by 1876 for Wallace to discover the land bridge, it remained circumstantial evidence because fossils of animals *from* the bridge were almost nonexistent. Very few were dug up in Central America during the land bridge's discovery, partly because there were few semi-arid grasslands, partly because there were simply few fossils. Lacking the big interior basins and plains of the continents, Central America has a meager fossil record. Its forests hide what fossils there are, and its heavy rains destroy exposed ones quickly. Using the bumpy bridge's fossils to envision how life has seethed across it has been a bit like trying to map Volcán Cacao's cloud forest through the mist.

The two times I've encountered Central American fossils more or less *in situ* are fairly typical. The first was while rafting the Pacuare River in Costa Rica, when a guide pointed to a fish fossil in a midstream boulder. I had about five seconds to examine it as the raft whizzed by. The second time was at El Castillo in Nicaragua, and the fossil was a tree trunk, perhaps a palm or cycad. Again I had only seconds to examine it because of the social context, which was even more complicated than a whitewater rafting trip. The fossil was in one of the homes to which El Castillo's Contra ex-mayor had led me and the unwary Dane on his goodwill tour. The house's owner said he'd dug the fossil trunk from his land nearby, but that was all I learned before the ex-mayor dragged us to the next house.

I'm an amateur, of course, but what I've heard from professionals is not so different. A geologist I met in Tegucigalpa had been exploring the Mosquitia for months in areas so remote they were unknown even to his Tawahka guides, and the animals had no fear of men. (I heard wonderful stories about such areas: of places where harpy eagles were so abundant that the local Tawahkas had to flee, and of strange corpses, half eaten by vultures, with one blue eye and one brown eye. When the eye of such a corpse was touched, it turned over in its socket, revealing another iris of a different color.) Although he looked for fossils the entire trip, the geologist had found only one: a tiny nubbin in a sandstone slab which he thought was an ammonite, an extinct, shelled relative of squid. I wouldn't have thought it was a fossil at all, and he wasn't sure.

In 1981, geologist R. C. Finch described the fossil situation in the central Honduran mountains: "The Guare beds are generally unfossiliferous, but a high organic content is indicated by the characteristic fetid smell of freshly broken surfaces. At some exposures a few highly fossiliferous beds have been found. One well-preserved fossil fish was found in a flagstone paving a coffee-drying patio in the town of El Nispero; unfortunately, neither the prospect of scientific fame nor cash inducement could part this fossil from its owner, and efforts to locate further specimens were fruitless." This was in one of the more productive fossil areas in Central America. In the 1970s, the nearby Esquias Formation yielded a femur which was identified as that of a hadrosaur, or duck-billed dinosaur, the only proof that dinosaurs lived in Central America. It dated from the Cretaceous period about a hundred million years ago.

Central America's fossil-hunting history has been correspondingly sparse. Oviedo may have glimpsed something prehistoric in 1541, when he described animal remains at the foot of a cliff. "I have never seen a beast with such fierce teeth, fangs, and claws," he wrote, and called the animal a "lynx," implying that it had a short tail and back legs. This suggests a saber-tooth, or possibly a ground sloth, which early naturalists sometimes mistook for carnivores because of their strong claws. Oviedo gave no indication that he was describing fossil bones, however. The modern idea of fossils didn't exist then, and evidently remained unknown to Francisco Ximénez two centuries later. When Ximénez saw stones in a church at Zacapulas that had "stamped in them leaves of trees and sticks and other plants . . . as though the stone had been wax," he didn't see them as evidence of prehistory, although he did speculate perceptively that they might have been formed by percolation and precipitation of water, as with cave formations.

In 1839, John Lloyd Stephens may have been the first to knowingly describe a Central American fossil, the remains of "a colossal animal . . . supposed to be a mastodon," in the bank of the Chinaca River a half mile from Huehuetenango. "The bank was perpendicular, about thirty feet high," he wrote, "and the animal had been buried in an upright position. . . . The impression of the whole animal, from twenty-five to thirty feet long, was distinctly visible." Stephens didn't collect or describe the bones, so there is no way of knowing what they were. "Mastodon" was a loosely applied word in the early nineteenth century, and a thirty-foot length sounds extraordinary even for a mastodon. It wasn't until two decades later that North America's first professional paleontologist, Joseph Leidy, definitely identified some huge molar teeth from Honduras's volcanic plateau as a mastodon's.

In 1886, a Mrs. B. F. Guerrero of Philadelphia showed Leidy other land bridge fossils. "The collection was obtained from the north of Nicaragua, but nothing further had been learned about it," Leidy wrote. "It mostly consisted of uncharacteristic fragments of bones, but among them were many interesting specimens referable to Megatherium, Elephant, Mastodon, Ox, Toxodon, and Capybara. The association of these is another illustration of the extension of the early South American Quaternary fauna into North America." Mrs. Guerrero's ground sloth, toxodon, and capybara bones seem to have been the first hard evidence that South American animals crossed to North America via Central America.

Central American fossils of organisms beside mammals have been even scarcer, and harder to interpret. In 1917, W. P. Woodring collected plant fossils in the Costa Rican Talamancas which paleobotanist E. W. Berry dated to the Miocene epoch roughly ten million years ago, and identified as belonging to extant tropical groups such as heliconians, figs, and laurels. Other botanists questioned his identifications, however, because the fossils were of leaves, tricky to classify. In 1987, botanist Alan Graham found that pollen grains from the shale matrix of Woodring's fossils were of different, more northern plant groups such as holly and heath. Woodring's site hasn't been rediscovered, so Berry's identifications can't be checked.

Some fossils have no connection to the land bridge because they long predate the existing continents. In the same year that Leidy described Mrs. Guerrero's collection, mining engineer Charles H. Rolke found fossil plants in a Honduran silver mine. Paleobotanist J. S. Newberry identified them as cycads and ferns about two hundred million years old, and observed that they were "another illustration of uniformity of the vegetation of the world during the Triassic Age," when plants worldwide held "so firmly to their original groups of characteristics, generic and specific, that wherever we open their tombs we recognize them as old friends."

The Bones from Gracias

Systematic digging of a Central American fossil site didn't come until after 1929, when J. C. Blick of Chicago's Field Museum identified mastodon bones found near the ancient colonial town of Gracias in southwest Honduras. From 1937 to 1942, the University of Chicago's Walker Museum sent expeditions there, and the Florida Museum of Natural History recovered more Gracias fossils from 1969 to 1980. They dug mastodon, camel, rhino, horse, and wild dog bones from steep riverbanks around Gracias, and also a few remains of plants, reptiles, and amphibians, allowing the first reconstruction of life in Central America about eight million years ago.

The Gracias fossils are well known to land bridge paleontologists, but they came as a surprise to me when I was in Honduras in 1992. Famous fossils are the exception—most are almost as well hidden in the thick strata of scientific journals as are their undiscovered counter-parts in the ground. With a day to spare in Tegucigalpa, I went to visit a Museo de Fauna at the University of Honduras and was excited to find the one-room museum's cabinets crammed with big, honey-colored mastodon, camel, and horse bones from "Gracias, Dept. de Lempira." I was so excited, particularly after the friendly young *dueno* told me there was lots more where that came from, that I got on a bus for Gracias early the next morning. In the center of the Miocene volcanic plateau, it seemed remote enough that some rumor of mastodons and camels might linger.

Gracias was remote. I spent a day riding up and down brushy valleys and pine-forested mountains, seeing more oxcarts than cars as Lenca Indians got on and off the bus in mid-forest. This took me as far as the mountain town of La Esperanza, an ancient place surrounded by green marshes and oak woods. Melodious chanting came from the church, and an immense purple jacaranda bloomed in the *zocalo*. Al-though it had a television, my *hospedaje* served a *comida corriente* of eggs, beans, and tortillas for breakfast, lunch, and dinner such as John Lloyd Stephens would have found in 1839.

No bus ran to Gracias next day, so I set out hitchhiking on the dusty roads. I got a hair-raising ride down a steep escarpment, and another through strange eroded canyons to a straggle of cinder block houses called San Juan, where the rides stopped. The only vehicle that passed was a La Esperanza–bound minivan so crammed that it looked like one of those toy buses with the passengers painted on the windows. I in-quired at a *tienda*, wherein teenage traveling salesmen pushed cosmetics "from Paris" to some women, and a dog reflectively gnawed cold tortillas on the doorstep. The women said a bus might come, sometime. I started walking. A couple of hours later, a heavily loaded bus came along, and I was able to squeeze onto the dashboard, with my back to many hairpin turns that the driver negotiated with ferocious boredom. The windshield was so cracked that I was surprised it stayed on. Campesinos in Stetsons bobbed up and down in unison, and a blonde woman nursed a baby in the front seat. Just before sunset, a huge peak appeared in the west, Celaque, Honduras's tallest mountain, beneath which is Gracias.

I'd been asking people about fossils on the way, without success. An opal miner on the bus from Tegucigalpa had never seen any during his diggings. He showed me his opals, red and yellow in a dark brown matrix, like hot embers. A campesino I met on the road near San Juan thought I was asking him about firearms, *fusiles*. I hoped to do better in Gracias, whose cobbled streets and quiet squares looked unchanged at least from the 1930s, but the very timelessness of the place seemed to have swallowed the past. The local forest rangers knew of fossils in the locality, mainly petrified wood, but not of any fossil-hunting expeditions. Nobody in town remembered the expeditions—not even the older people, which seemed strange. Considering their logistics, the expeditions must have had Indiana Jones aspects. One possibility remained. A Peace Corps volunteer, Charley Spence, told me the teacher at a nearby school collected fossils, and showed me a piece of petrified wood he'd given him.

I decided to walk out to the school and talk to the teacher. The way led over a heavily eroded plateau studded with pines and live oaks, likely fossil terrain, but I scrutinized the road cuts and stream banks in vain. The afternoon sun turned the ground into a bed of coals, and I felt terrible, having caught a virus in Tegucigalpa. I gave up on the school and crawled into the gallery forest of a stream for the rest of the afternoon. Fig, rose apple, and poro poro trees shaded sluggish water inhabited by whitish mollies and cichlids. Big marine toads plopped in and out, acorn woodpeckers called "*Kraaaa! Kraaa!*" in the pines, and a flock of parakeets flew shrieking overhead. Still idly hoping for bones, I followed the streambed downhill until it dropped over what must have made an impressive waterfall in the rainy season. A pile of leaves had accumulated at the edge, and, hearing a noise, I dug into them. Something yellowish slithered out of sight so quickly I couldn't identify it, but I kept digging to the bottom. A gray-green frog very like the leopard frogs of U.S. ponds crouched there, trying to beat the heat like me.

That night I visited the schoolteacher, Don Antonio Miranda, at his house in Gracias. He was a friendly, intelligent man, a little wary. He said he bought the fossils from campesinos, but didn't know where they found them. He knew nothing of past fossil hunting expeditions. He didn't show me the fossils he evidently valued most—wood turned into semiprecious stone—but brought out a molar and a big, eroded leg bone. The molar filled my hand, although it was only part of the tooth.

It looked like the mastodon molars I'd seen in the Tegucigalpa museum. Don Antonio called them dinosaur fossils, and when I told him I thought they were mammal bones, much more recent than dinosaurs', he nodded, then asked if I believed in "Darwin's theory of evolution." I answered that I thought fossils like his proved that evolution has occurred, although they didn't prove Darwin's theory of evolution through natural selection. I added that things like selective breeding of domestic animals had been used to support Darwin's theory.

"You mean, crossing animals?" he asked. I said yes, and Don Antonio said he'd heard of somebody recently crossing a rabbit and a cat. I said I doubted that. When he said it had been in the newspaper, I replied that you couldn't believe everything in the newspaper. He laughed. "You're like Doubting Thomas," he said.

In the Vaults

I had to return to the U.S. to learn more about the Gracias fossils. When I did, I felt as though I'd reached for a bone in a riverbank and pulled the bank down on my head. Olson and McGrew's article on the 1930s expeditions led me to Webb and Perrigo's on 1970s expeditions. Neither was more than a few pages in a journal, but the information they contained swelled in my brain like the Japanese paper pills that unfold into animals in water. It wasn't only around Gracias that bones had been found. A similar fauna of mastodons, camels, and horses had come to light near Corinto in northeast El Salvador. Much younger, Ice Age faunas including South American ground sloths and glyptodonts as well as North American deer and pumas had been found at Hormiguero in El Salvador and Yeroconte in Honduras. Fossils also had turned up in Panama, and I read Whitmore and Stewart's 1965 article about them. Bones from the Panama Canal's Gaillard Cut were dated as even older than the Gracias fossils, some belonging to mammals such as protoceratids and oreodonts, which reached their peak in the Oligocene epoch thirty million years ago and left no living descendants.

Each of these fossil faunas hinted at the once-living landscape of which it was a relic. The Panamanian Gaillard Cut assemblage was full of crocodiles' bones and coprolites (fossil feces), and broken bones of young mammals—perhaps the crocodiles' prey. Fossil wood was identified as that of *Schwartzia*, a tree still common in Panamanian rain forest. It evidently had been a hot, swampy coast, perhaps the southern tip of the long peninsula that eventually would become the land bridge. The Gracias assemblage also included fossil wood attributed to living tropical trees (the genera *Schmidelia* and *Gyminda*) but giant tortoises prevailed instead of crocodiles, and volcanic ash and mud sediments suggested a plain with active volcanoes rising from it.

I became mildly obsessed with Central American fossils, particularly the Gracias ones, because I had been there, and because they were such an odd mixture of familiarity and strangeness. The Hormiguero deer and pumas were familiar, and the Gaillard Cut's nose-horned protoceratids and pig-cow oreodonts were strange, but the Gracias animals were a little of both, like reality emerging from dream. The mastodons were gomphotheres, which had short trunks and tusks in their lower jaws as well as their upper jaws. The rhinos, of the genus *Teleoceras*, were low-slung creatures with stubby horns that probably lived in streams like present-day hippos. The horses looked like small, stocky versions of modern horses, but one genus, *Hipparion*, had three-toed feet instead of hoofs and the other, *Pliohippus*, sometimes had hoofs, sometimes toes. Oddest of all were the wild dogs, of the genus *Osteoborus*, which had high-domed heads and jaws so massive that they probably could eat large bones, like hyenas.

I found that artists' reconstructions of the Gracias animals were common, not because the Gracias fossils are well known, but because the same, or very similar animals lived in most of North America in the Miocene epoch. The Smithsonian in Washington, D.C. had a diorama showing gomphotheres, *Teleoceras, Pliohippus,* and *Osteoborus* running around the Texas plains. The Texas bones were found with Douglas fir and oak fossils, while San Francisco Bay Area fossil sites show that willows, sycamores, and chaparral grew there with gomphotheres and hippolike rhinos.

It's lucky that prehistoric Central American animals also lived elsewhere. If we had to depend on the land bridge fossils, we'd know much less about them. Or so it seemed to me, driven by obsession to see them in their obscure repositories. Their totality probably would fit in one construction site dumpster. As Gracias collector David Webb, curator of fossil vertebrates at the Florida State Museum in Gainesville, told me: "It's probably going to be dreadfully disappointing. Everything's so fragmentary. . . . When the American Museum of Natural History puts up a diorama or an exhibit of skeletons, they're going way beyond what I would see. I don't even necessarily want to see a whole skeleton when I'm going to measure each bone and look at the way the ends are hollowed out or whatever, muscle scars or other details. Then I like each bone separate and I like even a couple of broken examples just to see the variation. And that's unfortunately what you're going to see. Just drawers and drawers of broken bones. Most people expect the whole skeleton like you see in exhibits or the pages of a book, but those are highly exceptional. It's really scabby compared to picture books."

Webb was right about the trays of broken bones, but I felt excited anyway at getting my hands on the actual fossils of the evolutionary epic that I'd been thinking about for years—the basic materials, the bony relics. There was a ritual aspect. I had to get permission, and once it was granted, I descended (or ascended) into the bone vault, the paleontological underworld. Each vault was different. The one at the Florida State Museum was the least sepulchral, in a modern basement with adjacent offices. Webb, the only collector I was able to talk to at length, was helpful, but also preoccupied about the effects of a cold weather outbreak on the living horses at his farm. He could tell me little about Olson and McGrew's expedition in the 1930s. He had seen some home movies they had made on their boat trip to Honduras, but they apparently hadn't had time to film themselves digging. Local people had told them of a "Cave of the Vampires" near Gracias where blood dripped from the ceiling, but they'd found that the "blood" was just iron oxide. Webb didn't dwell on his own expeditions, except to say that the 1980s civil wars had put a stop to them. Salvadoran guerrillas had expelled his associate Steve Perrigo from a fossil site at gunpoint. Perrigo had returned to the site anyway, only to have the owner expel him at gunpoint for fear he'd cause trouble with the guerrillas.

"Every year since I keep thinking, 'Well, maybe we can go back and get somebody started again,' but it hasn't happened," Webb said. "You may have seen a picture of a whole skeleton of a little bat that Steve found there. It's in the same deposit with some bigger bones, sloths and other things. The sloths were actually two kinds that are new to science. And all this looks like one of the richest sites imaginable, by

Central American standards, and probably could be worked into something better, but it's just not a good time. That work needs to be done, and there's a lot more down through Panama."

At the Smithsonian, Gaillard Cut collector Frank Whitmore was snowbound by the same cold snap that hit when I visited. Another paleontologist conducted me through an unmarked door to a basement lab where the Panamanian bones were locked away. Many were plaster casts, the originals on loan elsewhere. The paleontologist was not interested in the fossils—he was a marine paleontologist—but was unwilling to leave me alone with them, so I got only a brief look. They'd let me look as long as I'd wanted in Florida, although an attendant had kept a discreet eye on me. At the imposing 1920s edifice of the Field Museum in Chicago, the attendant was so preoccupied with a crocodilian skull on his table that he took me up to the vault and left me alone for the afternoon. Huge, windowless, seemingly wall-less, its rows of gray metal cabinets receding to the vanishing point, it was one of the quietest places I've experienced.

I've seldom felt as ignorant as I did when I pulled out the museums' collection drawers. Only the typewritten labels connected most of their contents to what I thought I knew of Central American paleontology. Yet it was a stimulating ignorance, as at the Tikal campground in 1971. I had to look for myself; I couldn't just assimilate some processed data and move on. Once you've rummaged through drawers of them, fossils begin to be interesting and even beautiful objects on their own. Horses' teeth, the commonest objects in every collection I saw, resembled heaps of sickle-shaped agates—violet, blue, pink, and ochre. Sometimes they were embedded in yellow crystals, and bits of leg bone or jawbone often were studded with such crystals, red or transparent as well as yellow. Pieces of giant tortoise carapace resembled polished and figured jet jewelry. It wasn't only the mineral world that had acted on the fossils. Some fossil plant matrix, carbonized stem and leaf material embedded in pinkish sediment, was infiltrated with hundreds of present-day tree roots—the living feeding on the long entombed.

The fossils seemed the land bridge's basic materials in an ultimate sense, because Central America's eruptions, earthquakes, uplifts, and erosions had destroyed all but the most enduring parts. Of *Osteoborus*, the hyena-dog, only the bone-eating parts remained, sturdy molars and bits of jaw. Of horses and camels I saw only the running and grass-eating parts—leg bones and jaws and high-crowned, flinty teeth. Of gomphotheres, only lower jaws, tusk sections, and molars remained—the parts for scooping up and pulverizing roots and branches. (Gomphothere jaws are substantial even in fragments—I had trouble lifting a nearly complete one out of its drawer.) Of the low-slung but hulking rhinos, I recall seeing only one or two smallish teeth—of giant tortoises, only carapace fragments.

Only "lower" organisms have left great detail or entirety in Central American fossil beds (although more recent Ice Age assemblages do include some nearly complete large mammal skeletons). In San Salvador, I saw a National Natural History Museum display of exquisite fossil fish, frogs, and leaves from a volcanic ash lake deposit at El Sisimico. The Field Museum's vault had elves' catacombs of tiny mouse and bat bones dug from cave floors. Even the pulverized Gracias deposits yielded some small details. One drawer in the Florida State Museum contained a plastic capsule with part of the skull of a ranid frog from Gracias, perhaps a distant ancestor of the one I found above the dry waterfall.

The fish and frog fossils' detailed similarity to present organisms was somehow reassuring, although it didn't dispel a benighted feeling I got from the vaults. As Webb had said, the bits of large mammal bones and teeth seemed small tokens for the millions of years they represented. Museum dioramas are appealing because they are so bright and definite, like some eternal world of animist archetypes. Whether accurate or not, the reconstructed animals look preternatural against the vividly painted backgrounds of sunset skies, rolling hills, and smoking volcanoes. Sitting in the Field Museum vault with its dry scraps of mortality was more like being in a prehistoric landscape after dark, surrounded by unseen herds.

The Bones from Estanzuela

Probably the best public place to see the remains of Central American prehistoric mammals is at a leafy site just outside the little town of Estanzuela, Guatemala. Estanzuela is in the Motagua Valley, and frequent earthquakes shake loose fossils from Pleistocene river deposits there. One resident of the nearby town of Zacapa looked into his privy after the 1976 quake and saw a mastodon jaw grinning from the bottom of a new, five-meter-deep fissure. In August of 1971, six months after I passed through the Motagua, Harvard paleontologist Bryan Patterson began digging there. The bones he and others found were placed in a small museum in the mid-1970s, and remained pretty much as Patterson left them, with yellowing typewritten labels, when I returned in July 1995.

The valley looked different than I remembered it. July is in the rainy season, and the cactuses that had stood starkly in leafless brush of March 1971 now floated in billows of new acacia leaves. I reached the museum as it opened, a little before waves of schoolchildren swept in, and found the fossils neatly divided between North and South American species, with a slight South American predominance. The articulated skeletons of a *Cuvieronius* mastodon (a genus created by Henry Fairfield Osborn) and an *Eremotherium* ground sloth presided majestically. Horse leg bones and a tapir jawbone made up the rest of the northern contingent. Glyptodont shells, part of a toxodont skull, and the cranium and upper jaw of a horse-sized capybara completed the southern. As I looked at the beautifully preserved capybara skull, the museum's elderly attendant came over and touched it lovingly.

"This is a very rare skull," he said. "And that one," he added, pointing at the toxodont cranium, "was the first toxodont skull to be found in Central America." Toxodonts were among the "nine great quadrupeds" which Darwin found in Patagonia, and he thought them "among the strangest animals that ever lived." They are unusual in that their north-of-Panama remains have been found only on the land bridge, making them the exception to the rule of fossils being found mainly elsewhere. Even the relatively rich Estanzuela fauna manifests this rule, with its seven or so species. The museum had no bones of predators such as saber-tooths, for example, and I asked the attendant if carnivore fossils had been found.

"No," he said, "but this place is still full of buried bones. In the terraces down along the river you can find them anywhere. Children find them all the time. Sometimes they're half-buried under houses, so when they start to dig for them," he imitated a paleontologist scrubbing the ground with a whisk broom, "they come to a wall and have to stop.

So there's much more to be found, if the government would pay to look for it."

Despite their relative scarcity, known Central America's mammal fossils do say one thing with clarity. Only later faunas like Estanzuela's contain any South American mammals. All the earlier ones, like the Gracias and Gaillard, are of *North American mammals only*. Panama's Miocene mammals lived closer to Colombia than to the Great Plains, but they were the same species as in the Dakotas. Miocene fossils from a Colombian site called La Venta are all of South American mammals, like toxodonts and ground sloths. The Central American fossils confirm what the much more complete North and South American ones can only imply—that it has been a land bridge for several million years.

Yet the apparent clarity of this confirmation may be a result of scarcity and fragmentation. Known Central American fossils are not telling the whole story. There are far too few of them. They show us nothing of many other landscapes that must have existed during the past sixty-five million years. So far there are almost no Central American fossils from the early Age of Mammals, the Paleocene, Eocene, and Oligocene epochs. They also fail to show us most of the animals that must have lived with the gomphotheres and ground sloths of the extant faunas. Were there monkeys in the *Schwartzia* and *Schmidelia* trees of pre–land bridge Panama and Honduras, for example? As of 1996, there are no monkey fossils from Central America.

6

Biological Chauvinism

IN ITS SCHOLARLY WAY, the land bridge's discovery was rather like the engineering spectacle of the Panama Canal, with which it was historically contemporary. Fossil digging and canal building arose from similar exploratory and expansive impulses. The Panama Canal broke down a spacial barrier, and the discovery of the Panama land bridge broke down temporal ones. I imagine Buffon's and Cuvier's ghosts flitting in the wake of bone-hunter wagons, perturbed at the explosion of pet theories, but eagerly awaiting new vistas. Yet the vistas weren't all that new. If the canal did not end war and poverty, the land bridge's discovery did not end the prejudices with which science had first approached the question of intercontinental migration.

One of the few nineteenth-century evolutionists to visit Central America and write at length about it was Thomas Belt, the English mining engineer who recorded the legend of a lost Indian civilization on the Costa Rica's Río Frío. (He dismissed the legend, observing that Río Frío Indians were no different from others, except maybe poorer.) Belt had absorbed the latest biological thinking before he went to manage a Nicaraguan gold mine from 1868 to 1872. His *A Naturalist in Nicaragua* is a model of close observation and informed speculation that Darwin called "the best of all natural history journals that have ever been published."

Belt had no trouble identifying Central American organisms. He could tell not only between a turkey and a curassow, but between curassow species. Beyond that, his insights into the ecological relationships among Nicaragua's tropical forest and its entomology, geology, and ethnology were penetrating and original. "A ceaseless round of ever active life," he wrote, "weaves the forest scenery of the tropics into one monotonous whole, of which the component parts exhibit in detail untold beauty and variety." He saw that acacia ants live in symbiotic relationship with acacia trees, protecting them from other insects and eating special foods the trees produce for them. He discovered that leafcutter ants do not eat the leaves that he saw them carrying to their nests, but instead feed on a fungus that they grow on those leaves. Observing that organic acids leached downward by tropical rains had decomposed the bedrock under the trees to a depth of 200 feet, Belt recognized the forest's "immense antiquity." He also saw the changes within its apparent stasis, such as the burning by humans that was diminishing it. During his four-year stay, "many acres of the neighborhood of Pital were taken from the forest and added to the grass lands."

Belt was so accurate in most of his book that it comes as a surprise to read his political commentaries. "When Mexico becomes one with the United States," he wrote, "all Central America will soon follow. Railways will be pushed from the north into the tropics, and a constant stream of immigration will change the face of the country . . . and fill it with farms and gardens, orange groves, and coffee, sugar, cacao, and indigo plantations. No progress need be expected from its present inhabitants. . . . Nor will the Anglo-American long be stayed by the Isthmus, in his progress southward. . . . Not many centuries will roll over before the English language will be spoken from the frozen soil of the north to Tierra del Fuego in the south."

This headlong leap into chauvinism seems shockingly unscientific to a late twentieth–century reader, yet it wouldn't have surprised many in the nineteenth century. It would have seemed a sound, if imaginative and perhaps indiscreet, expression of well-established scientific principle. The principle was the same as Buffon had expressed in 1780: temperate Old World organisms were superior to tropical New World ones. Buffon had been old-fashioned in attributing this superiority, of men as well as other animals, to seniority and climate. The new evolutionary biology replaced such attributes with fitness. Whereas Buffon had seen an apparent absence of Old World organisms in South America as evidence of its inferiority, Darwin saw an apparent mass migration of Old World organisms into South America as evidence of its inferiority.

"I suspect that this preponderant migration from the north to the south," Darwin wrote in *The Origin of Species*, "is due to the greater extent of land in the north, and to the northern forms having existed in their own homes in greater numbers, and consequently having been advanced through natural selection and competition to a higher stage of perfection, or dominating power, than the southern forms." He added that the process was continuing with the establishment in the south not only of Old World men, but Old World weeds: "At the present day, we see that many European forms cover the ground in La Plata . . . and have beaten the natives, whereas extremely few southern forms have become naturalized in any part of the northern hemisphere." Wallace echoed Darwin in *The Geographical Distribution of Animals*: "The great northern continents represent the original seat of mammalian life and the region of its highest development," he wrote, "where the southern continents . . . have been isolated for varying periods, and after receiving an immigration of lowly forms, have developed and preserved these to a greater or lesser degree, according as they were more or less protected from the irruption and competition of higher types."

The unearthing of the "Great Faunal Interchange" seemed to substantiate such ideas. It appeared the interchange was more than a spectacle, that it was a kind of "triumph and tragedy" epic—a triumph for advanced northern organisms and a tragedy for primitive southern ones. The giant marsupial carnivores and placental ungulates that had dominated South America since the Dinosaur Age had disappeared from the fossil record by the Ice Age. Cats, dogs, and other carnivores had replaced the marsupials in the predatory niche, while deer, horses, camels, and peccaries had occupied the herbivorous niche of extinct liptoterns and pyrotheres. North American animals had conquered the south, it seemed, very much as Belt foresaw North American people conquering it.

Paleontologists drew dramatic pictures of an evolutionary "slaughter of innocents" as big-brained, highly adapted supermammals swarmed into a lost continent of evolutionary retardation. "The saber-toothed tigers . . . very possibly played a large part in the destruction of the giant herbivores which flourished at that time on the Pampas," wrote the New York Zoological Society's Madison Grant. "It would almost seem that the saber-toothed tigers were modified in their marvellous dentition for the express purpose of preying on these huge and thick-skinned animals."

Henry Fairfield Osborn, president of the American Museum of Natural History from 1908 until 1933, developed a theory of animal origins and migration that echoed Buffon's as well as Wallace's. "Northern Asia was the great center of animal population and of adaptive radiation into Europe on the west and into North America on the northeast," Osborn wrote in his *Origin and History of Life* (1917). He thought North and South America had been connected at the Age of Mammals' beginning, but then had separated, leaving the South American fauna to evolve a range of adaptation and diversity inferior to that coming from "the great center." Then, "in that Pliocene and early Pleistocene time the grandest epoch of mammalian life is reached: certain great orders like the probiscideans and the horses with very high powers of adaptation as well as migration spread over every continent except Australia."

Osborn's was the standard view of the Great Faunal Interchange for most of this century. "Centers in the northern hemisphere have been the places of origin for the principal advances in organization," intoned a 1951 biogeography textbook by W. C. Allee. "The groups whose adaptations or changes represented advances were enabled to enlarge their ranges and extend it to the south, at times driving more primitive forms before them." David Attenborough repeated this more entertainingly in his 1978 television series, *Life on Earth*. Standing before a windswept Patagonian cave full of fossil ground sloth dung, he spoke in his breathless way of "more advanced animals" from North America which "invaded south." He concluded, "As the populations mixed, northerners and southerners competed for the same food and territory. There were winners and losers, and most of the strange South Americans disappeared."

Triumph and tragedy compelled even those who didn't *like* the idea.

Also featuring a sloth cave in his 1977 best-seller, *In Patagonia*, travel writer Bruce Chatwin was ironic about the prevailing theory, calling it "this zoological version of the Monroe Doctrine." Yet when it came to describing the interchange, Chatwin used close to Osborn's and Grant's very words: "The mammals of South America developed odder and odder forms. . . . Then the land-bridge of Panama resurfaced and a host of more efficient, North American mammals, such as the puma and sabre-tooth tiger, rushed south and wiped out many indigenous species."

The Barnum Brown Expedition

Like earlier naturalists, Great American Interchange discoverers like Osborn and Ameghino didn't feel called upon to visit Central America in order to theorize about its evolutionary role. The circumstantial evidence on the pampas and prairies was compelling, and Central America's forests were daunting. O. C. Marsh, the first professional paleontologist to work in western North America, returned from his digs via Panama in the 1870s but apparently didn't look for fossils there, although he collected archaeological artifacts. Yet one of the liveliest, if oddest, accounts of "triumph and tragedy" emerged from an Osborn associate's expedition to Central America.

Barnum Brown may have been the greatest fossil hunter of the past century. Osborn said he was "the most amazing collector I have ever known. He must be able to *smell* fossils." Osborn sent Brown to Patagonia to look for early mammal fossils in 1898. In 1902, Brown discovered the first *Tyrannosaurus rex* in Montana, dragging its bones 124 miles across the prairie to the railroad on a horse-drawn sledge. In 1908, he found the *second Tyrannosaurus rex* in the same area. An octogenarian in the 1950s, he was still enthusiastically active, and when he heard that a crocodile hunter had found huge bones in a Petén river, he hurried there. His young second wife Lilian accompanied him and published a book about it in 1956.

Entitled *Bring 'em Back Petrified*, the book is a fascinating artifact of cultural as well as paleontological history. Hollywood's influence is discernible. Mrs. Brown is plucky, if squeamish, and solicitous of her absentminded, pipe-smoking husband, who has "staked his scientific reputation" on finding fossils. "Looking for bones in the jungle is one of the mortal sins of paleontology," she writes. "It simply *isn't done*. Which is why Barnum does it. He likes to find things where no one else will look for them." Brown spends his days examining rocks with a magnifying glass, and flings himself down with excited cries when he finds something, startling his native assistants. ". . . He examined it through the lens, then suddenly emitted a jubilant, 'FORAMINIFERA! Stand back, everyone. Nobody touch the rock, we've got *foraminifera!*' . . . Lolo threw Rufio a look of alarm. 'Is this bad? Are we get a disease?'"

The Browns spent a dry season at the Kekchi Maya village of Santa Amelia on the Rio Pasion, where they ran afoul of Kaa, a Lacandon *bruja*. Lilian's attempts to indoctrinate the village children with 1950s North American values infuriated Kaa. "I was careful to talk a great deal about their wonderful land of the Petén, and the great possibilities that were there if only they would learn to *develop* them—new industries, oil, lumber, cattle raising, farming. 'Someday,' I'd tell them, 'and even sooner than you children think, Santa Amelia will be a big town, with many people. You will all live in new houses with electric light and refrigerators, and have stores where you will buy lots of pretty things you see in these magazines. . . .'" The *bruja* also was displeased by the Browns' fossil hunting. Asked about bones, "she stared back in silence, arms hanging limp, fingers curling and uncurling like claws. 'It is best,' she croaked at last, 'to let the dead lie.'" When the Browns came back to their headquarters after a day of fossil hunting, they found their laboratory burned down. When they returned to Santa Amelia the next year to resume their dig, the village had disappeared into the forest, like the lost city of Tayasal. They couldn't even find a place to land their plane.

Yet the Browns did find fossils during their first and last Santa Amelia sojourn. After digging on land proved disappointing, Brown looked in the river and found a mastodon hip joint and a ground sloth brain case. He hired the townspeople to dive for bones, and they found fossils of prehistoric horses, saber-tooths, bison, camels, deer, and armadillos. "'Pixie,' Barnum said, at the end of an unusually profitable day, 'we've never come on a more *varied* fossil fauna in any of our expedi-

tions.' . . . 'How,' I answered, 'did so many kinds ever get into this
petrified zoo?'"

Lilian Brown then answered her own question in imaginative detail:

When polar air masses from the Arctic and Antarctic moved into the
temperate regions, everything with legs started trekking to warmer
climate. . . . No more bizarre group could be imagined than those
trekking north ahead of the cold. There were sabre-toothed marsupials with the physique of lions; pyrotheres that resembled elephants;
there were typotheres that would have fooled even a rabbit. . . . All
these travelers from the south were doubly grotesque because for
geologic ages they had remained isolated in what was the island continent of South America. While North America, Europe, and Asia were
evolving higher forms of life, this vast area to the south lagged behind
biologically, becoming archaic, inferior.

But during the Pliocene Age . . . the Panama region arched upward,
forming a land bridge. . . . The Isthmus of Panama served not only
as a migration route for northern animals heading south, but also as
an exit for the formerly isolated southern types. . . . But the northern
animal population . . . had a good head start . . . and its members
were well on their way towards the equator, and beyond. Their eventual appearance in South America must have been upsetting to the
inferior local animals, who, for the first time, were threatened by the
survival of the fittest. . . . Now, faced on the one front with competition from superior outsiders and on the other by approaching cold,
they couldn't stand their ground. They broke and ran to the north.
For long ages, the ancient anachronisms, north-bound from the island
continent, struggled along the lowland shelves to the east of the cor-
dilleran spine, working their way across the crooked neck of Central
America. Some, including the ground sloths, glyptodonts, and armadillos made good their escape and found a new life in what is now
the United States. . . . However, most . . . failed to survive very long.
The tiny Texas armadillo and the porcupine are the last of the strange
wandering southerners that made the trip to North America and
survived.

Most paleontologists thought that South American mammals spread
north not because the arrival of superior North American mammals
upset them, but for the same reason that North American mammals
spread south: because new territory became available. Barnum Brown

presumably would have agreed, although his evolutionary outlook also tended toward drama. (Walt Disney based the dinosaur extinction sequence in *Fantasia* on Brown's description of sauropod skeletons clustered around a prehistoric mudhole "as they made their last futile stand against fate.") Yet Lilian Brown covered the basic evidence for "triumph and tragedy." A South American megafauna *did* become extinct in South America, it *was* replaced by a North American megafauna, and the South American species that spread into North America largely became extinct there. If the mass extinction and replacement of a fauna isn't a sign of inferiority, what is?

Scott's Skepticism

Some evolutionists expressed doubts. W. B. Scott, Osborn's college friend and fellow fossil digger on the prairie, was one of the few early paleontologists to visit the isthmus. He traveled to Panama in 1911 and spent a week inspecting the canal "from end to end." He didn't look for fossils there, and seems to have been interested in the canal as much as an engineering feat as a geological excavation. Yet he did give some thought to the paleontological implications. "I gained an entirely new conception," he wrote in his autobiography, "of the geological history of the Isthmus and one which fitted very much better in the results of our work in Patagonia and in western North America than did the old account given by the French." In his definitive *History of the Land Mammals of the Western Hemisphere* (1937), Scott wrote that he didn't know why the South American megafauna had become extinct. "Many causes for extinction have been suggested, such as changes of climate, the onset of new infectious diseases, the 'struggle for existence' in competition with better adapted rivals, or enemies, and many others. It is probable that nearly all of the suggested factors, and many more that have not been thought of, have been real agents in the process, yet the combined operation of the various causes is not understood."

Scott's student George Gaylord Simpson called it "a tempting and indeed unavoidable conjecture" that the interchange caused the extinctions, but added that "it must be confessed that the evidence is not strong." In his *Splendid Isolation: The Curious History of South American Fossils* (1980), Simpson pointed to weaknesses in the triumph and tragedy brief. Marsupial carnivores apparently had disappeared from the South American fossil record long before dogs and cats arrived. Likewise, many South American ungulates seemed to have become extinct before North American ungulates crossed the land bridge. At least two South American ungulate familes—camellike macraucheniids and rhinoceroslike toxodonts—survived in South America as long as horses and elephants did.

One pioneer paleontologist not only rejected triumph and tragedy, but reversed it. The Argentinian Florentino Ameghino thought his fossils showed that South America, not Asia, had been the place of mammal origins and advancement. In the 1880s, when his brother Carlos found the fossils in Patagonia, it appeared that their rock strata were older than any others in which mammals had been found, so Florentino was logical in assuming that the South American mammals' uniqueness proved them ancestral to all others, including humans. Unfortunately, the rock strata weren't that old, although, like Columbus, Ameghino kept his cherished belief until death.

Ameghino's notion of Argentinian genesis was a respite from northern chauvinism, but it did no more than triumph and tragedy to explain the doubts Scott and Simpson raised. The doubts have persisted, as paleontologist Stephen Jay Gould pointed out in "O Grave Where Is Thy Victory," a 1982 essay published, with history's usual irony, in the American Museum of Natural History's magazine. Gould announced that quantitative studies of extinction rates by "a group of researchers centered in Chicago" had shown that mammalian migration north and south across the Panamanian isthmus had been about the same. "Members of fourteen North American families now reside in South America, representing forty percent of South American familial diversity," Gould wrote. "Twelve South American families now live in North America, forming thirty-six percent of North American families. . . . Native South American genera declined by thirteen percent between pre- and post-isthmian faunas. Native North American genera declined by eleven percent during the same interval. Thus, about the same number of families moved successfully in both directions and about the same percentage of native forms became extinct on both sides following the initial interchange. . . . The old story of 'hail the conquering hero comes'—waves of differential migration and subsequent carnage—can no longer be maintained."

One of the reasons that the old story could no longer be maintained was that it didn't take Central America sufficiently into account. It left out the fact that South American mammals, which largely were tropical because so much of their continent was tropical, were as successful in spreading into Central America's, and then Mexico's, tropical zones as North American mammals were in moving into South America. W. B. Scott had pointed this out in 1937: "Only a very small proportion of the mammals characteristic of each continent found their way into the other. . . . Between the two warm temperate zones extend the tropics, which acted as a vast sieve, holding back most mammals and allowing but a relatively small number of characteristically adaptable species to pass through."

7

Biological Relativism

M Y EXPERIENCE OF MAMMALS in Central America supports Gould's half-and-half migration model over the "triumph-and-tragedy" notion that the American biotic interchange constituted a victory for advanced northern organisms and a loss for primitive southern ones. Mammals of South American origin even seem to predominate slightly on a day-to-day basis. I've seen more South American agoutis and monkeys than North American foxes and squirrels, although all are common in suitable habitat. South American lesser anteaters and opossums are more commonly seen roadkills (by me, at least) than North American raccoons and rabbits.

This apparent predominance of South Americans may be illusory. Many North American mammals are nocturnal or secretive—especially the big, spectacular ones like jaguars and tapirs. Although no South American land mammals in Central America could be called big except the capybara and giant anteater, they're generally not elusive. Sloths are inconspicuous, but that is because they move so slowly through the treetops. Opossums, armadillos, and anteaters are as likely to ignore human intruders as elude them. I almost stepped on the first lesser anteater, or tamandua, I saw. It's not that these three can't move fast when they want, but they seem to live in a different time frame than

North American mammals. In fact, sloths, armadillos, and anteaters do have different metabolisms than other placental mammals, with lower average body temperatures.

Although South and North American mammal families may be about equal in Central America, North American *species* are more numerous. There are three anteater species, for example, but six raccoon family species. Central America's anteater species are the same as in South America, but four of its raccoon family species are mainly Central and South American. Gould observed in his 1982 essay that North American mammals generally have been more successful in evolving new forms as they've migrated than South American ones. "In North America, genera originally from South America evolved very few new genera, while North American forms were remarkably prolific in South America." This led him to wonder if "perhaps the conventional explanation is true in part, and North American forms radiated because they are, in some unexplained way, competitively superior to South American natives."

Such is triumph and tragedy's epic power that Gould almost seemed to have forgotten his 1982 challenge to it when he returned to the subject in a 1996 essay about sloths. The "flood of North American mammals across the new land bridge correlates well with the decimation of the native South American fauna," he wrote. "Fewer South American lineages managed to move north." Gould echoed Lilian Brown in citing the armadillo as one of a pitiful few southern survivors in the north, although he picked the opossum instead of the porcupine as his other example. "Most distinctive South American lineages simply died out," he continued, mistakenly including in his list of stay-at-home losers one group, "the giant and rapacious phorusrhacid ground birds," that *did* invade North America successfully. Gould concluded, "I so wish that this wondrously diverse and evolutionarily disparate fauna had survived—and I do blame the entirely natural rise of the Isthmus of Panama for triggering this particular biological tragedy."

Modified ideas of geographical superiority (or, to use a more scientific term, dominance) continue. When evolutionary biologist Edward O. Wilson described the Interchange in his book *The Diversity of Life* (1992), he didn't write of "more advanced animals" and "primitive forms." Like Gould a decade before, he noted that about the same number of South American mammal families crossed between the continents as North American. Yet he concluded that, "In general, where close ecological equivalents met during the interchange, the North American elements prevailed. . . . The mammals of North American origin proved dominant as a whole over the South American mammals."

Although Wilson acknowledged that "no one knows for sure" why North American mammals prevailed, he leaned toward the original Darwinian idea that the mammals of the larger Old World continents were fitter—"tougher competitors." He devoted several pages of his 1994 autobiography, *Naturalist*, to his fascination with the idea that there might have been "a main center of evolution on the land." He nominated not Eurasia but the Old World tropics as "the evolutionary crucible," citing the 1950s work of biogeographer Philip Darlington, who traced the origin of many "current hegemonic groups" such as dogs, cats, and deer to that region. Darlington's view pushed back the origin of North American mammals to, in Wilson's words, "the vast greenhouse region that comprises southern Asia, sub-Saharan Africa, and until recent geological times, much of the Middle East. The most dominant of the animal groups pressed on northward to Europe and Siberia, across the Bering Sea, a barrier periodically breached by the rise of isthmuses, and into the New World."

Yet ideas of Old World geographical dominance are hard to apply to much of biology and paleontology. It is easier to see superior fitness in the mammals that crossed the Central American land bridge than in other organisms. In some cases, neither North or South American organisms seem dominant. Many organisms from both continents get as far as Central America and simply stop. In other cases, South American organisms seem dominant, holding sway throughout Central America and far into Mexico. In still others, it's hard to see not only what is dominant, but what is North or South American.

Such details had not bothered the Comte de Buffon, who was uninterested in proving the inferiority of South American birds and fishes, "because they pass from continent to continent, and it would be nearly impossible to tell those belonging to one from those belonging to another." Buffon even attributed a certain superiority to South American reptiles, amphibians, and insects, since an inferior continent could be expected to produce superior kinds of inferior organisms. (From a chauvinistic viewpoint, this seems a superior example of Gallic logic.) Yet the sedentary Buffon's geography proved no more reliable with birds and fishes than with Panama's mountains. Land birds and freshwater fishes can't pass easily from continent to continent, and distinguishing between them is far from impossible. South America's land birds and freshwater fishes are highly characteristic, and markedly superior in diversity and beauty.

Europe and North America have little to compare with the fire-colored cock-of-the-rock, the turquoise-and-purple lovely cotinga, the fourteen-foot arapaima, and the electric eel. There is nothing on earth, not even in the Old World tropics, comparable to the Amazon Basin's over 3,000 known freshwater fish species or the Neotropical Region's over 3,500 bird species, nearly half those in existence. A few days' boat trip that I took on the Peruvian Amazon demonstrated ceaseless, casual superiority. A half hour of fishing landed two piranha species as well as various plant-eating piranha relatives and a bewildering succession of catfish with ornate markings, extravagant barbels or strange cries (South America has at least 1,200 catfish species). Nearly every fish caught was different. A continual diversity of parakeets, parrots, macaws, and other birds flew overhead. This was in an area settled as long as the Mississippi, not an isolated wilderness.

There's not much evidence that the land bridge's formation sent a wave of North American birds and fish into South America. On the contrary, South American birds may have invaded North America en masse, according to one interpretation. As ecologist Marston Bates wrote in *The Land and Wildlife of South America:*

> While siskins and perhaps a few other northern birds were working their way southward, tyrant flycatchers, tanagers, and hummingbirds went north to become, like the ubiquitous opossum, familiar inhabitants of lands as far north as Canada. Today, some of our most migratory land birds in North America belong to families that also occur, often in more varied forms, in South America—and this has led to the suggestion that such migrants may have been originally South American species which took to seasonally flying northward when the recession of ice ages changed the climate there.

Bates thought South America's rain forest had acted as a barrier to birds migrating from the north, and there must be truth in this. Yet both Central and South America have extensive mountains with habitats into which one would expect adaptable northern birds like jays, crows, titmice, and nuthatches to have spread. Most haven't. Jays have reached South America but are rather uncommon there; crows live only as far south as Nicaragua; and titmice and nuthatches haven't even reached Central America. During several days of trekking in the Peruvian Andes, the only birds of North American origin I recognized were water ouzels, the stream dwellers that were John Muir's favorites, and the white-headed South American ouzels were showier than the plain gray North American species. A few summer days in North American mountains usually turns up wrens, hummingbirds, tyrant flycatchers, tanagers, and vireos—all with South American centers of distribution, sometimes seasonal migrants from South America.

There is fossil evidence that some bird groups which now seem typically South American may have originated in North America and moved south. This doesn't involve songbirds, which have left almost no fossils, but larger birds such as storks and vultures. More such North American groups may have spread south than South American groups have spread north. The evidence is scanty and debatable, however, and triumph and tragedy doesn't apply. Although some South American groups like the "giant and rapacious" phorusrhacids became extinct, no huddled masses of primitive South American birds seem to have vanished before North American arrivals. "Primitive" tinamous, rheas, and hoatzins are surviving.

South American fish are demonstrably the only fish to have crossed the land bridge. They have crossed it very slowly, as one would expect of fish. Although the Amazon basin has the highest freshwater fish diversity in the world, Central America has fairly low diversity for a tropical region. Costa Rica has nearly 900 bird species, more than the U.S. and Canada, but only a little more than a hundred freshwater fish species. Almost all these fish are South American in origin, belonging to families that North Americans usually see in aquarium stores.

A tourist looking in a Central American stream and expecting an aquarium display will be disappointed. Even tropical fish look different in the wild than in brightly lit tanks, and a North American might think he's seeing what he'd see in an Ohio stream—some large bass or perchlike fish, some smaller sunfishlike fish, a variety of minnows, and some catfish or suckers lurking on the bottom. Yet the Central American fish are separated by hundreds of millions of years of evolution from the Ohio fish. No bass, perch, trout, sunfish, minnows, or suckers have spread farther south than the Isthmus of Tehuantepec, except where they've been artificially introduced. In Central America, what appear to be bass, perch, or sunfish are cichlids, the huge tropical group which includes angelfish, and what appear to be minnows or suckers are characids, the huge tropical group which includes tetras (and piranhas), or poecilliids, the huge tropical group that includes mollies. There are catfish, but they are South American ones.

I can write of fish with certitude because I have a tank of neotropical firemouth cichlids, sailfin mollies, and suckermouth catfish beside me. Their talents for claiming territory and procreating are impressive. The firemouths drive the catfish away from their fry by brandishing their gill covers like scarlet shields. The catfish flees, but is impervious behind armored scales, and needs little more than algae to thrive. The mollies sail imperturbably overhead, dropping dozens of liveborn young into the tank every few months. As far as the pet industry goes, there's no doubt as to which continent is the invader. Tropical fish dumped in North American waters have caused extinction of some native species, and feral cichlids now dominate south Florida waters. One common characid, the Mexican tetra, has been banned from pet stores because of its possible effects on native minnows. Even in the wild, characids and cichlids contrived to traverse mountains and deserts as far north as Texas and Colorado.

Wandering Continents

Are South American fish "in some unexplained way, competitively superior" to North American ones? The issue would be clearer if South America's fish were as uniquely South American as are its mammals. Buffon may have been wrong when he wrote that freshwater fish could "pass from continent to continent," but he had reason for thinking so, whether or not he knew it. Despite the over fifty million years of isolation which evolved its unique armadillos and anteaters, South America's

cichlids and characids have many close relatives in Africa—African cichlids and characids. As Buffon inferred, the issue of continental superiority is moot if a group of organisms can't be confined to one or the other.

Yet if cichlids and characids didn't get from Africa to South America
by swimming the Atlantic, how did they? The answer seems obvious
now, but would have seemed equally improbable to Buffon, Darwin,
or Henry Fairfield Osborn—which is one reason they could much more
easily entertain ideas of continental superiority than we. Buffon, Darwin, and Osborn thought, with most of their fellow scientists, that the
continents had always been in their present positions. They believed
continental outlines could have changed with sea level fluctuations,
thus creating intermittent land bridges, but that ocean basins and landmasses were more or less permanent. This belief remained prevalent
when the Barnum Browns were exploring the Petén, as evidenced by
a 1951 best-seller. "In spite of theories to the contrary," wrote state-of-
the-art young science writer Rachel Carson in *The Sea Around Us*, "the
weight of geologic evidence seems to be that the locations of the major
ocean basins and the major continental landmasses are today much the
same as they have been since a very early period of the earth's history."

The "theories to the contrary" had begun with German minister
Theodor Lilienthal's observation in 1756 that Africa's west coast and
South America's east coast would fit together like jigsaw puzzle pieces if
the continents were contiguous. In 1858, a man named Antonio Snider-
Pelligrini combined this fit with his own observations of close similarities between North American and European coal deposits to theorize
that continents might have been united in the past, then drifted apart.
Pelligrini was ignored, but when meteorologist Alfred Wegener took up
the "continental drift" theory in the 1920s, science paid enough attention to scoff. Wegener thought planetary rotation drove the continents
across the earth's crust like rafts, but measurements of rock strength
proved this impossible.

In the early 1960s, however, studies of the ocean floor showed it
wasn't the ageless basalt expanse Rachel Carson had described a decade
earlier. Sediments and crystallography proved that it was successively
younger on either side of clefts from which lava and volcanic gases
flowed. Evidently a new seafloor welled up continually from the earth's

mantle and spread out from the upwelling zones. This evidence of sea-floor spreading led to the theory of plate tectonics, which divides the planetary crust into an assemblage of rigid, basaltic plates resting on a semi-molten, plastic mantle about one hundred kilometers down. Plates are thought to form by emergence and hardening of mantle material in spreading zones, which appear not only in mid-ocean, but wherever the crust is thin or weak. Continents are "rafts" of granitic rocks resting on the basaltic plates, and as the plates move, the continents move. If a continent happens to lie directly above a spreading zone, the growing plates beneath it gradually pull the continent apart. Plate tectonics thus explains the jigsaw puzzle fit between Africa and South America.

Tectonic theory has explanations for much other planetary behavior. As plates grow out from spreading zones, they collide with other plates or slide against them. During collisions, continent-bearing plates tend to ride up over oceanic plates because the oceanic plates are denser. The oceanic plates are pushed, or "subducted" (led down) into the mantle. As they sink, pressure remelts the oceanic plate's rocks, and since heat rises, the molten rock returns to the surface as lava, forming volcanoes along the line of subduction. Other mountains arise as crustal material cracks and buckles under the stress of subduction, forcing blocks of continental crust upward. Earthquakes occur along these cracks, called faults.

Plate tectonics provides the most coherent explantion yet for the planet's geological behavior, although it is by no means proved. Its ultimate cause remains conjectural. Convection currents in the mantle may cause spreading zones by forcing mantle material to the surface where the crust is weak, but nobody has gone a hundred kilometers down to observe the convection currents. Still, convection currents may make smaller systems behave as theory says the earth's crust does. I saw this demonstrated early one morning in a Belizean hotel. As elsewhere in Central America, Belizean coffee is on the acidic side—the best beans go north. This acidic quality combined with the Belizean practice of putting condensed milk in coffee created a semisolid substance on the surface of my cup, and I was intrigued to see it divide into irregular patches that seemed to mark convection currents arising from the hotter coffee below. Some patches got larger, apparently rising from "spreading

zones," and some got smaller, apparently "subducting" under the growing ones. I suppose this "patch tectonics" would have subsided as the
coffee cooled, proving that convection had caused it, but I drank it first.

The plate tectonics answer to the similarity of Africa's and South
America's fishes is that until about one hundred million years ago both
continents were part of the supercontinent of Gondwanaland, whereon
lived both cichlids and characids. Plate tectonics' implications for land
bridges like Central America were the biological equivalent of the shift
from Newtonian to Einsteinian physics. In the old, static continent view,
a land bridge was like a valve, which might open or close, or be partly
closed by various filters such as rain forests or mountains, but which
had a certain mechanical stability. In the plate tectonics view, in which
not only continents and oceans but underlying crustal plates wander,
a land bridge is more like a vortex than a valve, a somewhat vague
potentiality which may have a clear mechanical entity at times, but
which may blur or dissolve at others, as everything continually shifts
in relation to everything else.

In the plate tectonics view, a land bridge like Central America doesn't
simply link the two continents it happens to connect, but others as
well. Scientists had speculated about other odd connections than that
between African and South American fish. In the 1930s, W. B. Scott
noted similarities between South American and Australian organisms.
Plate tectonics made such speculations inescapable, and land bridge
questions have become increasingly complicated. The question of where
organisms originated, for example, has become a kind of biological
musical chairs. As the geological clock ticks backward, continents circle
dizzily about the planet, and attempts to stop the clock and say just what
might have been happening at any particular time can be as awkward as
the rush for seats when the party music stops.

Marsupials are a case in point. Since they today live mainly in South
America and Australia, it would be convenient if marsupials had originated on a "primitive" southern supercontinent. In the 1960s, fossils
from the Bolivian Andes showed that marsupials similar to today's common opossum have inhabited South America since the dinosaur age.
Yet there are similarly aged marsupial fossils from North America and
Europe, and no similarly aged ones from Australia. Geological evidence
suggests that both Australia and South America drifted apart from the

supercontinent of Gondwanaland before the living groups of mammals evolved. Where did marsupials originate? George Gaylord Simpson concluded that marsupials probably did evolve first in North America, South America, Australia, or Antarctica, "but . . . we simply do not know which."

South America's ancient but ambiguous affinities with Africa have complicated the origins of two of the most characteristic "South American" mammal groups—monkeys and caviomorph rodents. The spider monkeys and agouti I saw at Tikal are typical members of these groups. Both appeared on the continent in the Oligocene epoch between thirty-four and twenty-four million years ago, and have evolved into dozens of families and genera: tamarins and marmosets as well as monkeys; capybaras, porcupines, guineau pigs, and viscachas as well as agoutis. Persistent anatomical characteristics (of the nose in monkeys and the jaw in caviomorphs) suggest that both groups evolved from just a few original migrants. South America was already an isolated continent when they arrived, so they probably did so by migrating across an island chain. What was at the other end of it?

Geology suggests that South America was closer to North America than to Africa for most of the past fifty million years, and that there were island chains between them. Yet biology suggests that South America's monkeys and rodents are more like Africa's than North America's (not least because North America doesn't have monkeys, although it had monkey ancestors like lemurs and tarsiers fifty million years ago). On the other hand, living African monkeys and rodents aren't very much like South American ones, although there are fossil African monkeys and rodents that more closely resemble living South American monkeys and rodents. Entire conferences have been devoted to South American monkey or rodent origins. "There are students on both sides of the argument," wrote George Gaylord Simpson, "so well-informed, so authoritative, and so evenly balanced in disagreement that anyone else can hardly argue against or for either view. A. E. Wood and B. Patterson have the ancestor of the caviomorphs hopping along islands from southern North America. R. Hoffstetter and R. Lavocat have them making the long (but then not quite so long as now) transatlantic hop from Africa. It is irrelevant that Wood and Patterson are North Americans, Hoffstetter and Lavocat French. Years ago I was on the North American side; now I am neutral, and await some really convincing evidence on either side."

David Webb told me in 1993 that paleontologists recently had found that South American monkey fossils are younger than had been thought, from the late instead of the early Oligocene epoch. "That weighs in favor of a North American origin," Webb said, "because there's no question that the Atlantic was continually getting wider, so the later it happened the wider the Atlantic was. It's just a longer boat ride from Africa in the late Oligocene. Primates abhor salt water—they're very fastidious little beasts that need lots of fresh water and lots of fresh food." Webb still was inclined to neutrality in the monkey wars, however.

For all their obscurities, mammal origins tend to be clearer than other organisms'. That South American and African fish are similar, for example, might lead one to expect that other freshwater animals would be so. Yet South American frogs have few similarities to African ones. South American frogs are more like Australian frogs. South American fish, on the other hand, have almost nothing in common with Australian freshwater fish, of which there are relatively few species, although the odd, ancient lungfishes live on both continents—and in Africa.

Biology's historical search for geographical origins has been a bit like Columbus's search for the Indies. Both Columbus and naturalists like the Comte de Buffon knew the earth is a sphere, but failed to realize the full dimensions of sphericality. The historical world of origins and destinations deals in straight lines—the routes of discovery voyages and conquest expeditions. The land bridge as valve functions within this paradigm. Yet there are really no straight lines on a spherical planet. The shortest distance between two geographical points could be achieved only by "digging to China," an archetypical child's daydream to which Columbus's voyages had a certain similarity.

The earth is not only spherical. It is mythologically alive, not a ball of inert rock but a dynamic system of plastic mantle and shifting crustal plates. Except for its still largely unknown cosmic origin, there are no clear beginnings and endings in such a system. The land bridge as vortex functions within *this* paradigm. Vortices are the epitome of circularity, of whirling motion from incalculable sources to unexpected outcomes. Triumph and tragedy is too simple for such a phenomenon, which consists not only of existing land, but of past land, past island chains, and even more tenuous links such as "sweepstakes distributions," whereby organisms make intercontinental journeys on birds' feet or driftwood. Animal migrations are circular wanderings, not discovery voyages or conquest expeditions.

The vortex story lacks the satisfying solidity of a tournament of mega-faunas, but it is more diverse, and perhaps more lively in its miniaturized way. Much of the megafauna is extinct, but many other land bridge organisms are very much extant, and their evolutionary stories reach back much farther into Central America's past than the megafauna's. Of course, little or nothing is known about most of them, and their multiplicity is daunting. I cannot even begin, for example, to tell the land bridge story of the most important land animals, the insects. Both I and the reader would have to be much better entomologists than perhaps yet exist to do that. Yet a good deal is known here and there about various plants and animals, and even the imperfectly glimpsed eddies and swirls of their deep pasts may give a sense of a vortex in motion, pulling bits of life north and south rather as a tornado pulls between earth and sky.

EVOLUTION

In their manner of eating and building the Indians of
the islands and of tierra firme are almost the same,
and the same is true of their bread, and of most fruits
and fish; but altogether in tierra firme are more fruits,
and I believe more kinds of fish, and many and very
strange animals and birds.

> Gonzalo Fernández de Oviedo y Valdés,
> *General and Natural History of the Indies*

8

The Bridge of Titanosaurs

P LATE TECTONICS BARELY had been invented when I first visited Central America in 1971, and I can't remember what if anything I knew about the subject. If I had known that plate subduction causes volcanoes, I doubt if it would have clarified my perceptions. It probably would only have added to my confusion. Like its landscapes, Central America's plate tectonics are unusually diverse. Beneath North and South America, a few vast continental and oceanic plates collide over enormous distances. Beneath Central America, a relatively larger number of plates jostle within a much smaller area. Geologists have mapped at least five crustal plates affecting Central America—the North American, Caribbean, Cocos, Nazca, and South America. Complications increase geometrically in such a vortex.

My first close encounter with Central American tectonics was on the Santa Elena Peninsula next to Costa Rica's Santa Rosa National Park in 1988, when biologist Daniel Janzen was encouraging visitors as part of a conservation campaign. Janzen is Thomas Belt's twentieth-century counterpart in some ways, having spent much of the past three decades studying Central American forest ecology. His long-term observations have greatly deepened Belt's intuitive perceptions of tropical forest complexity. He systematically confirmed Belt's observations about symbiosis between bullhorn acacias and their resident ants, for example, and his perseverance in this is evident in a 1987 PBS television documentary wherein he explains the acacia-ant symbiosis while the ants are stinging him. Janzen has accumulated so much information about the forest he studies that he's a kind of walking model of it, able to go anywhere and pick out some biotic thread that will lead into an entire network of historical-ecological relationships.

Of course, Janzen is not the only English-speaking naturalist studying Central American forest, as Belt virtually was in 1870. Yet he is also unusual in the degree to which he has gotten involved with the region's culture, and in this he is quite unlike Belt. Far from dismissing the potential of Central American governments for managing their own land, Janzen became an active proponent of Costa Rica's nascent park system. He wasn't the first North American biologist to do this, but his oddly extroverted personality (considering how much time he spends in the woods) made him particularly effective. Since the Costa Rican government lacked money to protect more land around Santa Rosa, he was financing it largely through his own contacts.

I'd come to Janzen's headquarters early one morning, and found him working at the computer that he kept in a tent inside his cinderblock house, presumably to protect it from multifarious forest mildews and damps. Plant and insect specimens in plastic bags festooned the ceiling, while two small, wild skunks foraged on the doorstep, making the place seem a high-tech wizard's cave. Although I was one of several visitors hanging around, he deftly routed me to the Santa Elena Peninsula, which was the main area that the park system needed to acquire at that time.

"You should take a look at that," Janzen said. "Nobody's ever studied its geology and vegetation, and they're real different from the stuff right around here." He said the peninsula was thought to have stood above the sea long before the existing land bridge, perhaps as long ago as the Cretaceous. "There might be dinosaur fossils out there for all we know," he added. I had seen the peninsula from the distance, a largely treeless jumble of yellow hills. I'd heard it had been the location of the airfield from which the CIA had been supplying the Nicaraguan contras, which hadn't been much of an attraction. Now it looked fascinating. I grabbed my daypack and started walking toward it while the morning cool lasted.

The landscape was like most of western Central America today, pastures dotted with remnants of the deciduous forest that grows where there's a yearly dry season. Santa Rosa has more forest than most places because it has been a park for two decades. Flocks of parrots and long-tailed flycatchers flew over a horizon dotted with feathery coyol palms. A troop of white-faced capuchin monkeys grimaced at me from a grove of guapinol and nispero trees, and a rabbit hopped across the trail. Monarch butterflies fluttered past, and I wondered if they were migrants from North America (Janzen later said they were a resident population). After a few miles, however, this landscape stopped as Santa Rosa's rolling volcanic upland ended in an escarpment that ran west to east almost as straight as a fence. Beyond it, a sunbaked, intricately eroded country of hillocks and sharp ridges stretched like a crazy quilt to yellow peaks. Low bunch grasses, odd little herbs and shrubs, and a scattering of gnarled nancite and *Curatella* trees replaced the tall jaragua grass and dry forest.

I've seldom seen a landscape change so quickly or oddly. Yet I did recognize something in this strange environment—chunks of black and red stone, glazed as though baked in a kiln, that littered the ground. The stones were peridotite, a material which comes from the earth's mantle, many miles under the planetary crust. It and related rocks such as serpentine rise to the surface only where the enormous stresses of shifting crustal plates force them upward. The Santa Elena peridotite came from a very different, much older place than the recently erupted volcanic rocks that bordered it. As Janzen had said, some tectonic event over a hundred million years ago may have forced it to the surface as part of an ancient landmass. After erosion wore that landmass away and covered it with sediments, the eastward movement of the Cocos Plate may have rafted it against Costa Rica's volcanic flank, and shoved it above sea level again. Erosion then would have removed the overlying ocean sediments and again exposed the ancient land surface.

Peridotite is infertile, even toxic, for many plants, one reason for the peninsula's sparse vegetation. As I walked on, I saw not a mammal or bird except for a hummingbird that briefly buzzed my yellow hat. The only animals were lizards, insects, and a small scorpion that emerged from a hole and quickly disappeared into another. The abrupt shift from the dry forest's fecundity to this strange emptiness was like a shift in time as well as space. Partly because of Janzen's mention of dinosaur fossils, it was like arriving on an island in the mososaur-haunted ocean of a hundred million years ago. I felt, in fact, as though I'd been transported back to the very beginning of the land bridge, to the first scrap of land that appeared between the continents as they began to converge.

Santa Elena's link with geological time struck me particularly, but all living landscapes have tangible connections to prehistory. The more one learns about the past, in fact, the more it echoes in the present. The landscapes where fossils are found often differ from the ones wherein the long-dead creatures lived, but not always. In some ways, living landscapes are truer to prehistory than the museum dioramas that recreate vanished organisms. They have what the dioramas don't, the entire context in which extinct megafauna lived—bird calls, plant smells, wind in the trees. Such places may give a feeling for even those times of which there is little fossil evidence, like the land bridge's first appearance.

Of course, there are limits to imagining the past in the present. Although the Santa Elena Peninsula may have been part of a Cretaceous landmass, it probably was in the middle of the Pacific rather than between North and South America. Tectonic plates can raft land halfway across the ocean in a hundred million years, and organisms change much more quickly. "There's a problem with judging just by what survives," David Webb told me. "Every epoch you see a whole new suite of big animals, because we have a good solid record of mammals in every continent. But what we can't say is what their ecological needs were in terms of living species. I mean, the Gracias rhino's got damned little to do with anything living in the New World, and not all that much with the rhinos that still live in Sumatra and Africa. It's just a different beast altogether." Even "judging by just what survives" is not easy, particularly with less conspicuous creatures than rhinos. If Gonzalo de Oviedo tried to comprehend Central America's flora and fauna today, he might get as discouraged as when he threw up his hands over the "almost *in infinito* subject" of its lizards in the 1500s. Much more is known than in Oviedo's time, but that doesn't necessarily make comprehending seven percent of the planet's biodiversity easier. Sometimes it makes it harder, because less can be ignored.

Oviedo chose well in throwing up his hands over lizards. A walk through a lowland rain forest can seem a saurian funhouse, with lizards popping up ubiquitously, sometimes startlingly. On the ground, eight-inch, yellow-and-blue-striped *Ameivas* seem to dart away at every footfall, and less agile but equally colorful skinks of the genus *Sphenomorphus* wriggle aside. In the underbrush, a flash of red or yellow catches the eye, the distended throat pouch of a lanky *Anolis* lizard, of which there probably are half a dozen species in the vicinity. Every tree trunk seems to have at least one tiny *Gonatodes* day gecko in residence, hopping about like an animated bark chip. If the path runs near water, there are periodic splatterings as basilisks imitate Christ, and the occasional hearty splash as a four-foot iguana bails out of the treetops. These are the common lizards. Something stranger may appear, blinking furtively: a foot-long *Corytophanes* with a casqued head absurdly disproportionate to its gangling body, or a stout *Sceloporus* spiny lizard with glistening blue scales.

The lizards' evolutionary backgrounds are even more bewildering than their present abundance. The blue-and-yellow *Ameivas* belong to a group called teiids, which is now confined to South and Central America except for a single genus in North America. But fossils show that teiids lived *only* in North America and Asia a hundred million years ago. Anoles, iguanas, and basilisks belong to a group (formerly called the iguanids but now more or less nameless because herpetologists are so confused about it) which today occurs only in the Americas, except for a few species in Fiji and other Pacific islands like the Galápagos, *and* seven species in Madagascar. The Pacific island "iguanids" are thought to have arrived there on flotsam from Central America. Nobody knows how the Madagascan "iguanids" got there.

Similar complications apply not only to lizards, but to most Central American organisms. Not all are as ubiquitous, mobile, and ancient as lizards, of course, but many are more so. It's very hard to generalize, although generalization is necessary if the land bridge's story is to be more than a flotsam of scientific names drifting on a sea of tectonic jargon. Anyway, living evidence is all that exists for the evolutionary pasts of most Central American organisms. As David Webb said, the fact it's there doesn't necessarily make it useful. Finding out about, even *finding*, many Central American organisms can be very difficult. Yet there's enough living evidence to fill millions of dumpsters, and often the evidence is eloquent.

Early Travelers

We'll probably never know just where or when, but there *was* a time when the first bits of a land bridge appeared, as South America inched toward North America. The continents had quite distinct plants and animals then, around eighty million years ago, derived from the former supercontinents—Gondwana and Laurasia. Temperate and subtropical forests of gymnosperms and hardwoods grew across both continents: pine, bald cypress, oak, and magnolia in North America; podocarp, auracaria, southern beech, and winterbark in South America. In those forests lived Gondwanan and Laurasian versions of mammals, birds, reptiles, amphibians and invertebrates—and dinosaurs, also quite characteristic. North America's late Cretaceous dinosaurs were *the* dinosaurs of popular legend—tyrannosaurs, horned ceratopsians, duck-billed hadrosaurs. Central America's lone dinosaur fossil, the hundred-million-year-old Honduran femur, belonged to a typical North American kind if it was a hadrosaur as is thought. South American dinosaurs are less famous, and may have been "old-fashioned" compared to their Laurasian contemporaries. Common late Cretaceous dinosaur fossils in South America are of sauropods, the long-necked, long-tailed *Brontosaurus*-like group usually associated with the earlier Jurassic period.

South America still was close to Africa, but a spreading zone was active between the two continents, and the Atlantic was widening. Another spreading zone existed in the mid-Pacific, particularly in the vicinity of today's Galápagos Islands, where a convection "hot spot" erupted vast amounts of magma onto the ocean floor. The oceanic plate produced by this Pacific spreading zone, the Farallon Plate, collided with the North and South American continental plates, forming a subduction zone along the west coast of both continents. A volcanic island arc arose between them, and this arc may have allowed some plants and animals to cross between South and North America. It even may have formed an early land bridge.

In the late Cretaceous, some striking similarities between North and South American organisms appeared. Paleontologists are unable to make clear distinctions between the tropical forests that then covered southern North America and northern South America. Early paleobotanist E. W. Berry thought he had identified identical late Cretaceous tree fossils in Kansas and Argentina. Later paleobotanists like Peter Raven and Daniel Axelrod questioned this, but affirmed that tropical trees which may have originated in Gondwana grew as far north as Wyoming and Washington, D.C., by the Eocene epoch, fifty million years ago. These included genera still common in the tropical Americas, like *Podocarpus, Luhea* (guacimo), and *Bombacapsis* (pochote). Other common tropical trees like fig and laurel may have moved from North America southward.

Many living plants could be relics of an early land bridge. Little palmlike cycads of the genus *Zamia* that grow in forests from Florida to Brazil are a good example, since they are ancient gymnosperms that coevolved with dinosaurs beginning in the Triassic period. Other cosmopolitan relics are less primitive. The cactus family began as leafy trees in Cretaceous South American rain forest, where such species still occur. The family evolved its bare, thorny forms as it spread north and south into drier parts of both continents. Today, Central American cactuses grow as free standing prickly pears and "organ pipes" in dry areas and as vines and epiphytes in rain forest.

In Panama, I met a Smithsonian biologist, Steve Mulke, who was studying a grass called herbaceous bamboo, *Pharus latifolia*. A knee-high, canelike plant with broad leaves, the species is common on the neotropical rain forest floor. Mulke said it is almost identical to the earliest grass fossil, probably from the Cretaceous, and to a species living in African rain forest today. Even some trees have changed little since Africa and South America separated. In drier Central America forests grows a leguminous tree, guapinol (*Hymenaea courbaril*) which extends through tropical South America and the West Indies. Recognizable by its silvery bark, and because its leaves are paired like deer hoofprints, Guapinol has one of the oldest fossil histories of tropical tree genera.

Thirty- to twenty-five-million-year-old invertebrates, frogs, and lizards have been preserved in amber, fossil *Hymenaea* resin, from the Dominican Republic and Chiapas. Guapinol has a close African relative which looks like it and grows in similar habitats. The living African species is very like the fossil American one which produced the Dominican Republic amber.

Fossils suggest that some dinosaurs moved between the continents in the late Cretaceous. A sauropod called *Alamosaurus*, related to the South American *Titanosaurus*, was common from Utah to Texas, where it left numerous footprints in creekbeds. A hadrosaur named *Kritosaurus* left fossils on both continents, and got as far south as Argentina. Dinosaur migration doesn't seem to have been massive, judging from the very fragmentary evidence. Tyrannosaurs, for example, don't seem to have spread south, which is interesting in the light of the "triumph-and-tragedy" notion of biotic interchange. One might liken South America's "old-fashioned" sauropods to ground sloths, and North America's tyrannosaurs to saber-tooths. If North America's dinosaurs were so up-to-date, so "highly evolved," why didn't they swarm south and replace archaic South American dinosaurs?

One animal group does seem to have swarmed south en masse. The distribution of the teiid lizards I mentioned earlier suggests they crossed a land bridge from North America in the Cretaceous. Fossil teiids were common in Cretaceous North America, and began appearing in South American strata of the subsequent Paleocene epoch. Some living South American teiids are very like North American fossil teiids of eighty to sixty-five million years ago. Teiids then became extinct in North America, however, a strange variation on biotic interchange which guanacos and vicuñas would repeat sixty million years later when their North American forebears died out. Nobody can explain why a lizard group which apparently was thriving enough in North America to spread into South America should have died out on its continent of origin, but it happened. North America's living teiid lizards, the racerunners and whiptails of the genus *Cnemidophorus*, spread there from the south much more recently.

Early mammals seem to have moved between the Americas. Three similar marsupial groups lived on both continents. The Patagonian fossil bed that yielded the dinosaur *Kritosaurus* also contained a tooth of a very early placental mammal called a condylarth, a group that vaguely resembled hoofed dogs and lived mostly in North America and Asia. Central America's living fish also may be evidence of an early bridge, according to ichthyologist Gary Bussing. Although mainly belonging to South American groups like cichlids and characids, they are different enough from South America's fish to suggest a long isolation. Common Central American cichlids—the convicts and firemouths of aquarium stores—belong to different genera than common South American cichlids—aquarium store oscars and acaras. So cichlids may have crossed to Central America on the Cretaceous bridge, and later been cut off from their home continent.

The most successful early traveler may have been a little, primitive snake called *Coniophis*, which left widely distributed Cretaceous fossils in North and South America. It evidently was very like the living South American false coral snake, *Anilius*, a harmless scarlet-and-black species so primitive that it has vestiges of hind legs under its skin. Early snakes are thought to have been burrowers, and *Anilius* remains one. Two other ancient, burrowing groups of creatures that still inhabit Central America might have spread between continents on a Cretaceous land bridge. Although there's no fossil evidence, they seem so odd and archaic as to be vestiges of such a hoary event. Since both groups mainly live in the southern hemisphere, it's likely they spread from south to north.

The oldest and oddest are the onychophorans, also called "velvet worms," although they aren't worms. They have cylindrical, segmented bodies like worms, but they also have antennae and multiple, clawed legs like centipedes. They're so odd they are classed in their own phylum, which has existed at least since the early Cambrian period, 540 million years ago. Several were preserved in the famous Burgess Shale of the Canadian Rockies, among the earliest fossil deposits to show animals' soft parts. One of these looks so weird that paleontologists named it *Hallucigenia*, although part of the weirdness, it later turned out, was due to the fact that they were looking at the creature upside down. Such early onychophorans lived in the ocean, but their descendants somehow have adapted to land without changing their outward appearance much. The group is so old that the mere three million years during which the present land bridge has existed seems a very short time for them to have made the momentous move from South America.

Their presence on the West Indies suggests that they started moving north much earlier.

Confined to moist habitats because their thin skins dehydrate easily, onychophorans live mostly underground, although they also occur in treetop epiphytes. I once found one in a rotten log in Costa Rica's Caribbean rain forest. It was a beautifully subtle yellow-ochre color, with a violet undertone, and I'd never seen such a velvety texture on an animal. I couldn't resist touching it. When I did, a whitish fluid spurted from the creature's head, quickly acquiring the stickiness of glue on my fingers. Onychophorans use this glue for hunting as well as self-defense. The six-inch creature squirted my hand twice more, then retreated partway down a hole, and decided the danger was past; at any rate, it stopped. I found another a hundred meters away that day; these two remain the only onychophorans I've seen in years of turning over Central American logs. They were in the same habitat as zoologist Ivan Sanderson described for a Haitian onychophoran in 1935: "large bodies of very finely divided wood mould which was bright red in color."

The other burrowing travelers are called caecilians, and are amphibians like frogs, although they are limbless. As with snakes, caecilians apparently lost their limbs by taking up a burrowing life—some extinct species had vestigial hind legs. All except a few aquatic species live underground, and push their way through the soil with their snouts. They have tiny or vestigial eyes, and find their earthworm prey with sensory tentacles on the snout. There are dozens of caecilian species in South and Central America, but they're very seldom seen, although they may come to the surface on wet nights. Francisco Ximénez saw them in dung pits, and called them two-headed snakes, "although only one end is the head, but they are so alike that only when they move does one know which it is."

Two groups of caecilians live in Central America today. The subfamily Dermophiinae occurs from Mexico to western Panama, the subfamily Caeciliainae mainly in eastern Panama. The Dermophiinae are absent from South America, whereas the Caeciliainae live throughout the tropics of that continent. Immunological tests show significant chemical differences between the albumin of the two groups, and suggest that they have been evolving in isolation for about fifty-seven million years. According to herpetologist Marvalee H. Wake, this may indicate the time at which an early land connection between the continents was severed. Presumably, today's Dermophiinae evolved from South American ancestors after crossing the Cretaceous bridge, while the Caeciliainae of eastern Panama (as well as a newly discovered small species of Caeciliainae in southern Guatemala) arrived much more recently over the present one.

The Devil's Tail

Central America may have another relic from possible early land bridge times that is not a living organism or even a fossil. The late Cretaceous, of course, saw the end of the dinosaurs (except for the closely related birds), and a cause of their extinction may have been collision of a Mount Everest–sized asteroid with the earth. The resultant explosion of dust and gas could have temporarily changed global climate enough to exterminate large animals like non-bird dinosaurs, and some small ones like certain kinds of foraminifera, while allowing other creatures to survive. Physicist Luis Alvarez developed the asteroid theory in the late 1970s when iridium, an element rare on earth but common on comets, was found in sixty-five-million-year-old sediments worldwide.

A crucial bit of evidence sought by asteroid proponents has been a sixty-five-million-year-old crater big enough to hold the asteroid that caused the catastrophe. Such a crater would be hard to find, because erosion and sedimentation would obliterate most signs of it within a few million years. Some ancient craters have been advanced as dinosaur-slayers, however, and one of the best known is in northern Yucatán surrounding a town named Chicxulub, Yucatec Maya for "the devil's tail." In 1990, geologist Alan Hildebrand analyzed rock samples from test drillings at Chicxulub and found a layer of fractured rock that interrupted the otherwise uniform limestone strata at a depth of 1,000 feet. It contained "shocked quartz"—crystals which could have been shattered by the enormous force of an asteroid impact. In 1991, NASA scientists interpreted a semicircle of sinkholes around Chicxulub as evidence of a slump in the buried rim of a crater roughly 180 kilometers across.

If an asteroid landed at Chicxulub, generating shock waves that traveled around the world, tsunamis hundreds of feet high, and enough atmospheric dust to plunge the earth into years of "global winter," it certainly would have disturbed the local wildlife. Yet it is hard to imagine just what this would have meant to a land bridge's comings and goings. A bull's-eye in the center of a Cretaceous isthmus might have stopped them temporarily by digging a "path between the seas," not unlike that which 1950s "peaceful atom" enthusiasts proposed to dig with nuclear blasts in Panama or Nicaragua. Judging from the limestone sediments of its location, however, the Chicxulub crater originated at sea. Even if the asteroid had ploughed a huge trench across a land bridge, such a local effect would have been minor compared to worldwide extinction of entire classes of animals. Anyway, today's caecilians and cichlids suggest that an early land connection ended about eight million years later than the Chicxulub crater's formation.

I happened to pass through the Chicxulub area during my 1971 loop. If anyone had told me I was looking at the cause of dinosaur extinction, I would have been nonplussed. Dry season Yucatán seems the antithesis of such drama—rocky and dusty, but hemmed in by prickly scrub, without even the scenic barrenness of desert. I rode on the back of a Pepsi truck across the invisible, yet-unsuspected crater to a village on the coast. A Texan I'd met in Merida had arranged a trip with fishermen there, but the wind was blowing too hard. I spent two memorably sleepless nights in a ruined customs shed as the wind flung sand in my face and rattled the tin roof. In the daytime I loitered around seasonally dry lagoons and mangrove swamps where the only apparent fauna were skittish white-winged doves.

Dinosaurs were the last thing on my mind. Of course, that was before 1980s theories of dinosaurs as agile bird relatives instead of wallowing reptilian ones. I still associated dinosaurs with misty King Kong landscapes of bogs and tree ferns, not with the salty, windblown scrub surrounding a Maya village where baseball was the reigning enthusiasm. Judging from less romantic 1980s ideas, however, that Yucatán coast probably was very like the Cretaceous one from which the asteroid's fall might have been visible. Central America's only dinosaur bone, the Honduran hadrosaur femur, came from limestone sediments suggesting a landscape of coastal lagoons and windblown scrub.

9

The North American Tropics

THE SECOND TIME I went to Central America, in 1987, it was with almost as vague a notion as on my 1971 trip. After working for months on a conservation book project that allowed no time away from the desk, I hungered to *experience* some natural wonder as I scribbled of extinctions, endangerments, and species recovery plans. I'd researched a little about Costa Rican national parks on the project, which had set me to daydreaming of gaudy neotropical birds, so I decided to go there. A field guide to Costa Rican birds didn't exist then, but I bought Ridgley's Panamanian guide, and gloated over it like a jewel thief at Tiffany's window. Those rubies, emeralds, sapphires—that glitter of gold, irridescence of opal, sheen of turquoise and lapis lazuli—soon they would be mine.

Costa Rica's Monteverde Cloud Forest Preserve gratified my lust so quickly that it almost seemed suspicious, as though the *Instituto Costaricense de Turismo* had mustered every gaudy bird at trailside to please the jaded ecotourist. The lush forest within yards of the visitor center was packed with them. A red-headed barbet with a green back and a yellow belly perched near an orange-bellied trogon with a green head. A prong-billed barbet with a bluish bill and a bright ochre head perched near a violaceous trogon with a yellow belly and a blue head. A flock of black-thighed grosbeaks with chrome yellow bodies flew past, and a bright chestnut squirrel cuckoo ran up a tree trunk. Azure-hooded jays with red eyes and indigo backs squawked and skulked in the understory. I felt as though I'd stepped into the jacket art of a Latin American magic realist novel.

When I read more about tropical forest, however, I found I'd have been as likely to see gaudy barbets, trogons, grosbeaks, and cuckoos in a Southeast Asian or African forest as in Latin America. The species would have been different, but Old World barbets and trogons look very like those in the New World. Afro-Asian and American trogons, for example, are all colorful dove-sized, long-tailed birds that spend much time sitting on branches making hooting and clucking sounds. I did see many solely Latin American birds at Monteverde—emerald toucanets, keel-billed toucans, three-wattled bellbirds—but I was surprised how much Old World influence there was. There's really nothing surprising about it, however. After the Cretaceous link between North and South America ended, Central America evolved as part of a North American tropics for over fifty million years.

A "North American tropics" seems a contradiction in terms today, when Central and South America share tropical ecosystems very different from North America's overwhelmingly temperate ones. Yet North America was about half-tropical or subtropical during much of the Age of Mammals, particularly in the early epochs, when forests containing camphor trees, palms, and figs extended up the coasts to Alaska and Labrador. Since land bridges linked North America to Eurasia for much of that time, the North American tropics had many "Old World" characteristics. Little prosimian primates which still live in Africa and Southeast Asia left many early fossils in North America—goggle-eyed tarsiers and long-tailed lemurs. Ancestors of dogs, cats, and horses appeared among soon-to-disappear condylarths and uintatheres. The North American tropics must have been as majestic as Africa's or Asia's today. Its appearance as Cretaceous cosmopolitanism declined was a major evolutionary event.

By the end of the Cretaceous, continued spreading of Pacific seafloor had thrust the island arc which may have formed the early land bridge to the northeast. The Antilles, which today arc from Florida to Venezuela, may be remnants of it, judging from ancient creatures that survive there. One such creature, one of the most primitive living mammals, is the solendon, a long-nosed, shrewlike creature whose closest relatives are in Madagascar. The crust beneath the Antilles then broke off from the Farallon Plate to form a new one, the Caribbean Plate, and the Farallon Plate began subducting under the Caribbean. A new volcanic island arc formed between South America and North America's southern end, which then consisted of a peninsula including present-day Chiapas, Yucatán and Belize and an "exotic terrane," including parts of southern Guatemala, Honduras, and Nicaragua. Like the Santa Elena Peninsula, the exotic terrane may have been rafted eastward in the Pacific until it collided with southern North America. The Motagua Valley marks the border between it and the original peninsula.

The Farallon Plate's subduction under the Caribbean Plate continued through the next fifty million or so years, as though a ponderous mixmaster was at work between the continents. Where it encountered the less dense, continental crust of Guatemala and Nicaragua, the Farallon slid relatively smoothly into the mantle, although erupting and exploding volcanoes evidenced the turmoil below. Where it encountered the Caribbean Plate's equally dense, oceanic part, it behaved more untidily, smearing ocean floor and exotic terranes from the west onto newly created volcanic islands in the east. Limestones compressed from abyssal muds, and pillow basalts erupted from undersea volcanoes, appeared on island coasts. Southern Central America slowly emerged.

Various islands thrown up by the mixmaster may have grown big enough for some plant and animal migration during the early Age of Mammals—the Paleocene, Eocene, and Oligocene epochs. Yet the early island arc never seems to have formed a real land bridge like today's, as increasing differences between North and South American organisms showed. In the Paleocene epoch, the two continents had significantly, if not entirely, different mammal faunas. A subtropical forest fauna in what is now Wyoming included cow-sized pantodonts with five-toed feet and long tails, dog-sized taenidonts and condylarths, and a variety of early primates, rodents, and carnivores. Similarly aged fossil deposits in Patagonia had dog-sized condylarths and pig-sized notoungulates, as well as various edentates—animals like living armadillos and anteaters—and marsupials.

Fossils suggest the few Paleocene mammals that traveled between the Americas were South American. Jaws found in late Paleocene strata in Wyoming are thought to be of armadillolike edentates, and another Wyoming jaw is of a small notoungulate, a creature faintly like (but unrelated to) an overgrown guineau pig. Nobody knows why Paleocene South American mammals may have spread north while North American ones failed to go south. Edentates and notoungulates may have been somehow superior to insectivores and pantodonts, but they had become extinct in North America by the end of the subsequent Eocene epoch, so the apparent dominance was temporary. There's still much to be said for edentates and notoungulates, which hung on to their Paleocene beachhead for millions of years. Notoungulates survived to evolve the toxodonts, which left their bones in Estanzuela on the way back north, and edentates are recolonizing North America now in the form of the nine-banded armadillo, which spread from Mexico to Kansas in the nineteenth century, and also got to Florida somehow. In 1984 I saw a nocturnal woodland near Daytona which crawled with armadillos, snuffling and rooting like tiny pigs. They were thick as woodlice under a log, but nimbler, bounding off like rabbits if I got too close. The woodland contained many tree genera that lived in Paleocene Wyoming—sabal palms, magnolias, oaks—so it was a resonant evolutionary echo.

Tapir's Gourds and Rainbow Cichlids

Cretaceous cosmopolitanism continued to fade through the Eocene and Oligocene epochs from fifty-eight to twenty-four million years ago. These epochs are almost as mysterious as the Paleocene because so few Central American fossils are known from them. Still, organisms increasingly resembled today's. Fossil pollen from Eocene and Oligocene strata in Panama mainly belongs to plant groups that still live there. An Oligocene fossil fauna from Guanajuato in central Mexico included a tapir and two rodents, one of which may have been related to squirrels, the other to agoutis. So, living organisms may tell us something about what was happening then.

One way cosmopolitanism faded was that originally South American organisms in Central and North America diverged from their southern relatives. A major plant family is an example of this divergence. The

catalpas, or *Bignoniaceae*, are almost as important as legumes like guapinol in neotropical forests, with over 600 species, mainly of trees and
vines. One of the largest, oldest genera is *Tabebuia*, which includes some
of the loveliest forest trees, with trumpet-shaped flowers that can turn
the canopy solid red, yellow, orange, or pink. Tabebuias are widespread
and diverse in South America, and probably evolved there in the Cretaceous, although they now occur throughout Central America and the
West Indies too. They are rather "normal" trees in that most species are
large, with insect-pollinated flowers and wind-dispersed seeds. Several
other groups of catalpa family trees are distinctly odd, on the other
hand, and these occur mainly in Central America.

The most common is the genus *Crescentia*, the gourd trees. These
small trees bear purplish flowers directly on their trunks, and the bat-
pollinated flowers mature into grapefruit-sized fruits which large animals eat. An even odder genus is *Parmentiera*, also small, bat-pollinated
trees with whitish flowers on their trunks. *Parmentiera* fruits are elongated instead of spherical, and have common names like "tapir's gourd"
and "candle tree." Over a dozen species occur in Central America, and
most are so restricted in range and habitat as to be almost wraithlike.
Candle tree (*P. Cerifera*) grows on a single limestone outcrop in central
Panama. Tapir's gourd (*P. Valerii*) grows mainly on Volcán Cacao in
northwest Costa Rica.

When I visited Volcán Cacao in 1988, I noticed a gray-barked,
knobby little tree in a pasture. It had a chestnut-colored fruit growing
on its trunk, and when I looked at the tree a few days later, the fruit
had doubled in size. Daniel Janzen identified it as tapir's gourd (*jicaro
de danta* in Spanish), and said the species had been known from only
a few herbarium specimens before he'd found it to be fairly common
on Volcán Cacao. It hadn't seemed common to me despite a week of
walking around there. When I started to look, however, I found several
of the little trees with eighteen-inch fruits like giant cucumber-potatoes
growing from their trunks. I noticed one because a hummingbird was
hovering at its flowers. They grew beside trails I'd been walking several
times a day, and I was nonplussed that I'd missed such strange-looking
plants. It was as though they'd crept up and planted themselves since
my previous passage.

Botanist Alwyn Gentry thinks *Crescentia*, *Parmentiera*, and another genus (*Amphitecna*) are descended from a Tabebuialike ancestor which spread north into Central America around the end of the Cretaceous, then evolved in isolation after the early interchange ended. According to Gentry, "Many Gondwanan taxa have a similar distributional pattern with a strongly differentiated group of species or genera in Mesoamerica, obviously derived from South American ancestors." It's unclear why Central American trees became so "strongly differentiated." There had to be bats to pollinate gourd trees, and large animals to eat their fruits, but there were large animals and probably bats in Eocene South America as well as Central America. Alwyn Gentry has suggested that the big Tabebuialike ancestor may have evolved into little gourd and candle trees by the strange process of neoteny, whereby populations under stress compensate by reproducing when still immature in size. Shifting fault blocks and rising volcanoes would have created a rapidly-changing, broken landscape full of microclimates in Central America—a more stressful one than the ancient basins of the Amazon and Orinoco.

Broken terrain probably influenced a group of animals which diverged from South American ancestors. Despite their antiquity, cichlids are a marginal fish group in South America's great river systems. Big characids like piranhas and pacus, and truly giant fish such as arapaimas and arawanas, dominate those. During my days on the Amazon, I didn't see any cichlids in the seemingly endless variety of fish pulled from the river. There are a lot of South American cichlid species, but most live in specialized habitats like oxbows and backwaters. In Central America, cichlids are the main freshwater fish, and a few species even live in offshore reefs. I've rarely looked in Central American waters without seeing at least one cichlid species immediately. They've filled most ecological niches, from algae grazing to large fish predation, and dominate even the biggest rivers and lakes in sheer numbers.

The dozen or so cichlid species of Lake Petén Itzá dazzled French explorer Arthur Morelet when he collected them in 1847. "Here the same species frequently changes color several times," he wrote. "Almost all the different species have some marked peculiarity in color, while our freshwater fish are only of neutral tints." Central America's cichlids are all recognizable by bright colors and complex behavior—they form pair bonds and guard their eggs and fry. They're bewilderingly diverse in other ways, however, ranging from the lunk-headed "guapotes," which grow nearly a meter long, to elfin "mogas," which rarely exceed a few inches. It's likely that such variations on the theme of colorful, perch-shaped fish have evolved—in the absence of competition from South America's more diverse fish fauna—as faulting has chopped Central America into a maze of isolated watersheds. It's equally likely that nobody will ever figure out exactly how this occurred, at least not from the welter of living cichlids.

I've kept four species of similar small size, all with different but overlapping distributions, all increasingly characteristic the more I've watched them. Tricolor cichlids (*Parapetenia salvini*) have wicked snouts and blood red patches on their azure-speckled yellow sides. They are thought to resemble the "primitive" cichlids that first colonized Central America, and act like it. Nervous but fierce, they charge around uncomplicatedly, like cichlid lowbrows. Any bite-sized fish that gets in their tank disappears with astonishing speed. Firemouths (*Thorichthys meeki*) are more cagey about their aggressions, swaggering and puffing out scarlet gill covers in ritualized displays. Black-and-white banded convicts (*Archocentrus octofasciatum*) will attack a hand put in their tank while they have fry—which is most of the time, since a pair will breed successfully under almost any circumstances. Ochre-and-green rainbows (*Herotilapia multispinosa*) are considered among the more highly evolved species because they have special plant-eating teeth. They are surprisingly peaceful compared to their relatives, except when they're in a breeding mood. Then a pair turns bright yellow-and-black, like football players, and chases about knocking heads.

Lost World Survivors

Despite its diverging cosmopolitans, Central America probably had a very different tropical flora and fauna than South America by the Oligocene epoch. Although cichlids prevail, its biggest, fiercest freshwater fish today is the gar, a barracudalike, horny-scaled creature that has inhabited North America virtually unchanged since the Paleozoic era. Central America's gars live in lowland lakes, rivers, and estuaries as far south as Tortuguero, but look just like those found in the Mississippi, although they're a different species. They were among the commonest fish I saw caught at San Carlos, where the San Juan River flows out of

Lake Nicaragua. Many were over a meter long. During their breeding season, the bottoms of the lake's tributary streams are strewn with gar eggs.

As I discovered at Monteverde, many of the neotropics' most spectacular creatures are North American tropical relics. The largest neotropical forest mammal, Baird's tapir, is very little changed from animals that lived in North American and Eurasian forests of the Eocene and Oligocene. Tapirs behave as though the Oligocene had never ended, evading the modern world with ponderous but ghostly obliviousness. They can move through lowland swamps or mountain slopes with impressive speed and quietness for such large animals. In undisturbed forest, their horsey smell and three-toed tracks may be everywhere, but like quetzals they're not easy to see. Thomas Belt never saw one during four years in the Nicaraguan rain forest.

One might say that the *most* spectacular neotropical bird is a North American relic, at least, the most spectacular Central American bird is. This is the resplendent quetzal, the irridescently plumed and crested, emerald and scarlet species whose name means "precious plume" in the Nahuatl language. Male quetzals' tail feathers may be twice as long as their bodies, and were reserved to adorn pre-Columbian nobles. After the conquest, the quetzal became almost as legendary as the lost city of Tayasal. Francisco Ximénez described it in 1722, but evidently didn't know it well because he promulgated two still common misconceptions—that quetzals always die in captivity, and that their nests have two entrances to accommodate their long tail plumes.

"All the way from the frontiers of Tabasco I had heard of the marvelous beauty of this bird," wrote Arthur Morelet, who traveled across the cloud forests of Guatemala's Verapaz Province in 1847. "My curiosity was so much excited by what was told me that I endeavored, but in vain, to classify it from the description." Quetzal habitat remained so remote that the species wasn't scientifically described until the 1850s, and Alexander Skutch was the first to record its life history in the 1930s. Quetzals still are not easy to see, as the birds have disappeared with the forest from much of their former range. Even where they're common, it's tricky to get a good look at them. The first time I saw one, a male in full breeding plumage appeared immediately in response to a taped call, but the forest shade made his feathers look gray. Later the same day, I

saw eight quetzals feeding in a laurel tree, but they were too busy fluttering around after the fruits to strike any travel poster attitudes. Since
then, I've seen mainly glimpses.

Quetzals don't look quite like any other living birds, which suggests
they've evolved relatively recently, perhaps since the highland regions
they inhabit arose in the Miocene epoch. Underneath their tail plumes
and head crests, however, quetzals are really just fancy trogons, like
the ones I first saw at Monteverde, and live very much as do their
shorter-tailed cousins in Eurasia and Africa, eating mainly fruit and
nesting in tree holes. They are rarer than ordinary trogons because they
are less adaptable—more specialized to the cloud forest habitat in which
they've evolved. Some of the ordinary trogon species are commonly seen
in settled farmland and even towns and cities, but quetzals seldom are.

Both tapirs and quetzals have spread into tropical South America
since the present land bridge formed, and have evolved new species
there. The list of other "Afro-Asian" creatures that have become part of
the neotropics via the vanished North American tropics is long. Often
in Central America I've felt I'd wandered into the pages of Kipling's *The
Jungle Book* as much as Hudson's *Green Mansions*. Central American
forests are full of cuckoos, for example, an Old World bird family which
has undergone what evolutionists call a "secondary radiation" in the
New World. Neotropical cuckoos are almost as devious about parasitiz-
ing other birds' nests and generally complicating natural history as their
Old World counterparts. They have a strange penchant for looking and
acting like other animals. The chestnut-colored squirrel cuckoo I saw
at Monteverde, for example, is long-tailed and climbs around in trees
like its namesake, and there are cuckoos called "anis" that look and
behave like grackles and blackbirds.

I once came across what appeared to be a small grouse strutting
around with its tail feathers spread in riverside rain forest. This was
surprising, since grouse don't live south of Arizona, and as it turned
out, it wasn't a grouse at all. It was a pheasant cuckoo, a rare species
that lurks in thickets and lays its eggs in the nests of birds such as
flycatchers. I don't know why these cuckoos resemble pheasants or
grouse, neither of which live within their Mexico-to-Argentina range.
Perhaps they're mimicking other vaguely grouselike birds such as wood
quail or tinamous, which do live within their range, but I don't know

what function this would serve. The vaguely chickenlike roadrunners are also cuckoos, and live in drier parts of Central America. They have smaller relatives called ground cuckoos and striped cuckoos, which run around in rain forest and savannas.

Not all relics of the North American tropics belong to Old World groups. North America evolved many endemic tropical organisms. The collared and white-lipped peccaries of Central American wilderness are descended from ancestors that diverged from the Old World pigs after crossing into the New in the Eocene or Oligocene. The porky smell peccaries exude, which hangs very strongly in humid forest air, demonstrates the relationship even without a look at their snouts and trotters. The smaller collared peccaries, which range into the southwestern U.S., are almost as common as white-tailed deer in Central American forests, and get quite used to hikers and biologists in protected areas. Francisco Ximénez had a pet peccary that insisted on accompanying him to Mass. The larger white-lipped species is more aloof, and runs in troops which are formidable adversaries to predators. Biologist Archie Carr described one in Nicaragua: "There was a sea of them, maybe a hundred, possibly three hundred, and the rustle and patter of their hard little feet was all about me like the rain drops of a sudden shower." In response to an injured sow's scream: "Suddenly there was a new sound from the band. It was the deep rumbling blood-voice, half roar, half snarl, of a hundred boars ready to fight. The awesome theme was picked up at first one point and then another, until we were nearly surrounded by a wall of sustained and utterly menacing sound."

As common as the trogons in Central American woods is another green or blue, long-tailed, clucking and hooting group. These are the motmots, jay- to crow-sized birds named for the calls of one species. A Wyoming fossil proves they have been in North America since the Oligocene. They are confined to the neotropics, although they resemble Eurasian birds called bee eaters—both nest in holes they dig in earth banks. Motmot tails give them an exotic look because the feather barbs fall out of the upper part, making them "racquet-tailed." Like trogons, they are among the few showy forest birds which persist in city parks and suburbs, where they can be surprisingly inconspicuous despite their beauty. I've stood a few meters from a loudly calling broad-billed motmot and not seen it.

The blue ocellated turkeys that surprised me at Tikal on my first land bridge visit are certainly relics of a lost world, since turkeys are solely North American. Fossils of turkeys more like the ocellated than the present U.S. species are common in Pliocene and Pleistocene California deposits, including the La Brea tarpits near Los Angeles. Even the large cracid family which now lives mainly in tropical South America may have originated in the north. Its members—guans, chachalacas, and curassows—are more like Eurasian pheasants than South American rheas and tinamous. A twenty-one-million-year-old fossil guan has been found in Nebraska.

The first time I saw great curassows, at a stream in Costa Rica, it was like something out of *The Arabian Nights*. I'd never heard of curassows, so when a coal black male with an ornately curled head crest and a lemon yellow, bulbously knobbed bill appeared in the underbrush and led a file of grayish females to a pool a few meters away, I felt as though sitars had begun to play among the pochotes and guacimos. The big birds' behavior also gave an Old World impression, although less romantically than their appearance. The males flapped their wings like roosters, and the females twitched their tails and clucked like hen chickens. In fact, curassows tame easily. As I waited at Palacios airstrip after my Plátano River trip, a young male strutted around, scratching at the grass. When an old man started to walk across, it ran after him, pecking his bare feet. The man shouted and waved his arms, and the curassow cocked its head as though pleased with the effect.

Unpredictable Amphibians

Magnificent as are the mammals and birds of the lost North American tropics, the most remarkable survivors are a group of animals that most people never see, even though they are the most abundant vertebrates in many forests. These are the tailed amphibians called salamanders. We know that salamanders come from North America because fossils of some of the big kinds that live there today—sirens and hellbenders—go back to the Jurassic. Asia and Europe also have them, but North America has so many that it might more justifiably be called "land of the salamander" than "land of the eagle."

A strange thing about salamanders, considering how ancient and diverse they are, is that they are almost entirely temperate zone animals. None of the many Eurasian salamanders extend into the tropics. In fact, only one salamander family does: the plethodontids, also called the lungless salamanders because, paradoxically, they have dispensed with lungs while developing a largely terrestrial way of life. They breathe through their skins. Whereas older salamander families continue to lay their eggs in water in the traditional amphibian way, many plethodontid species lay them on land, the embryos passing through their tadpole stage in the egg and emerging as tiny copies of their parents.

Plethodontids probably evolved in temperate North America in the Cretaceous period. The more primitive ones, those that lay their eggs in water, still live in eastern North America. Today's temperate zone plethodontids are a fascinating lot, ranging from almost wormlike slender salamanders of the Pacific coast to the colorful green and red species of the Appalachians. Yet there's something conservative and predictable about them. They may be found in odd places like treetops and caves (I found one under the garbage can in my garage), but the vast majority seem to spend most of their time under rocks or logs. They are very easy to find for this reason, to the extent that turning over a log or rock in any North American woodland is likely to reveal a lungless salamander. I've found dozens, of several species, during a half-mile walk in northern California.

Odd things happened, however, to the plethodontids who took the unprecedented salamandran step of wandering below the Tropic of Cancer. They became very successful, diversifying into over 150 species that live in most habitats from Mexico to Brazil. They also became, at least in my experience, very unpredictable. As I mentioned earlier, I've spent years turning over rocks and logs in Central American forests. In the process, I've found exactly two lungless salamander species. Both, moreover, were in very chilly environments—at about 3,000 meters on Costa Rica's Talamancas and Guatemala's Altos Cuchumatanes—so both were living more like temperate zone plethodontids than tropical ones.

The traditional, temperate under-a-log life evidently doesn't work for salamanders in the tropics, perhaps because there are too many salamander-eating creatures looking under logs—snakes, coatis, grisons, tayras, cacomixtles, and armadillos. Central America's plethodontids apparently have gotten around this problem by living *inside* things instead of under them. Zoologist Ivan Sanderson described this habit in Belize in the 1930s, when only about thirty Central American salamander species were known. Having turned over a cohune palm log "and found nothing but a toad underneath," he began pulling the log to pieces and found snails, insects, crabs, a lizard, a scorpion, a whip scorpion, and a harvestman. "These were intriguing finds, but in capturing them we had caught occasional glimpses of some black and shiny things that shot across our field of vision and disappeared once more into the stringy mass of the rotten palm trunk. . . . We conferred and decided to capture one by working from both ends of the palm at once. This had the desired effect, and when we reached the center . . . we found that we had a new kind of newt." (Sanderson misnamed the creature: newts are a nontropical salamander family.)

Herpetologist David Wake, an authority on Central American salamanders, once showed me a selection he had brought back from a 1985 trip to Costa Rica. There were bluish *Oedipina* salamanders so elongated they looked like worms. To find them, one must dig, or take apart palm trunks as Sanderson did (that was the genus he found). There were elfin *Nototriton* salamanders, which have prehensile tails and live in the moss mats of the cloud forest canopy. Wake arranged a row of them on a string, like tiny acrobats. There were robust *Bolitoglossa*, species of which live in just about every microhabitat in the forest—bromeliads, orchids, tree holes, and inside, instead of under, fallen logs. Central American genera also include inch-long *Parmivolge* salamanders that live in leaf litter, and *Chiropterotriton*, *Dendrotriton*, and *Pseudoeurycea* salamanders that live in bromeliads. There are at least eleven genera, including nearly half the entire world's salamander species. Wake thinks they evolved such great diversity because the varied, ever-changing Central American landscape fragmented populations into isolated groups that become new species.

I had never looked for Central American salamanders when Wake showed me these, so I was not as impressed as I should have been by his ability to find them. He has found thirty salamanders in a single bromeliad, and twenty-one species in a sixty-kilometer Costa Rican mountain transect. On a subsequent trip to Costa Rica, I found no salamanders at all, and began to admire Wake greatly. Turning over logs at every chance, I found frogs, snakes, scorpions, and tarantulas, but no salamanders. I didn't find them in bromeliads, moss mats, or tree holes, either. I'm not the only one who has been frustrated by tropical salamanders. In the 1950s, Archie Carr wrote plaintively of searching for them in Honduran cloud forest bromeliads. "We hauled them down, one after another, dumping upon our shivering persons the quart or gallon of cold water that each contained and finding not one single vertebrate animal. Of invertebrates there were only some sow bugs, an occasional centipede, several scorpions (one of which stung me), and swarms of ants (nearly all of which stung me)."

Wake professed mild puzzlement at these failures. "I, too, have my problems," he wrote me, "but usually manage to find them. My most recent trip to the tropics was to Chiapas. I took a group of Mexican biologists into a patch of woods behind their research station, where they had no idea salamanders occurred, and we found nine animals out at night. What is generally successful is going out on moist nights, or when there is light rain, and working low banks, often unvegetated, with a flashlight." Yet, on another trip to Costa Rica, I found a salamander that Wake had missed despite two weeks of looking. Daniel Janzen had invited him to explore Volcán Cacao for salamanders in 1987, but Wake and his assistants had found only two species, although one turned out to be new to science. In 1988, I decided to visit Volcán Cacao because Wake told me about his trip and made it sound so interesting, despite its salamander scarcity. When I got there, Janzen told me to look out for salamanders, and I did so as I climbed the volcano one morning.

Volcán Cacao's upper slopes are so densely overgrown that climbing them was more like being in the forest canopy than under it. I soon found myself several meters off the ground as I tried to get over bamboo tangles and moss-covered small trees whose branches were as thick near the ground as at the treetops. I couldn't see anything but fog and foliage, except when a break in the clouds revealed the flowery rain forest of the lower slopes. Uncomfortable as it was, this aerial hiking worked for finding salamanders, or at least a salamander. I was at eye level with big bromeliads that would otherwise have been above my head, beautiful plants, bright green striped with pink, or red-striped dark green. I peered into dozens, and saw purple worms and green spiders, but no salamanders. Finally I sat down to rest where a patch of sunlight had broken through the fog. Glancing into one of the bright green bromeliads, I saw a chocolate brown, silver-spangled salamander which I managed to catch despite its surprisingly energetic wriggles. When I took it to Janzen, he said it was different from the ones Wake had found. He sent it to Wake, who pronounced it *Bolitoglossa subpalmata*, one of the commoner Central American salamanders, except that they generally are larger than mine, and don't live in epiphytes. No others had been found at Cacao, so it was difficult to be sure of its species. Wake told me in 1995 he was still unsure, and "to complicate matters, I am about to break up *subpalmata* into several species."

Since then, I have looked into a lot of bromeliads, but haven't found any more salamanders in them. Probably if I'd looked as hard as I did on Volcán Cacao, I would have. The problem with looking for salamanders that live *inside* things is that one often must take apart their habitat to find them. As these habitats are already being taken apart by farmers and ranchers (many former forest transects where Wake found dozens of salamander species in the 1970s are now pastures), doing it just for curiosity isn't constructive. But I still look out for salamanders, in an idle way, because I can't resist the fascination of finding such beautifully formed little creatures. The prettiest one I've found was in one of the most beautiful places, under Pico Bonito in northern Honduras. Climbing a path uphill from the Bonito River, I kicked a rotten log, which split, revealing a large salamander whose back was mottled a deep red like the river boulders. The red was on a cream-colored background; the legs and belly were bluish black. It was as resplendent in its way as a quetzal. Wake told me it might have been *Bolitoglossa dofleini*, although science will never know because I left it alone.

Living in one of Central America's most lushly tropical habitats, that salamander was like an advertisement for its family's unprecedented success in colonizing hot countries. It is a success which remains hard to explain, although tropical plethodontids have other special traits beside living inside things. They are entirely land-breeding, and all catch their small invertebrate prey by flicking out an especially adapted tongue, rather as frogs do. (*Bolitoglossa* means "mushroom tongue.") They can protrude the tongue for one-third their body length and retrieve it with prey attached in less than one-hundredth of a second. They can also move their heads so quickly that the tongue seems to flick sideways. Lowland salamanders like the Rio Bonito one have webbed feet that serve as suction cups, allowing them to spend their nights hanging upside down on leaves or vines, waiting for prey. David Wake thinks these traits help them to prosper in the diverse tropics, where water-breeding salamanders might succumb to teeming aquatic predators, and less efficient feeding methods might not compete with the many other predators on small invertebrates.

Still, it's hard to see how these factors alone could account for such a conservative creature as the salamander suddenly overrunning an entire new biome. (Sixty-five million years is fairly sudden in salamander evolution.) Land-breeding and mushroom tongues are by no means unique to tropical plethodontids—in fact, all western North American plethodontids breed on land, and most have mushroom tongues. Yet the tropical plethodontids have spread not only throughout Central America but throughout tropical South America. If any group of organisms can be said to have triumphed, it is lungless salamanders. They seem to have done so, moreover, without tragically replacing any "less fit" native South American tropical salamander equivalents, although this competitive aspect of their unique migration is little known.

Mountain Pine Ridge

Not all traces of the North American tropics are as elusive as salamanders or tapirs. There are places where entire landscapes echo the Eocene and Oligocene, particularly the northern Caribbean region from Belize to the Mosquitia. Its complex of Caribbean pine woods, swamps, and hardwood forest seems a warmer version of Florida, and fossils show that such a tropical ecosystem, inhabited by tapirs, occupied southern North America thirty million years ago. Mountain Pine Ridge at the north end of Belize's Maya Mountains can seem a lost world of North American tropical echoes. The mountains' granitic core forms a plateau rising from the coastal plain in steep escarpments from which thunder thousand-meter waterfalls. Caribbean pine, several oak species, bayberry (*Myrica*), palmettoes, cycads, and tree ferns grow on its top—a vegetation different from the more Amazonian hardwood forest below the escarpments.

Yellow orchids bloomed in sunny glades of dumb cane grass and tiger bush fern when I was there in March 1994. Standing on the edge of an escarpment, I looked across a deep, forested gorge at one of the waterfalls. Flat boulders bordered its top, and something white sailed down the gorge and landed on them. I turned my binoculars on this, and saw it was a king vulture, one of the black-and-white-plumaged, red-yellow-and-blue-headed birds that dominate other vultures in the neotropics. Another, brownish dot landed next to the first, an immature king vulture. Although still widespread in Central American forest lowlands, king vultures are not a common sight, but the more I looked at the boulders, the more I saw. There must have been a dozen on the waterfall boulders, strutting about like Maya nobles on a plaza. Occasionally, one would take off and ascend in widening gyres until it was out of sight, perhaps gliding away to look for carrion on the coast, or even in Guatemala or Mexico. It seemed a sight from another time.

The streams at Mountain Pine Ridge are strange. Where springs rise along the banks, they are bordered by hanging bogs of sundew and yellow-flowered bladderwort, carnivorous plants mainly confined to the temperate northern hemisphere. The water runs clear and deep over honey-colored granitic sand, but is poor in nutrients and sparsely inhabited. The streams are among the few I've seen in Central America without cichlids, which apparently haven't been able to ascend the escarpment onto the plateau. The only animals I saw in them were little black-spotted poecilliids and the tadpoles of a frog which lives only in the Maya Mountains, *Rana julianae*. These tadpoles are very large, and flattened in shape, perhaps as an adaptation to the fast-flowing streams. They graze algae from the rocks with suckerlike mouths.

As I walked beside one stream, Tiger Creek, I kept hearing plopping sounds, probably the adult frogs, although I never saw one. I might have been walking beside a Florida creek. The genus *Rana*, which includes the common bullfrog, is mainly an Old World and North American genus. The only other animal I encountered there was a mammal with a big head and naked tail which crossed the path and disappeared in the tiger bush before I could identify it. It perhaps was a rat, a modern enough creature, but among the plateau's tree ferns and cycads it had an archaic look, as though it might have been a solendon, the ancient insectivores which may persist among the Caribbean pines of Cuba and Hispaniola.

If it was a rat, it probably belonged to a North American group that has been almost as successful at tropical evolution as lungless salamanders. The cricetids are a rodent family that includes most of the little furry creatures of North America—grasshopper mice, deer mice, pack rats, voles, muskrats. Like lungless salamanders, the cricetids moved into the tropics, possibly during the Oligocene, and took advantage of habitat diversity to evolve even more variation. Fossils of at least six different branches of the family have been found in Central America, and today they live in trees and on the ground, in forest and grassland, in highlands and lowlands. Some are aquatic, catching fish like minuscule otters. Costa Rica alone has twenty-eight cricetid species, including at least four tree-dwelling genera and two aquatic species. "We normally collect about a dozen rats to every other mammal," wrote Ivan Sanderson in Belize, "and sometimes have as many as thirty distinct species at the end of a trip."

Like lungless salamanders, cricetid rodents also have spread into South America, where they've evolved even more species than in Central America. Cricetids further resemble salamanders in seeming to disappear into tropical habitats. North American cricetids are so easily found as to be a nuisance. On many camping trips, deer mice have found *me*, absconding with food or gear, moving into my backpack or car to build nests. Of Costa Rican cricetids, Daniel Janzen and D. E. Wilson wrote, "none are widespread and abundant." My glimpse of a rat on Mountain Pine Ridge—if it was a rat—was the only time I remember seeing a possibly cricetid rodent in the neotropics. Trapping is the only reliable way to find them.

The near invisibility of such creatures seems exemplary of the North American tropics' distant, obscured character. It really *is* a lost world, and my attempts to evoke its echoes can only go so far. For example, monkeys are so typical of tropical forest that one would think the North American tropics must have had them, perhaps with similarities to Old World monkeys, as with tapirs and trogons. But no fossil monkeys are known from North America, and living Central American monkeys belong entirely to South American groups. Eurasian kinds of prosimians like tarsiers and lemurs were common in Eocene North America, as I've said, but they became extinct in the Oligocene. David Webb told me that one Oligocene tarsierlike primate called *Margarita* from Texas was "a really strange, progressive one," suggesting that it *could* have evolved into a monkey—but there's still no evidence that it did. There is still no way of even imagining what lived in the post-Oligocene trees.

The North American tropics didn't end with the Oligocene. Much of the continent retained a warm climate right through the subsequent Miocene and Pliocene epochs, until the glaciers formed. There are more Central American fossils from those later epochs, but we don't know much more about the North American tropics' end than we do about the beginning. We may know less about it than we do about the dinosaurs' extinction. Dinosaurs definitely ended with a bang of some sort. The North American tropics ended with a whimper of still insoluble problems, of mysteriously disappearing North American tarsiers and equally mysteriously appearing South American monkeys.

10

Gourd Trees and Gomphotheres

I ENCOUNTERED ANOTHER unexpected thing during my 1987 "gaudy bird–watching" trip to Central America. Most of what I'd heard and read about Costa Rica emphasized its greenness and lushness. A few hours' drive from lush Monteverde, however, I found myself in a forest that looked like New England in December except that the temperature was in the nineties. This was the dry deciduous forest of Guanacaste Province, where many trees drop their leaves during the rainless season that prevails from October to May on most of Central America's Pacific coast. Dry deciduous forest like Guanacaste's covered as much of Central America as rain forest when Europeans arrived, and it probably has been there much longer than the rain forest that presently grows along the Caribbean. Most of Central America's rain forest genera live in South America too, but many dry forest organisms are endemic to Mexico and Central America, suggesting they evolved before the present land bridge formed.

Today's dry forest may have originated as a result of climatic changes that overtook North America as the moist, wooded Oligocene ended. Global climate cooled and dried in the subsequent Miocene epoch, and much increased volcanic activity in western North America enhanced the effect, uplifting the continental interior and cutting off ocean moisture. Great Plains fossils show a shift from woodlands and savannas to open grasslands as shrub-browsing, three-toed horses were replaced by larger, two-toed equines with high-crowned teeth that let them graze on silica-rich grasses. Volcanic activity also increased in Miocene Central America. The ash and lava plateau that now covers much of Guatemala, El Salvador and Honduras arose, and the climatic causes of today's dry season may have become prevalent then.

Central American fossils also suggest a drying climate although, as usual, less clearly than with continental fossils. As I've said, the late Miocene Gracias animals were the same genera found in Miocene beds from California to Kansas: *Teleoceras* rhinos, *Rhynchotherium* gomphotheres, *Procamelus* camels, *Neohipparion* and *Pliohippus* horses, and *Geocholone* tortoises. The horses and camels had molars well adapted to chewing tough prairie grasses, and this suggests that the region was a warmer version of the grasslands that spread across North America at that time. Yet the deerlike protoceratids common in the somewhat earlier Gaillard Cut fauna in Panama were mainly forest animals that had declined in North America as forests shrank after the Oligocene. Their abundance in Panama suggests that area was still forested, and that Central America was a last resort for them. The two horse species of the Panama fauna—*Anchitherium* and *Archaeohippus*—were also leaf-browsing species, although the big *Diceratherium* rhinos and hippolike oreodonts that lived with them were more adapted to the savanna.

Central American grass fossils are very rare. As I mentioned earlier, Miocene fossil leaves found in Costa Rica in 1917 were of forest trees. That deposit also contained fossil spores from club mosses, ferns, and other shade-loving plants, but no grass pollen. Miocene pollen from the Panamanian Gatun formation indicated moist-temperate or subtropical forest with bayberry, walnut, and alder. Both these floras probably grew close to the Caribbean, which probably was wetter than western Central America then, as now, but the few plant remains found in western fossil beds like Gracias also are poor in grassland species.

Gracias plant fossils found in the 1930s suggested that the animals lived in lusher surroundings than their northern relatives. Everett Olson wrote that palm and hardwood remains showed that "the environment was not greatly different from that represented by the hardwood rain forests or the broken periphery of those forests today, and that conditions were quite different from those on the great plains to the north at about the same time." Olson also thought the Gracias horses were smaller than North American ones because their environment had less grazing land than the Great Plains. Olson and McGrew's plant identifications were tenuous, however, being made from fossil wood in river gravels. I couldn't find their specimens in the Field Museum in Chicago, and I didn't have any better luck with the "fossil fragments of the wood of *Schwartzia*, a legume that still grows in the area" that Frank C. Whitmore had found in Panama. As far as I could gather, David Webb and his coworkers had found no recognizable tree species among their 1968 to 1977 Gracias plant fossils.

"It wasn't very exciting to my paleobotanical friends," Webb told me. "It was pretty cheesy preservation . . . little carbonized films of material, although I can see where a good botanist could identify it." It certainly wasn't recognizable to me—mats of pinkish or blackish fibers still in their pebbly matrix. "These things are interesting when you can get them," said Webb. "I wish we had more botanical stuff coming out of Honduras and points south." It is odd that plants, so much less elusive than mammals in life, should become so much more so in death.

The Gracias animals could have lived in surroundings not so different from today's western Central American mixture of lowland dry forest and highland wet forest. Many living forest plants demonstrate long adaptation to big browsing animals, like the odd little gourd trees. Daniel Janzen and ecologist Paul S. Martin have cited thirty-six tree and shrub species in northwest Costa Rica that could have coevolved with a megafauna of gomphotheres, horses, and rhinos, including acacias, nancites, figs, persimmons, coyol palms, guapinols, and zapotes. The plants tend to produce massive crops of large, sweet or otherwise attractive fruits which fall to the ground when ripe, and either large, thick-coated seeds resistant to large animals' teeth or small seeds which can pass through an animal's gut undigested. These traits certainly seem adapted to attracting large animals which will eat a lot of fruit, swallow many seeds in the process, then defecate the seeds far from the parent tree.

Janzen described how this works with gourd tree fruits: "Horses break the hard shell in their mouths and swallow the ball of seed-rich pulp with eagerness and little chewing. A tethered range horse may eat ten to twenty of these fruit balls in a meal, twice a day. Within two or three days its dung is rich in seeds, which germinate into hundreds of healthy seedlings with the first rains." Janzen and Martin cited similar relationships between fruit-bearing trees and African animals, in both forest and savanna. Gourd trees, they wrote, "would not look out of place in Nairobi National Park in Kenya."

Crooked Tree

Some of this equivocal Miocene world seems to linger in Central America's wetlands and savannas, which can be both lush and dry at different times. A trip I took at Crooked Tree Lagoon in Belize to see a jabiru stork nest might have been in a landscape of nine million years ago. There was a Miocene plenitude about it. Soon after the rainy season's end, the lagoon was a sheet of shallow water choked with waterweeds and bordered with scrubby logwood and freshwater mangrove. Cabomba and water lily flowers rose above the surface, sometimes so thickly it seemed like a meadow. Cichlids swarmed in the weeds, particularly tricolors, much larger and vivider than their aquarium counterparts, with magenta bellies. The "*pok, pok*" sounds as they struck at surface insects and the squawks of coots and jacanas made the hair on my arms prickle. More snail kites, black-collared hawks, and yellow-headed vultures than I'd ever seen circled overhead, and higher up were ospreys. Our guide showed us a limpkin sitting on its nest in the logwood, and three speckled jacana eggs on a lily pad, the "nest" of that genus.

We passed out of the lagoon into a winding creek where small Morelet's crocodiles glided, and wading birds (boat-billed, tiger, and little blue herons, and snowy and great egrets) thronged a purple-flowered darkwood tree. The creek soon entered a wider lagoon, one of the biggest expanses of open shallow water I've seen. Zebu cattle and great blue herons stood in it, and flocks of black-bellied tree ducks billowed at the horizon. It was strange to see the cattle grazing placidly hundreds of meters from dry land—it made them seem less domesticated. I doubted the little crocodiles got a chance to eat a zebu very often, yet if Crooked Tree becomes a fossil deposit, it may not be so different from the Panamanian Miocene beds with their crocodile coprolites and ungulate bones.

It seemed unlikely that this wetland would turn to dust in a few months, but that is what happens most years when the rains stop and the water evaporates. It began to seem more likely when we landed the boat, however, since we had to drag it over newly exposed mud to tie it to a tree. We then walked, first through a cattle-bitten but fairly thick woodland of cohune palm, hog plum, poisonwood, guanacaste, gourd tree, and ceiba. There might also have been *Schwartzia* and *Gyminda* trees, but I've had no more luck finding living specimens than fossil ones. A coati foraged in the grass, and brown jays scolded. A big black and yellow indigo snake raced across our path, paused under a bullhorn acacia, then vanished into mucky ground where orange flint nodules lay among limestone fragments.

The muck soil and woods ended abruptly in a sunny expanse of white sand grown with wildflowers and grass like broomsedge. We'd entered Caribbean pine savanna, and the gnarled little pines were every-where, mixed with live oaks and small savanna hardwoods—nancites and yahas. It was a little like stepping from Venezuela into Arizona. Several pine and oak trunks were studded with acorns, and I heard the familiar "*kraaa, kraaa*" calls of the acorn woodpeckers who'd stored them there. Meadowlarks sang, and a covey of bobwhite quail fled into the grass, heads bobbing comically.

The stork nest was a massive stick pile on the branch of a dead pine. One of the black-and-white, red-throated adults was in attendance, and pretty soon the two chicks popped up, their white pin feathers dishev-eled, their beaks hanging open in the late morning heat. The adult shifted about, clicking its bill softly. Our guide, a young Belizean whose family owned the land, said there was always an adult there to keep snakes and vultures away. The stork and its chicks seemed prepared to sit and be stared at all day, like museum specimens, as indifferent to time as though made of skin stretched over clay. The big, ungainly bird, with its clublike bill and bare red throat, gave the landscape a satisfying gravity that somehow reminded me of lifting a gomphothere skull out of a drawer—of perceiving evolution with the muscles as well as the mind.

The storks were really no more ancient than the herons, ducks, and coots with which they shared Crooked Tree, but their size and grotesqueness made them seem so because it echoed those qualities in the vanished rhinos and protoceratids. And storks were an integral part of the clumsy, heedless megafaunas that rampaged across the Miocene. The marabou storks of Africa and Asia still scavenge on big game carrion with hyenas and griffin vultures, and probably had New World counterparts which squabbled with vultures, condors, and bone-eating *Osteoborus* dogs over rhino scraps. Indeed, genetic studies have shown that storks had common ancestors with the New World vultures and condors. Like most living storks, jabirus feed less gruesomely—on small aquatic and savanna animals. Yet they still need big, heedless expanses to live. Only a few dozen jabirus survive in Central America, breeding in the biggest wetlands.

The Great Eruptions

Heaps of rhino and camel bones entombed in Great Plains ash beds suggest that Miocene eruptions were of a magnitude beyond anything in human memory. Complete, still-articulated skeletons indicate the animals died in entire herds, probably suffocated by the corrosive ash. In Central America, fossils are too fragmentary to provide evidence of mass deaths, but when I showed a rock from near the top of Volcán Celaque near Gracias to a geologist, he said it was rhyolitic, typical of explosive volcanoes. Although Miocene volcanoes are long extinct, one can get a sense of their grandeur from the top of very much alive Volcán Masaya in the Nicaraguan Depression.

Masaya has been active almost continuously since murderous Pedrarias called it "a giant mouth of fire that never ceases to rage." Benzoni wrote that a Dominican friar, "thinking there was gold within," had lowered a bucket on an iron chain into the crater and tried to scoop some out. "The bucket and part of the chain was consumed with fire," however, and "a flame rushing out had nearly killed the monk and his companions." It remains the only volcano in Central America where molten magma is visible at a crater bottom. In the 1970s, Time-Life writer Don Moser watched "a pool of lava that was sloshing to and fro" at the bottom of the active crater, Santiago. "At a temperature of about 1,300 degrees Farenheit the incandescent rock looked as liquid as water, and surged like surf against the wall of the shaft."

In early dry season, 1993, I climbed to the crater past tumbled lava fields and occasional boulders thrown out during its last big eruption. Bare-branched frangipani trees with trumpet-shaped white flowers grew out of the lava, and pink orchids bloomed on their trunks. Masaya isn't very high, but the view across the Depression is sweeping. I saw little sign of civilization in the distant lowland, and it wasn't hard to imagine shovel-tusked gomphotheres, striped horses, guanacolike camels, and big-jawed wild dogs among the guapinols and gourd trees. As I neared Santiago, billowing sulfurous vapors seemed redolent of ancient, buried things. I crossed a recently extinct crater floored with gray ash and tussocks, where teiid lizards mated and black vultures perched on lava shards, then circled around to where I could see into the lava well. Occasional cascades of stones rumbled down its walls. When steam obscured the sun I could see lava at the bottom. It didn't "slosh to and fro," but it glowed red, and rhythmic sounds came from the shaft. "*Whuff, whuff, whuff . . .*" They never stopped, as though an enormous animal was breathing.

The old lava that fans from the Masaya craters is honeycombed with caves—winding tubes formed as molten magma streamed through hardened flows. I walked into one just below Santiago Crater. The entrance was unimposing, a jumble of rocks where the roof had collapsed, but the tube dipped quickly into utter darkness. Pale red tree roots snaked along the floor, and the ceiling was laced with rootlets from which water steadily dripped. Bats were plentiful, and I saw and heard them clearly because the roof was only a few meters high. A tiny individual with the bulldog face of an insect-eater clung to the ceiling a little below the entrance, and I disturbed more as I moved deeper. They formed a cloud behind me, silhouetted against the light, but when I turned off my flashlight and waited, they came to roost again. I glimpsed a group of pink-snouted fruit-eaters clinging together like tiny winged piglets before my light drove them back to flight.

The bat flutterings dwindled as the tunnel curved and the daylight faded. The walls constricted, then opened out again, then curved again. The darkness was as silent as the bone storage vault at the Field Museum, but the breathing sounds from the lava well seemed to reverberate in my head. I was feeling a little feverish. The floor sloped steadily down, and I kept going until the cave constricted again and dropped away into a jumble of rocks. I suspected that I had passed branching tunnels. When I turned back, the way looked unfamiliar, and I was glad when I heard bats again.

Outside the cave, I climbed above Santiago to the inactive San Fernando crater, which has grassy sides and a forested floor. Red salvia bloomed in the yellowing grass. As I stood on its rim, plaintive hoots and whistles came from the trees at the bottom. When the sun went behind the vapor cloud, a beautiful thrushlike song rang out, then stopped as the cloud passed. Tropical birds seem to specialize in haunting calls, and they sounded particularly so at Masaya because birds were almost the only numerous wildlife. The sole four-legged creature I saw (other than lizards) was a variegated squirrel. Except for the occasional coyote and deer, large animals have disappeared from most of the heavily populated Depression. Masaya is a national park, but years of neglect during the Contra war encouraged poaching.

I did find one ecosystem of teeming herbivores and cruising predators at Masaya. A caldera lake from a long-ago explosion lies a few hours' walk from the active volcano, bordered with lava cliffs on one side and woodland on the other. When I went there one blistering, windy morning, the shallows teemed with fish. At the surface, the red dorsal-finned males of a mollie-like poecilliid pursued drabber females, and slender, sand-colored gobies rested on rocks, swiveling their eyes and occasionally darting after small prey. A little deeper, large schools of bluish-gray, banded fish grazed algae from the lava, probably midas cichlids (*Amphilophus citrinellum*), the commonest cichlids of Nicaraguan lakes. Smaller, black-and-white convict cichlids roamed among them, like zebras in a wildebeest herd, and occasional smaller, darker fish darted out territorially from rock crannies. These were "mogas" (*Neetroplus nematopus*), among the most pugnacious Central American cichlids at the same time they're the smallest. They also live by grazing algae, the miniature rhinos of Depression lakes. Above all this herbivory swam one or two elongated, speckled fish with powerful underslung jaws and baleful orange eyes—"guapotes" or jaguar cichlids (either *Nandopsis managuense* or *N. Dovii*), the top predators among cichlids. They patrolled furtively, sometimes chased away by the midas cichlids. Occasionally one would dart at an insect on the surface.

This ecosystem is less irrelevant to Miocene megafaunas than it might seem. Even more diverse cichlid communities are a feature of today's megafauna-rich African savannas, inhabiting the lakes of the Great Rift Valley. Cichlids seem peculiarly suited for the alkaline, fertile lakes that form in such places, and African Rift cichlids and Nicaraguan Depression cichlids have bizarre traits in common. Midas cichlids have a tendency to develop grotesquely enlarged lips, which evidently help them to graze algae and small animals from the rocks. Also, a certain percentage of midas cichlids are not the usual bluish gray, but a brilliant red-gold color. I glimpsed one in the lake at Masaya. This erythrism may give the fish a selective advantage in attracting mates in dark and turbid lake water. Both red color variants and enlarged lips can be found in various African rift cichlid species as well as in other Central American cichlids, and the existence of the traits in both suggests that they have been in their genes a very long time. Cichlid populations like today's probably lived in the pools and streams wherein the bones of Gracias rhinos and gomphotheres began the fossilization process.

Of course, today's Nicaraguan lakes formed much later than the Miocene. The diverse fish of Laguna de Masaya, in particular, seem to be a historical phenomenon. When Oviedo visited the lake in 1529, he found the water "so warm that nothing but intense thirst could have induced me to drink it," although it became potable when cooled. "It seems to me that this must be on a level with the fire that burns in the crater of Masaya," Oviedo wrote. "Only one species of fish, as small as a needle, is found there. . . . I asked the *Cacique* why they did not bring fish from other places and put them in? He replied that they had done so several times, but the water rejected them, and they died, diffusing a fetid odor, and corrupting the water."

Twilight of a Tropics

Increased volcanic activity in the Miocene may have enlarged Central America's land area. By its end, migration between the Americas began to increase after some fifty million years of isolation. Fossils show that amphibians and reptiles were moving in both directions, probably by "waif" dispersal, crossing water gaps on floating plants, or by swimming. Common, warty *Bufo* toads moved from South to North America, as did *Cnemidophorus* whiptail lizards, teiids returning to their family's original home. North American land tortoises appeared in South America, champions of waif dispersal as their presence on the Galápagos Islands shows, and indigo snakes did also.

A fossil Miocene parrot, *Conuropsis*, has been found in North America, perhaps an immigrant from the south. By the late Miocene, eight to five million years ago, at least three mammal species had crossed the Panama water barrier. Argentina has yielded fossils of a North American mammal, a raccoon relative called *Cyonasua*. Also, the bones of two ground sloths with names like a pair of villains in one of Shakespeare's Athenian tragedies, *Pliometanastes* and *Thinobadistes*, have been dug up in Florida and California. Despite the vast evolutionary gulf between them, the raccoon relative and the ground sloths may have been rather similar superficially. All were the size of small bears, and probably had a shuffling, flat-footed gait. One can imagine a *Cyonasua* and a *Thinobadistes* paddling past one another off some remote mangrove islet of the Panama swamps, grunting truculently to guard their rights of way. Living raccoons and sloths are good swimmers, and bad-tempered when jostled. The three pioneer species did well in their new homes, judging from their wide distribution, and must have thrived in Central America too, although they left no fossils there.

At the same time as sloths were spreading into North America, many large native animals were disappearing, such as rhinos and bone-eating *Osteoborus* dogs. In fact, North America underwent the largest post-dinosaur megafauna extinction at that time. "In the late Miocene," David Webb has written, "climatic deteriorations destroyed the large browsers of North America as the extensive midcontinental savannas gave way to steppe. . . . Mixed feeders and even grazers, including peccaries, horses, rhinos, antilocaprids, and gomphotheres were decimated." Smaller, opportunistic herbivores such as rodents apparently replaced many of the large ungulates in the new grasslands.

Scarcity of fossils makes it hard to say how the late Miocene extinctions affected the North American tropics, which had begun to withdraw south toward Mexico and Central America by that time. Yet as the Pliocene epoch began, Central America would have looked increasingly familiar. Deer, dogs, and cats resembling today's species were moving south, and older Central American groups had begun to resemble present forms. Tropical weasel family genera such as tayras, grisons, and giant otters were much as they are today, as were raccoon family animals like coatis and kinkajous. Surviving mastodon, horse, and camel species continued to share Central America with tapirs and peccaries. The twilight of the North American tropics certainly was more like today's world than the Miocene had been, with its hippo-rhinos and bone-eating dogs. It may have been more like the present than the subsequent Pleistocene epoch. Without South American toxodonts, megatheres, and glyptodonts, it would have seemed less exotic.

Costa Rica's Guanacaste Province perhaps echoes southern Central America five to three million years ago. South American monkeys and agoutis probably didn't live there yet, and mastodons, giant tortoises, and wild camels certainly did live there. Yet its mosaic of dry and wet forest, and much of its diverse wildlife, perhaps hasn't changed all that much. The Pliocene impression is enhanced by semiwild horses which the Costa Rican Park Service runs on its lands to help reproduction of megafauna-dependent native trees.

I had a close encounter with a horse on my salamander-collecting trip to Volcán Cacao in Guanacaste National Park. It wasn't even semiwild, a morose whitish creature, but it was untamed enough for me, since I was expected to ride it to the biological station at the volcano—my first horseback ride. The ranching family that managed the station took it for granted I would ride, and I did, except on two particularly steep slopes of which even the horse seemed afraid, although it negotiated them nimbly once I dismounted. Most of the way was easy, the path rolling over foothills of wind-rippled bunch grasses, a terrain largely created by ranching. The border between foothill grassland and volcano forest was curiously abrupt. We came to a streambed with a steep slope on the other side, and huge trees replaced bunch grass with hardly a seedling in between. Janzen said this is because most forest seeds are distributed by forest animals, which seldom wander into grassland. A wall-like density of shrubs enclosed the trail within the forest, and it grew so steep and muddy that I dismounted again. Knowing its destination was near, the horse hurried ahead almost happily

As I got acquainted with the Cacao forest in the next week, I was

struck by its differences from the Caribbean rain forests I'd seen. Buttress roots and lianas and other epiphytic plants were not prominent,
nor were leafcutter and army ants. Despite monkeys and toucans, the
overall impression was far from Amazonian. It was almost always chilly
from rain and mist, and the wind blew so hard at night I thought the
station bunkhouse might become airborne. Janzen told me the kind of
forest at Cacao used to grow between 800- and 1,500-meter elevations
all along the Pacific coast, but has been replaced by farmlands or settlements, a replacement that began long before Columbus. "This is just
one example of the many kinds of very peculiar trees we think grow
in this forest," he said of tapir's gourd in the 1987 PBS television documentary. "But the problem is we don't know anything about it. This
forest is very different from any other forest that's ever been studied in
Costa Rica, and we simply don't know what sorts of things are living
here."

Many of the plants I saw at Cacao belonged to the plant families that
E. W. Berry thought he recognized in Miocene fossils in Costa Rica. Figs
and laurels were common, as were heliconians, pipers, melastomes, and
club mosses. These are all very widespread neotropical plants, but in
the mist-laden winds that hid them from the sun and tossed their leaves,
they seemed from another time. The only forest like Cacao's that I've
seen is at El Imposible National Park in El Salvador, which grows at a
similar elevation and distance from the Pacific. It also has a wall-like
density and lushness of shrubs. El Imposible is less pristine than Volcán
Cacao, and lacks many native mammals, but it has little trees of the
tapir's gourd family and several endemic plant species.

Cacao's animal life was elusive. The station manager's son thought
that there were no jaguars or pumas because he'd never seen them, but
when I mentioned this to Janzen, he pointed up the trail and said: "I've
seen fresh jaguar shit right there." Even common animals appeared
and disappeared phantasmagorically. Coati troops showed only upraised
tails as they filed through the underbrush, and blue-crowned motmots
and collared trogons seemed to materialize like Cheshire cats out of
the yellows and reds of hotlip and heliconia flowers. The fauna also
bemused a group of aquatic entomologists as they searched for stream
insects. A longhaired graduate student with the obsessed gaze of the
dedicated field collector told me they seemed less diverse than he ex-

pected in tropical rain forest. Some were abundant, such as caddisfly nymphs which had cut so many circular leaf pieces to make their cylindrical cases that the fallen leaves in the streambed looked like swiss cheese, but such an abundance of one species is more typical of temperate than tropical ecosystems.

A few days later, I met the graduate student again at Cerro el Hacha, a biological station in the dry forest at Volcán Cacao's foot. The lowland dry forest is almost as endangered as Cacao's wet forest—Janzen has estimated that about two percent of it remains intact in Central America. Yet even these remnants have the fierce vitality of tropical lowlands generally. The graduate student found Cerro el Hacha wild enough: "worse than Africa." He was staying in an abandoned squatter's shack full of lizards, four-inch scorpions, and eight-inch cockroaches, and his first night there he'd come down with a fever and vomiting, "the worst night of my life." He was assigned to collect insects in the park's remotest part, near the Nicaraguan border, by loading a mule with gear and traveling around to streams at night, an unnerving prospect. The dry season wind moaned and blustered, and *terciopelos* (fer de lance) and *cascabels* (rattlesnakes) haunted the foothills. This was in 1988, and occasional distant gunfire intensified the spookiness.

Lowland vitality teemed during a 1990 walk I took into Santa Rosa National Park's Cañon del Tigre. It was early rainy season, and the forest had put out new leaves after standing bare from October to May. It looked like a temperate forest in spring, except that no wildflowers grew on the forest floor, and many more tree species occurred than in the most diverse temperate forest. I saw two dozen belonging to eighteen families along one curve of path. They were all shapes, sizes, and colors—thorny pochotes, sinuous gumbo limbos, *madroños* with flaking strips of orange and white bark, *jinotes plateados* with wrinkled, silvery, reddish-warted bark —but all had a leathery drought-resistant look. Also responding to the rains, newly-hatched lizards swarmed in the leaf litter, and snakes had come out to eat them. A brown, flat-headed vine snake (*Oxybelis aeneus*) hard to distinguish from the pink-flowering creeper on which it twined had just caught a small anole.

As I passed into a glade of gourd trees, dry forest endemics flew across the path—sky blue birds with long tails and showy black head plumes. I'd have thought them quite exotic if I hadn't known they were jays, with the exotic name of "white-throated magpie jays," but not much different in character from the denizens of U.S. backyards. Magpie jays have larger vocabularies than northern jays—they make a variety of plaintive squeaky sounds as well as scolding squawks—but the nosy, acquisitive behavior that accompanies the noise is the same. The species lives only along Mesoamerica's dry Pacific side from northwest Costa Rica to northwest Mexico. In the grass by the trail were other endemics, emerald green young ctenosaurs belonging to a lizard group which also lives mainly on the land bridge. Occasionally a blackish adult dashed in front of me like a portly miniature dragon.

As the trail dropped down the Cañon del Tigre's walls, the forest became desertlike, with cactuses standing on basalt columns, but tall evergreen guapinols, nisperos, and espavels covered the floodplains at the bottom. An indigo snake whipped across the road, one of the Pliocene travelers from North to South America. The snake looked huge, carrying its head two feet off the ground and moving with impressive speed, yet it seemed odd that such crawling creatures should be more mobile geographically than swift-flying magpie jays. Successful crawling migrations have been a general theme of land bridges, however, from onychophorans to snakes, as though the ground is a more conductive environment than the trees or the air. There was certainly no scarcity of crawlers. In the leaf litter by the trail, a little Omega viper (*Bothrops ophrymegas*) was just finishing another anole, working its jaws to engulf the back legs, and a striped snake called a *guardacamino* wriggled past.

A side trail onto a ridge passed from the dry forest into the Santa Elena savanna, which was livelier than it had been in the dry season. Little yellow lilies, purple peas, and a white, avens-like flower bloomed in the bunch grass. A nighthawk fluttered before me in a broken-wing act, and I saw its gray, faintly mottled eggs, like pebbles on the red peridotite. The ground was already infernal in the late morning sun, and I retreated so the bird could return and shade the eggs. The heat was so overpowering that when I came to a pool in a steep rivulet, I climbed in. It was a relief, but I was not to escape the lowland's ferocity even there. Dozens of little crayfish pinched me, and bigger ones advanced ominously, claws outstretched. A nesting oriole scolded from an overhanging branch, ready to buzz my head.

I returned to the canyon bottom, and spent the afternoon in the dry bed of the Nisperal River, surrounded by larger but gentler animals. Collared peccaries wallowed in the sand, drowsily squealing and clacking their teeth. A white-tailed doe and fawn appeared and sat by them, then a flock of guans. I'd seldom seen such a companionable assemblage of wild creatures. Downstream, a white ibis, a little blue heron, a bare-throated tiger heron, and a tricolored heron hunched over a pool, while a pair of ctenosaurs copulated on a branch, and a flock of big yellow-headed parrots muttered "*gwawa, gwawa*" in the canopy. In the sky, a black vulture, a crested caracara, and a king vulture circled, one above the other.

As I walked back in the evening, flocks of parrots, parakeets, and fork-tailed flycatchers flew over, and spot-bellied bobwhites and Inca doves rocketed out of the jaragua grass. A laughing falcon called triumphantly somewhere: "*Guaco! Guaco! Guaco!*" Laughing falcons mainly eat snakes, and that one must have had a full crop. When I passed a thicket of prickly, fragrant *Jacquinia* bushes, a thrush-sized, black-and-blue-masked bird hopped from the roadside onto a low branch, eyed me, and then instead of flying jumped back to the ground and ran off. It was another of Central America's cuckoos, a lesser ground cuckoo, which acts like a miniature roadrunner although it looks like a songbird, and has a geographical range like those of magpie jays and ctenosaurs.

Near sunset, I stopped at a waterhole. Horses were drinking, and approached to examine me as I sat on a knoll under some trees. One had a rusty streak of blood on its neck, perhaps a vampire bat bite. When the horses left, a coati came to drink, then a little whitetail buck, then a pair of rabbits. All approached the water skittishly, drank hastily, and departed. Thickets of pink-blossomed mimosas covered much of the bank, and the wind tossed their branches noisily. A coyote appeared, drank, glanced around, drank again, and crept into the mimosas. Yellowish, short-haired, and long-eared, with a doglike tail, it didn't look much like a furry temperate zone coyote, more like some archaic savanna creature. Turkey vultures circled low and perched in nearby trees. Some big purplish pigeons landed, then flew away without drinking as though sensing something amiss. The coyote stayed in the mimosas, but nothing else appeared.

Darkness fell, as it really does fall in the tropics, and I heard hyenalike sounds in the distance—more coyotes. I started walking again as clouds

raced past a bright moon. A large animal galloped away in the underbrush, leaving a horsey smell, probably a horse, possibly a tapir. My
flashlight reflected a red dot on the path, like a glowing marble. When
I got closer, it disappeared, and something fluttered around my head—
a bat, I thought, or a small owl. Then, from the length of its wings, I
realized it was a parauque, the tropical whippoorwill I'd first heard at
Tikal. As I followed it with my flashlight, I could see its red eyes in
the air. It flew directly at me, like something in a nightmare, glowing
orbs racing at my head, then was gone, veered away. Every few meters I
came to another one. Each waited, transfixed, then flew up and fluttered
around my head. When I turned my light into the forest, I could see
more parauque orbs, while the green sparks of wolf spider eyes and
the occasional ruby embers of scorpions' eyes flecked the ground at
my feet.

11

The Seaway

TWO GOOD PLACES to get a sense of what the land bridge's opening has meant for the planet are not entirely on land. They are small coastal national parks in southern Costa Rica—Manuel Antonio on the Pacific and Cahuita on the Caribbean. Both parks have little coves with crescent beaches backed by swampy rain forest where the "*pete pew!*" of the chestnut-backed antbird is heard. Otherwise, they are very different. Steep headlands of sedimentary and volcanic rock overlook the coves at Manuel Antonio, while Cahuita's are bordered by heaps of bleached coral fragments which clatter like crockery when walked on. Thirty-four reef-building coral species occur at Cahuita, but there are no coral reefs at Manuel Antonio. Big flocks of brown pelicans, frigate birds, and brown boobies are usually visible offshore at Manuel Antonio, but fewer seabirds occur at Cahuita.

Differences are even more noticeable underwater. At Manuel Antonio, clean yellow sand beaches drop away quickly into water often greenish tan with sediment, in which objects appear and disappear as in a mist. Persistent tidal currents pull the swimmer back and forth past jumbles of boulders that support few corals but plenty of fish—sergeant majors, blue tang, grunts, blowfish. At Cahuita, beaches are littered with detritus from the turtle grass beds that extend toward the reef, and snorkelers crawl rather than swim over the shallow beds, but the water is so clear that the grass looks fluorescent green. Here and there are sandy hollows where miniature reefs have become established, with green sponges growing among brain and fungus corals. Fish teem in such hollows, many of the same kinds as at Manuel Antonio, but others are different, such as coral-eating parrotfish.

Cahuita and Manuel Antonio are echoes of an evolutionary event that preceded the land bridge and its biotic interchange, and that may have affected the planet more. This was the closing of the deep seaway that had existed between the continents since the Eocene. The closure had impacts on marine life at least as profound as the land bridge's on terrestrial life. It caused the extinction of many marine species, and evolution or migration of many others. It *may* have changed global climate catastrophically. Scientists have speculated that seaway closure diverted to the north a major ocean current that had flowed through the intercontinental strait. The diverted current may have become the Gulf Stream, and, as it carried moist tropical air over the North Atlantic, the Stream may have greatly increased precipitation at higher latitudes. That in turn may have helped cause the ice ages as increased snowfall accumulated into glaciers.

The land bridge perhaps was more a side effect of the seaway's closure than vice versa. For one thing, the seaway closed not from the process of island arc formation that had been thrusting up land between the continents since the Cretaceous, but from an *interruption* of that process between western Panama and South America. During the Miocene epoch, the Farallon Plate divided into two smaller plates, the Cocos and the Nazca. (Like continents, plates divide when a spreading zone opens in their midst, pushing the new plates thus formed away from each other.) The Cocos Plate kept moving in the same northeastward direction as had its "parent," and so kept subducting under the Caribbean Plate from Guatemala to western Panama. Powerful volcanic activity continued in the area, as it does today. The Nazca Plate, located under eastern Panama, began moving in the same direction and at the same speed as the Caribbean Plate, and thus stopped subducting under it. Volcanic activity was greatly reduced, as it remains today.

It seems paradoxical that *reduced* volcanic activity should have caused the final link in the land bridge. Yet, as one plate dives under another, subduction produces deep ocean trenches as well as volcanic island arcs. An end to subduction meant that the Mid-American trench along eastern Panama's Pacific coast disappeared because the "mixmaster" was no longer digging it. The inactive trench filled with sediments, and the ocean became much shallower. By eleven million years ago, nonvolcanic islands began to appear in eastern Panama and Colombia's Chocó Basin as pressure along fault lines pushed up ridges from the water. Over the next few million years, the region became an archipelago.

As islands continued to rise, erosion deposited deep sediments on the relatively quiescent sea bottom, and the Chepo, Chucunaque, and Chocó basins between the islands gradually filled with silt. By the mid-Pliocene epoch, four million years ago, remaining seaways were no more than fifty meters deep. By the late Pliocene, about three million years ago, the Caribbean and Pacific were so different as to suggest that the former straits had become the lowlands which now extend from the Canal Zone to the Chocó. The land bridge was finished, waiting for its intercontinental passengers. Yet the sundered Caribbean and Pacific coasts already had been changing for millions of years as the deep seaway formerly connecting them had shoaled.

The seaway closure's effects were clearer to early evolutionists than those of the land bridge. Slow to discern Central America's land migration role, Darwin was well aware of a former seaway's possibility. In *The Origin of Species* he wrote: "Dr. Gunther has recently shown that about 30 percent of the fishes are the same on the opposite sides of the Isthmus of Panama, and this fact has led naturalists to believe that the Isthmus was formerly open." Darwin wasn't convinced of this, and Thomas Belt also had doubts, noting that the Caribbean and Pacific coasts had only fifty seashells in common out of a total of over three thousand known species. "So remarkably distinct are the two marine faunas," Belt wrote, "that most zoologists consider that there has been no communication in the tropics between the two seas since the close of the Miocene Period, whilst the connection that is supposed to have existed at that remote epoch . . . is disputed by others equally eminent."

By 1876, however, Alfred Russell Wallace was using his land bridge and its relatively recent biotic interchange as proof of a former seaway. Wallace also noted that the seashells of "the Pacific shore of tropical America" are more like those of the Caribbean or even West Africa than those of the Pacific Islands, and concluded that "during the Miocene Epoch a broad channel separated North and South America."

Uncertainty persisted about the location of the "broad channel." The

Nicaraguan Depression long attracted seaway theorists. Its low altitude and great lakes suggested that at least part of it recently had been under the sea, as did the presence of usually saltwater fish in Lake Nicaragua. "Sometimes, when in shallow water, we saw a pointed billow moving away from the boat, produced by some large fish below," wrote Belt, "and I was told that it was a shark." By the time Archie Carr visited the lake in the 1950s, it was known that not only sharks (bull sharks, *Carcharinus leucas*) but sawfish and tarpon lived in it. The sharks often reached six feet and had a reputation as man-eaters, and the sawfish (shark relatives with serrated snouts) could weigh as much as 700 pounds. It was generally believed that the fish had become landlocked after an arm of the sea was cut off, and Carr thought the lake shark's man-eating reputation showed this, since seagoing bull sharks aren't known to attack humans. Confined to a lake, a six-foot shark might evolve unusual food preferences.

In the 1960s, however, lake bottom geology studies failed to turn up marine sediments, showing that the lakes formed from inland subsidence along fault lines and never were connected to the sea. Then ichthyologist Thomas Thompson demonstrated that the sharks, sawfish, and tarpon are not landlocked, but migrate back and forth between the lake and the Caribbean in the San Juan River. Sharks tagged off the Costa Rican coast appeared in the lake, and lake-tagged sharks were caught again at the San Juan's mouth. When I was in El Castillo in 1993, big jumping fish were a frequent sight in the San Juan rapids. They probably weren't sharks or sawfish because overfishing has decimated them, but they may have been tarpon or other marine species that migrate up the river, such as *robalo* and *roncador* (snook and grunts). In San Carlos on Lake Nicaragua, I saw a newly caught tarpon that filled half a rowboat, and piles of *robalo* and *roncador*.

There may have been straits through Nicaragua, or through Tehuantepec, at times during the past sixty million years. Both were part of the continental landmass, however, so neither could have been as deep or long-lasting as the Darién seaway. The rhino and horse fossils from Panama's Gaillard Cut show that it was Darién that isolated North from South America until the Pliocene. Darién was the "broad channel" that Alfred Russell Wallace had referred to.

Seashells

It's not surprising that the Central American seaway was discovered before the land bridge. Marine animals, particularly seashells, always have played a more important role in paleontology than land animals, albeit a less popular one. Seashells were the first fossils to be recognized as such, because they are easy to find and often closely resemble the shells of living species. The very concept of evolution depended heavily on seashells, because early paleontologists found them the most reliable indicators of changes in organisms through time. They could measure the ages of rock strata best by the changes in their abundant and varied fossil shells.

Marine snails and bivalves are ready-made fossils. They live in the sediments wherein they are fossilized, unlike most vertebrates, and are tremendously abundant. Francisco Ximénez noted that rock made of "*conchas del mar*" was the main source of lime in colonial Guatemala. In 1850, Professor C. B. Adams of Amherst University collected 38,920 specimens of 376 snail species and 2,860 specimens of 157 bivalve species during a six-week trip to Panama, mostly within a few kilometers of his Panama City hotel. Seashell abundance is easy to overlook because they seem nondescript, passive creatures, but the animals within can be surprising. Although many live as one expects snails or clams to, by grazing algae or filtering plankton, many do other things. Common tropical marine snails called cone shells are predators, for example, harpooning fish with poison darts.

Yet even seashells are not an infallible key to the evolutionary past. In Central America there are large gaps in *their* record. Fossil shells are more abundant and reliable from the Caribbean than the Pacific, where plate subduction destroys sediments. Tectonic activity also seems to have destroyed most early seashell fossils. There are land plant fossils from the Jurassic period, but no seashells, and those from the subsequent Cretaceous and Paleocene are sparse, like the Mosquitia geologist's ambiguous "ammonite." Seashells are common from later epochs, but they become so common that they overwhelm the nonspecialist with long lists of genera, which may be one reason the seaway hasn't caught the popular imagination as the land bridge has. I've never seen a museum exhibit that dramatized it, and marine fossil displays seldom refer to it. In 1993, the Managua National Museum had a Pacific coastal plain whale skeleton from the time of the Gracias fossils, but not even its species was known.

Still, paleontologists have used marine fossils to draw a picture of the seaway and its eventual closure. According to the picture, first drawn in the 1950s by W. P. Woodring and redrawn in the 1980s by Edward J. Petuch, most Central American coastal waters had a similar fauna from the Eocene epoch until the Pliocene. This fauna largely was a product of the strong east-to-west ocean current that ran through the Panama seaway. Because the current caused upwellings of cool, nutrient-rich water, animals that like such conditions predominated, including a great diversity of mollusks, which fed by filtering detritus and plankton from the water. Reef-building corals, which like warm, clear, relatively quiet water, were less common.

Mollusk evolution is so leisurely that relics of this ancient fauna have lingered in parts of the Caribbean where deep water upwellings continue. Examining mollusks caught by trawlers and divers off Venezuela and Colombia, Petuch discovered a number of species that are virtually the same as animals "thought to be extinct for millions of years and known as fossils from around the Caribbean." Since local conditions are unchanged from the Miocene, the animals have remained, Petuch wrote, "in a sort of evolutionary stasis, neither becoming extinct nor evolving into new, morphologically different species complexes." The Honduran Bay Islands also have pre–land bridge relicts. Huge coral reefs lie off the islands today, but deep cliffs drop off suddenly outside them and plankton-feeding fish are abundant, indicating nutrient-rich upwellings. Mollusks similar to those in the Venezuela and Colombia relict pocket live in deeper waters. *Falsilyria* is one, a rotund, pinkish little sea snail with what look like 1950s-style abstract decorations on its shell. A common genus north to Florida in the Miocene, it now occurs only off eastern Honduras and Nicaragua.

In 1986, a diver found a new, endemic *Falsilyria* species living ten meters deep on the sandy bottom off the Bay Island of Utila. When I snorkeled off Utila in 1993, it seemed remoter and stranger than the shallower reefs of Florida or the Virgin Islands. Its reef lay in such deep water that I had to swim alarmingly far out to reach it, and the huge staghorn corals seemed to arise not from a sandy bottom but from unplumbed blue depths. A barracuda about my size hovered undisturbed by my hurried passage, and a school of blue tang vanished in midwater, as their color matched that of the grotto into which they descended. With cold, dark currents pulling me through the staghorns, there was none of the sunny calm of shallower reefs.

The entire northeastern Caribbean from Honduras to Yucatán is a vast relic of time before the land bridge. Then a backwater unaffected by the seaway current, it was the one part of Central America's coast with extensive coral reefs, and it still has them, to put it mildly. The Belize barrier reef is the New World's biggest, second only to Australia's, and is the only place except the South Pacific with atolls, great circular reefs enclosing shallow lagoons. To fly over the Belizean coast at jetliner height is to see life differently than humans usually do. What on the surface would be a travel poster scene of beaches and palms is transformed into a vast, greenish brown film, less a scattering of discrete organisms on the elements of sky, land, and water than a collective element itself. At light plane altitude, the distinction between organisms and elements—visible if ambiguous from a jetliner—can break down completely. Passing over the Hol Chan Marine Reserve in an air taxi, I wondered how a collection of boats had come aground on the mudflats of a marshy estuary, then realized that the boats were anchored over the same four-meter-deep reef where I'd been snorkeling the day before.

The reef can be disorienting even from sea level. When I snorkeled at Long Cay near the system's seaward edge, the corals were ten meters below me but distinct in miniature because of the water's clarity. I saw the reef "landscape" in a way that I never have in undersea films. Stony ridges and winding ravines dissected the sea bottom, and fish sheltered in corals like birds in a forest canopy. A tight blue tang school dived and disappeared among the branches like a flock of hyacinth macaws. A yellowish moray eel that looked four meters long slithered like an anaconda along a ridgetop, dove into a crevice, reappeared, and disappeared into another. At the edge of this "plateau," a deep canyon dropped off, enhancing a slightly nightmarish sense of floating in midair. When I drifted over the indigo darkness at its edge, I saw hundreds of big fish hovering in the current that ran along it, the silvery, streamlined fish of open waters. Their bodies were black against the yellow reef margins, but they flashed and glittered when they drifted out over the canyon's ultramarine.

I think the blue of the outer Belizean reef was the deepest, purest blue I'd ever seen. The light was so intense that when I landed on neighboring Half Moon Cay and walked into the low forest there, the sunlight dappling the ground appeared a weird fluorescent red. Froglike sounds and chickenhouse smells wafted down from the treetops, made by a roost of the red-footed boobies and magnificent frigate birds that had been circling overhead as we approached the cay. When I climbed the Belizean Audubon Society's observation tower above the canopy, the colors had the intensity of a dream—the white of the boobies' plumage, like laundry spread out to dry, and the black and scarlet of the male frigate birds.

Despite its huge size, the present Belize reef isn't very old. Most of it was land when sea levels were lower during the last glaciation. Yet a reef system fringed that land, and even older reefs fringed every coast of the northern Caribbean at least as far back as the Eocene. Such antiquity can seem to trivialize tectonic contingencies like land bridges. When I snorkeled among the teeming, confiding fish of Belize's Hol Chan Reserve, I might have been in the Mesozoic Tethys Sea of a hundred million years ago. The nurse sharks and rays that swam obliviously among the staghorn and brain corals doubtless looked and behaved much as their ancestors did before the Atlantic seafloor began to spread open, when the Tethys lapped Laurasia's south shore. Even the more recent bony fish—the big groupers, gray snappers, and grunts that thronged the snorkeling boats like friendly horses in hope of food handouts—had similar ancestors in the Tethys.

The Seaway Closes

Yet the ancient Tethyan fauna did change in the late Miocene, as the Darién and Chocó waters gradually shallowed. Shoals probably had begun to obstruct the east-to-west current through the seaway by five million years ago. Without the current's cool-water upwellings, conditions throughout the Caribbean became less like those on the Pacific, where strong offshore currents and upwellings continued. Seashells have provided a way of dating the seaway's final closure. Particularly useful have been foraminifera, the fossils that excited Barnum Brown during his Petén expedition. Foraminifera are protozoans whose limey cases, microscopic seashells, cover the sea bottom in huge deposits and are thus reliable indicators of changes in ocean conditions. Paleontologists have used them, along with other evidence, to estimate the closure at about three million years ago.

Seaway closure affected marine life in complicated ways. Biologists once thought it caused a mass extinction of cool-water mollusks in the Caribbean, and many such mollusks did disappear or survived only as the "living fossils" Edward Petuch has found. Recent studies suggest, however, that Caribbean mollusks actually became more diverse after the land bridge formed, perhaps because a greater diversity of shallow-water habitats became available. Corals suffered more than mollusks. Although only the north Caribbean had big reefs in pre–land bridge Central America, a number of coral species lived along the south Caribbean and Pacific coasts. They survived in the Caribbean after the land bridge formed, but became extinct in the Pacific. Corals on Central America's Pacific coast today are descended from East Indian and Polynesian corals, which probably arrived fairly recently as drifting larvae. Other Indo-Polynesian animals have colonized Central America's west coast, such as the brown and yellow sea snakes that live in drifts of foam and seaweed.

The seaway closure's most significant evolutionary effect was on animals that *didn't* go extinct. Many such animals, particularly mobile ones like fish and crustaceans, were able to adapt to conditions on both sides of the land bridge. They no longer could mate with their counterparts on the other side of Central America, however, and this became a grand natural experiment in speciation, the evolution of new species in isolated populations. Biologist Nancy Knowlton has described how the seaway's closure seems to have affected one common group, the pistol shrimps (*Alphaeus*). Pistol or snapping shrimps are colorful tropical crustaceans that live in bottom crevices, which they defend by snapping their enlarged claws at rival shrimps or other enemies. The resultant popping sounds are as common in Central American waters as crickets on land.

Knowlton and her coworkers captured and identified pistol shrimps from both sides of Panama. They then paired Pacific and Caribbean shrimps which looked enough alike that they might have descended from a single pre–land bridge species, although all are presently classified as different species. As was to be expected with different species, few of these trans-isthmian pairs mated successfully and produced eggs. Some got along amicably, despite their reproductive failure. Others fought, sometimes so violently that they tore off each other's claws. When Knowlton analyzed the shrimps' genetic material, she found more similarity in the pairs that got along than in the pairs that fought. The amicable pairs tended to come from near-shore, shallow-water habitats, while the hostile pairs came from deeper waters, suggesting that the hostile pairs had been evolving separately several million years longer than the amicable pairs. The gradual shoaling of isthmian waters that began over five million years ago would have separated deep-water habitats long before the opening of the land bridge divided the amicable shrimp pairs' shallow-water habitats three million years ago.

It's perhaps as impressive that "twin" species on opposite sides of the land bridge have remained as similar as they are over three million years as that they have changed. There are plenty of reasons for them to have changed. The Pacific and Caribbean coasts are very different today, as Manuel Antonio and Cahuita demonstrate in their miniaturized way. From the Belize barrier reef to the San Blas archipelago, Caribbean waters tend to be clear, warm, and full of gaudy fish, as long as fishing pressure is not too heavy, in which case they can become depressingly empty. Without rich nutrient upwellings, the Caribbean's food webs are made of slender threads. From the Tehuantepec estuary to Panama Bay, Pacific waters tend to be turbid, cool, and full of fish that are drabber, but more dependable in their abundance, although factory trawlers can impoverish even them.

Manuel Antonio and Cahuita don't represent all of the coasts, however. The Pacific has some small but diverse coral reefs, particularly off islands, where waters are clearer, and the Caribbean has stretches such as Costa Rica's Tortuguero, where long beaches drop into deeper waters. When I visited Nicaragua's Mosquito Coast, it seemed as turbid and windswept as the Pacific, although Central America's second most important coral reef system, the Miskito Cays, lies fifty kilometers offshore. The bays that punctuate both coasts tend to have characteristics all their own.

The Gulf of Panama is virtually a small sea, with its own system of tides because tectonic uplift has left it very shallow. At Isla Taboga, about twenty kilometers offshore from Panama City, a wide expanse of algae-covered rocks separates land from water at low tide, and the shallows are opaque with silt when the tide is moving. The rock-bottomed deeper waters there reminded me of Long Island Sound more than the Caribbean, except that sergeant majors and mullet swam in them rather than porgies and cunners. The island's main tropical spectacle is above water. When I climbed to a clifftop on the uninhabited northern side in February 1993, I found hundreds of brown pelicans nesting in the canopy of a forest below the cliff. I'd heard there was a pelican rookery, but I hadn't expected the ungainly birds would be sitting on big rain forest trees, and diving for fish in the waters below.

Tides in the shallow, meandering Caribbean bays can be almost imperceptible, although they can change enough to strand unwary sailors, as Columbus discovered when he tried to escape the Belén estuary. At Almirante Bay off Isla Colón, I watched needlefish and silversides from a dock as I've watched sunfish in New England ponds. The water was so still at dusk that big fishing bats were a common sight, skimming over to snatch small fish from the surface. Sometimes they came into the room and glided silently around the ceiling fans.

A bay habitat the coasts both have is mangrove forest, and the seaway's closure has caused differences between Pacific and Caribbean ones. Four genera of the salt-tolerant trees—red, white, black, and buttonwood—occur on both coasts, but the Pacific's red mangrove is a different species from the Caribbean's, and the Pacific has another genus, the tea mangrove. Because high Pacific tides leave mangrove roots exposed longer to air, they tend to have limited faunas. When I was in mangroves on Nicaragua's Pacific, the tide had receded out of sight, leaving bare mud below prop roots on which lived mainly large snails, a kind of Salvador Dalí forest. At the Cuero y Salado Wildlife Refuge on Honduras's Caribbean, the water was so high and the mangroves so lush that I saw no sign the tide ever exposed the mud. The place defied my preconceptions of mangrove swamps as the low, spindly habitat one sees in the Florida Everglades. Black mangroves formed a thirty-meter green wall above the Cuero and Salado rivers, and many other plants grew among them—swamp ferns, huiscoyol and royal palms, spider lilies, and small, palmate-leaved trees called *zapatons*. With Pico Bonito in the background, it looked like climax rain forest.

Coastal Megafauna

I saw small American crocodiles at Cuero y Salado, and the refuge also has a breeding manatee population. How did the Panama seaway's closure affect such creatures—the marine counterparts of iguanas and tapirs? It doesn't seem to have affected the American crocodile, although the species is mainly coastal. It swims between Caribbean islands, and the great size it can attain seems typical of seagoing creatures. (The biggest wild reptiles I've seen were American crocodiles reclining loglike at Costa Rica's Carara Biological Reserve, where six-meter-long individuals survive.) Yet American crocodiles also can live far up rivers; Thomas Belt found "many that were not less than fifteen feet in length" in the San Juan River and Lake Nicaragua. Continued freshwater gene flow between Caribbean and Pacific would explain why the species has failed to "twin" and still lives on both coasts.

Continued gene flow across the land bridge would have been impossible for fully marine animals, and some seem to have "twinned." The green sea turtle, the herbivorous genus whose meat and cartilaginous *calipee* were coastal staples for most of history, has a Caribbean species (*Chelonia mydas*) and a Pacific one (*C. Agassizi*). On the other hand, some marine species such as hawksbill turtles are the same on both sides of the land bridge. Either they evolve more slowly than their relatives, or somehow contrive to keep their genes flowing between the oceans without benefit of a Panama seaway.

The land bridge's formation seems to have affected manatees in a more complex way than crocodiles or sea turtles. The West Indian manatee was abundant in the Caribbean when the Spanish arrived. Dampier considered it second only to the green turtle as a provision for pirate ships, and recorded that he had known two Miskito "strikers" to bring aboard two manatees every day for a week, "the least of which hath not weighed less than 600 pounds." The manatee's former Caribbean abundance isn't surprising. Distantly related to elephants, they live on the aquatic grasses which carpet Caribbean estuaries and reefs, a bountiful food source. There are fewer sea grasses on the Pacific coast, and one would expect there to be fewer manatees. In fact, there are no manatees on the Pacific, and there is no evidence they ever lived there. Dampier was surprised at their absence from the Gulf of Panama.

Far from "twinning" after the seaway closed, manatees seem to have lived only in the Caribbean. This raises the possibility that they were absent from the Central American coast before the seaway closed, and that its closure allowed them to move in. Manatees can't tolerate cold water. They crowd into warm springs or power plant outlets to survive Florida winters. When the seaway was open, the cool water current between the continents may have stopped them from spreading north, even though the Caribbean north of Honduras would have been perfect for them. Fossils show that manatees evolved in African and South American waters about thirty million years ago, yet North American manatee fossils appear much later. The earliest definite ones of the living manatee (*Trichechus*) are from the late Pliocene in Florida, about the time the seaway was closing.

The manatee may be a neglected champion of the supposedly long-vanquished southern side in the "triumph-and-tragedy" epic. If it is a land bridge migrant, it is the largest surviving one, much larger than the biggest North American survivors, the tapir or the spectacled bear. Although defenseless against human hunting, it somehow managed to outlive tougher land mammals such as gomphotheres, and today shows considerable resilience when protected. I looked out a Miami airport hotel window in 1995 and saw a three-meter manatee feeding placidly on the waterweeds of a golf course canal below.

The manatee's championship did have a North American challenger until recently. A similar-sized seal lived in the Caribbean when the Spanish arrived, the monk seal. Dampier saw seals sunning on the Alcranes Islands off Yucatán, and they bred on Swan Island north of Honduras. Monk seals evidently lived all along Central America's coasts before the seaway closed. Seals can live in colder waters than manatees, so the deep currents of the seaway would not have been a barrier to their movements. Their bones have been found in southern California strata just below those of post–land bridge animals like ground sloths. They had disappeared from Central America's Pacific when the Spanish arrived, however, and were much less common than manatees in the Caribbean. Like Petuch's seashells, they seem to have been a dwindling seaway relic. Hunted as a source of oil, the Caribbean monk seal largely had disappeared by 1800, and is now considered extinct, although Hawaiian and Mediterranean species survive precariously.

The manatee may not be the only South American dark horse. A recent discovery suggests that another large coastal mammal may have taken advantage of seaway closure to invade the north. When biologist Thomas Carr conducted aerial surveys of Mosquito Coast lagoons and estuaries in 1992, he was looking for manatees. He found encouraging numbers of those, but made even more sightings of animals he hadn't been looking for. On 136 occasions, Carr and accompanying observers saw South American river dolphins (*Sotalia fluviatilis*), a species generally thought to live no farther north than Venezuela. Carr was able to make a firm identification by dissecting a stranded carcass.

These dolphins, which look like miniature bottle-nosed dolphins with yellowish gray backs and pink bellies, live throughout the rivers and coasts of tropical South America east of the Andes. When I was on the Amazon, they were an almost continual presence along with the much larger Amazon river dolphin (*Inia geoffrensis*), an entirely freshwater species. The big Amazon river dolphin is a very strange creature, pinkish white and nearly blind, with a long beak and a definite neck. It may be more like primitive cetaceans than saltwater dolphins, and hearing it rise to breathe at night on a narrow forest tributary several kilometers from the river was like returning to the Miocene. Yet it was just as strange in a way to see troops of the little bottlenoselike *Sotalia* porpoising up the river near Iquitos, Peru, over a thousand kilometers from the Atlantic.

Given their ubiquity on the Amazon, one would think river dolphins would be a common sight in Central America if they are there. Sightings had been recorded in Panama and Nicaragua before Carr's, but not well documented ones. Yet, as Carr noted, "the relative abundance of dolphins suggests that their occurrence is regular rather than incidental to this part of Nicaragua." Perhaps this is an example of a land bridge migration still underway, and there will be South American river dolphins in the Gulf of Mexico someday. Perhaps there already are.

12

The Bridge of Megatheres

THE THREE MILLION years since the land bridge opened is a long time, but not so long compared to the more than fifty million years of continental isolation before it. In fact, the earth has not changed that much since the seaway closed. We call our world the Holocene instead of the Pleistocene, but it's still the Ice Age. The temperate zone continental glaciers have barely disappeared, and probably will return, whatever we cause in the way of global warming. We may narrow or flood Darién by melting some of the polar ice caps, but not deep enough to carry an intercontinental current that can recapture the Gulf Stream and make the North Atlantic less snowy.

Central America had its glaciers, and they left clear, if little-known, marks. On the north side of the highest ridge on Guatemala's Altos Cuchumatanes, I found a cliff-ringed bowl that was very like cirques in the California mountains. A small glacier must have formed there, although my guide, Dr. Guzmán, said he'd never seen even a snow flurry on the plateau. Below the ridge, we passed a grassy mound from which a spring flowed, rare in the plateau's karst landscape, where surface water sinks into the limestone. This suggested that the mound was a moraine—a heap of gravel and soil left by a retreating glacier. A water-filled depression below the mound looked like a glacial kettle, a place where ice buried in the moraine had melted, causing it to slump. The moraine and kettle appeared fresh, as though the last glaciation had retreated a few years before instead of fifteen thousand.

The boggy valley below the mound, the Llanos de San Miguel, was littered with boulders and floored with slabs of limestone bedrock as flat as tabletops, more signs of glacial passage. The boulders were erratics that the ice had plucked from the cirque and carried downhill, and the slabs looked like glacial pavement, rock scraped smooth as ice flowed over it. They lacked the scratches usually left by a glacier's passage, but those probably had eroded from the soft limestone since the ice melted. Guzmán said there were flat slabs, boulders, and mounds on other parts of the plateau—I read later that the Cuchumatanes glacier covered a hundred square kilometers.

Central America's other glaciated region is its other highest massif, Chirripó, where the marks of ice are even clearer. Fully exposed to Caribbean trade winds, the Talamancas get more precipitation than interior plateaus like the Cuchumantanes, although snow never falls at Chirripó either. Downpours came every afternoon and evening I was there, and it drizzled for much of the mornings as well. Ice hundreds of meters thick must have accumulated during the last glaciation, and its flow cut Chirripó's granitic ridges into a classic alpine landscape which looms strangely above the dense cloud forest on most of the Talamancas. Climbing from the epiphyte-laden trees below 3,000 meters into the glaciated zone was like stepping from a Frederick Church jungle scene into an Albert Bierstadt Rocky Mountain panorama, a battlement of peaks, cirques, and talus slopes so ice-scoured that it hurt my eyes. Scratches on granite pavement were barely eroded, and moraines were good-sized hills. Water was everywhere, as though the glacier was still melting. It glittered in tarns (Lago Chirripó, the largest and highest, is twenty-two meters deep), stood in boggy pools, and rushed away in almost subterranean streams cut into the moraines.

Geologists took a surprisingly long time to notice Central American glaciation. Richard Weyl seems to have been the first to describe Chirripó's, in the 1950s, and the Cuchumatanes' wasn't discovered until 1968. Thomas Belt may have been the only early naturalist to remark on glacial signs, and he was wrong about them. While exploring silver mines in the Ocotal River region of the Nicaraguan highlands, he thought he saw "evidences of glacial action . . . as clear as in any Welsh or (Scottish) Highland valley . . . the same accumulations of unstratified sand and gravel, the same transported boulders that could be traced to their parent rocks some miles distant." He concluded that all Central America above 2,000 feet had been covered by ice, and that this had caused the extinction of animals such as horses. He thought other species had survived "on lands now below the ocean, that were uncovered by the lowering of the sea caused by the immense quantity of water that was locked up in frozen masses on the land."

Belt mistook stream-deposited landscapes for glaciated ones, but his general impression that the landscape had changed catastrophically in the past few million years was right. A tectonic uplift that prevailed throughout the Americas at the end of the Pliocene may have raised Central America's mountains and plateaus even higher than today's nearly 4,000 meters. As with the Miocene's volcanic explosions, we aren't sure why that uplift occurred so suddenly and widely, although there is a theory as to the Talamancas' origin. One of the most spectacular tectonic phenomena operating on Central America may have raised them. The Cocos Plate passes over a "hot spot," a convection upwelling of heat from the earth's mantle, at the Galápagos in mid-Pacific. As it does so, the heat changes the plate's structure, and this causes a 200-kilometer-wide, 2,000-meter-thick "welt" in it. The plate continually carries this welt northeastward, and shoves it against Central America at the Talamancas. Lighter and thicker than the rest of the plate, the welt subducts less easily under the Caribbean Plate, and this apparently has lifted the Talamanca granite. The welt, called the Cocos Ridge, also seems to have stopped volcanic activity south of Volcán Irazu by choking off magma vents.

As I've said, it was the subsidence of plate subduction in Darién that caused the land bridge, not this tectonic uplift. Yet the uplift evidently contributed to the Great American Biotic Interchange by allowing cold climate organisms to spread south—and north—through environments like the Cuchumatanes and Talamancas. A rain shadow effect from the rise of the wall-like ranges also may have helped grassland and savanna organisms to migrate through Central America.

We still don't understand that much about how the biotic interchange passed through Central America, however. If the interchange was a triumph-and-tragedy epic, for example, one might have expected a kind of Oklahoma Land Rush start, with saber-tooths and dire wolves lining up at Darién to bag the first unwary liptoterns and macraucheniids. Yet known fossils suggest that migration across the bridge was slow for a long time after Darién became land. Although the seaway is thought to have closed three million years ago, most land animal fossils demonstrating intercontinental migration date from about 2.4 million years ago or later. This apparent slow start may be an artifact of the fossil record, with important migrants leaving no fossils, or fossils not yet found. (There are, predictably, no Central American fossils dating from 3 to 2.4 million years ago.) It's also possible that something hindered migration when the land bridge first opened. Panama and the Chocó may have been too swampy and heavily forested for plains-dwelling animals like toxodonts and horses to cross. Yet fossils don't show rain forest or swamp animals crossing the bridge early, either.

The fossil record improves dramatically in late Pliocene strata. It shows that skunks like Central America's present-day hog-nosed skunks had reached Argentina at that time, about 2.4 million years ago. So had peccaries and cricetid rodents, the cryptic North American rats that had diversified in Central America. Llamas, horses, saber-toothed cats, and bears appeared in Argentinian strata slightly later. South American animals migrated north in about equal force. The late Pliocene Palm Spring Formation in the southern California desert has yielded bones of glyptodonts, armadillos, ground sloths, and capybaras as old as the Argentinian llamas and horses. There even are Central American fossils confirming migration at about this time. The late Pliocene El Sisimico lake beds of El Salvador have yielded ground sloth fossils as well as those of North American animals.

The interchange hit its full stride (in the fossil record, at least) in the early to middle Pleistocene epoch from two to one million years ago. Mastodons of the genus *Cuvieronius* appeared in Argentina, the South American "elephants" that pleased Cuvier by refuting Buffon. We can be sure they got there via Central America because they've been found at places like Estanzuela. Other venerable North and Central Americans first fossilized in South America at this time were dogs, including the still living *Canis*, coatis, tapirs, and deer. South America continued to send imposing creatures north, including two other ground sloth families, giant anteaters, and the rhinoceroslike toxodonts. The most impressive were the truly gigantic ground sloths of the megathere family, some of which stood six meters tall, and a genus of predaceous, flightless birds (*Titanis*). These were the "giant and rapacious phorusrhacid ground birds" that Stephen Jay Gould's 1996 essay said "simply died out" after the land bridge opened. Fossil *Titanis* found in Florida were three meters tall, with large hawklike heads and bills.

Coastal Plains and Savanna Corridors

Although the Ice Age may have begun later than the first big wave of migration, the Pleistocene's half dozen or so glacial interludes must have affected the interchange greatly. David Webb has written that most of the mammal groups that migrated between the continents were "grazers that lived in large herds and are best known in settings of open woodlands or grassland savannas." As Belt surmised, lowering of sea level during full glaciation broadened coastal plains, and this would have made it easier for such animals to cross the bridge. I got a sense of how drastically Pleistocene sea levels fell when I visited Blue Hole, a 300-meter-wide sinkhole inside Lighthouse Reef atoll on the Belize reef's outer edge. It took three hours to get there by motorboat from Ambergris Cay, itself an hour from the present mainland.

Sinkholes are steep, usually circular pits caused by surface subsidence as ground water erodes underlying limestone. When divers from Jacques-Yves Cousteau's *Calypso* expedition explored the Blue Hole pit in 1971, they found huge stalactites and stalagmites which proved it had been on dry land, since such structures can't form underwater. The stalagmites on the bottom, 120 meters under the Caribbean's present surface, showed that sea level had been at least that much lower. Belize's coastal plain would have been over twice as wide then as now. When I was there, the sunny rim made good snorkeling, with big parrotfish, black angels, and triggerfish swimming among profuse corals, and little thimble jellyfish dancing at the surface like swarms of golden bees. The depths looked deathly dark and cold, a watery grave for unwary ground sloths and mastodons, although Cousteau's divers found no bones in it. Cousteau thought the ceiling had collapsed after sea level rose again.

Fossils have been found on offshore islands. The Panama City Science Museum has Pleistocene mastodon molars from the Gulf of Panama's Pearl Archipelago, showing the Gulf was land during glaciations. In the Caribbean, a land tortoise shell has been found on the Honduran Bay Island of Utila about fifty kilometers offshore, and freshwater turtles and land iguanas still live there. When I arrived on Utila, one of the large, gray iguanas lounged beside the airport runway, as though awaiting transport back to the mainland. I asked a biologist if it was an endemic species, and he said Honduran reptiles hadn't been studied enough to know.

The widened bridge's most spectacular surviving relics are tiny frogs which live on islands of Panama's Bocas del Toro province, where Columbus sought his Indian passage. About an inch long, the frogs belong to a species, *Dendrobates pumilio*, common from western Panama to southern Nicaragua. On the mainland, it is called the strawberry frog since most individuals have red, black-speckled heads and torsos. Their gaudy skin is poisonous, so they pursue an ingenious life history unhindered by predators. A male calls to attract females, and when one approaches, leads her to a curled leaf or other sheltered spot and deposits sperm. She lays her eggs with the sperm, and they incubate there. When an egg hatches, the female carries the tadpole on her back to water in a bromeliad or treehole, and afterwards may return and feed it by laying infertile eggs in the water.

In Bocas del Toro, these frogs are just about any coloration *but* black-speckled red. When I was on Isla Colón, near La Gruta, the woods resounded with the "*zeet, zeet*" calls of a *D. pumilio* that was apple green with brown polka dots and yellow legs. The calls were misleadingly loud for such tiny creatures, and the green coloration camouflaged them, unlike their mainland relatives, but I was able to locate an individual which was calling persistently to another nearby. On Isla Bastimentos, the next island over, bright orange frogs were even more common, or easier to see. They seemed to drip from the branches in one banana plantation. Other morphs are yellow, blue, even white, and ten color varieties have been counted in all. They probably evolved as the post-glacial rise in sea level isolated populations, and *D. pumilio* also has evolved differences of size, behavior, and poisonousness on different islands. Biologists Charles W. Myers and John W. Daly have called it "a leading candidate among all vertebrate animals for the title 'most variable species.'"

Drying climate that accompanied glacial interludes in the tropics may have been as important for migrating herds as widened coastal plains. On coasts and interior valleys, forest may have withdrawn into areas called "refugia" where moisture remained adequate to support it, and savanna or thorn scrub may have formed grassy corridors for wandering herds. Ten-thousand-year-old pollen from lake sediments in the Petén and Belize is of grasses and other nonforest plants, and there is living evidence of former savanna-scrubland corridors. Typical animals are scattered through the Americas as though their distribution was once continuous, but has been interrupted by forest since the last glaciation. The tropical rattlesnake occurs in dry or savanna parts of Central America from Mexico to Costa Rica, then reappears in Venezuelan and Colombian savannas. The green jay and vermilion flycatcher occur in brush from the southern U.S. to northern Central America, and reappear in northern South America. Dry land plants like mesquite have similar distributions.

Many dry land organisms have failed to spread between continents, however. North American ground squirrels and jackrabbits don't occur south of the Mexican plateau, although tree squirrels and cottontail rabbits have spread to Brazil. South American dry land animals such as tuco-tucos (ground squirrel–like rodents) and maras (jackrabbitlike rodents) have never spread north, whereas forest-dwelling porcupines and agoutis have. The available evidence from the *last* ice age doesn't prove there was a savanna corridor all the way through Central America. Ten-thousand-year-old fossil pollen from Panamanian lakes is not of savanna plants as in Belize, but forest trees. This doesn't prove there were never savanna corridors through Panama, but it does suggest that there wasn't one during a glaciated period which perhaps was like others.

The complexity of such phenomena makes looking for echoes of Pleistocene savannas in present Central America difficult, although it has a certain allure. Savanna floras are engagingly simple compared to the thousands of tropical forest species that riot nearby, particularly for a temperate zone naturalist like me, versed in California oak savannas and grasslands. But the problem with seeking Pleistocene echoes in Central American savanna or scrub plants like Caribbean pine, live oak, gourd tree, acacia, and cactus is that they were savanna and scrub plants long before the Pleistocene. The same is probably true of many or most of the "lower" animals found in savannas or scrub.

The majestic assortment of big mammals and birds that distinguished the Pleistocene is almost completely gone from the rain shadow valleys of Honduras and Guatemala today, although the valleys probably still look much as they did during the Pleistocene. This is particularly true of the cactus-spiked, mountain-walled Motagua Valley which has produced so many mastodon and glyptodont bones. One must go to the little museum at Estanzuela to see their relics, however. The most one may see in the way of living Ice Age savanna corridor mammals is the odd armadillo or hog-nosed skunk. There may be cricetid rodents around too, but they almost certainly will remain invisible in the bushes.

Highland Corridors

Uplift and glaciation definitely cooled Central America's climate, and today's vegetation demonstrates a colder past better than a drier one. As I've said, fossil pollens show that North American alders, walnuts, and bayberries lived as far south as Panama in the Miocene epoch. The rise of Miocene volcanoes allowed such species to spread south, along with the conifers, oaks, magnolias, and other temperate species that now cover Central America's plateaus and peaks from 800 to 2,000 meters. Further Pliocene uplift followed by lowered Pleistocene temperatures probably turned most of the land bridge above the coastal plains into the Californialike landscape that surprised me when I first arrived in Chiapas. This vast temperate expanse would have offered migration opportunities different from those of lowland savanna corridors. The spectacled bears and vicuñas that now inhabit the Andes would have traveled it. Porcupines must have followed it north from the Andes, where they still have close relatives.

Migration opportunities weren't unlimited, however. Many temperate organisms never crossed the border between the old, continental land north of the Nicaraguan Depression and the new, oceanic land south of it. When I was driving through the Depression with Jacinto Cedeño, he pointed to tiny dark dots in ravines below the summit of Volcán Cristobal. "Those are *ocote* pines," he said. "That's as far south as they grow." In fact, no conifers ever spread naturally south of the Depression, as though the north's most venerable trees disdained to set root on the upstart oceanic lands. The last large mammals to move onto the land bridge, bison and mammoths, also spread only as far as the Depression, suggesting an affinity for the conifer forests that stop there, although, as David Webb writes, "One can only guess at the elaborate interactions that must have occurred between large herds of herbivores and tropical American vegetation."

Northern Central America's highlands always have impressed travelers with their abrupt contrast to the tropical lowlands. Thomas Belt found the "social groups" of Nicaraguan ocote pines and oaks "fresh and new" after the rain forest, but mining engineer William Wells felt "inexpressibly sad" in "the dreary solitudes . . . silent but for the murmur of the breeze in their tops" of Honduran pines. Archie Carr thought Honduran groves of liquidambar, a deciduous hardwood that occurs north to Appalachia, "curious and somewhat eerie. . . . Although we knew well the tears of fragrant balsam and the deep-toothed leaves and prickly, spherical fruits on the ground, there was nothing familiar in the continuous towering canopy or in the mid-day twilight beneath it, or in the stately columns that marched out evenly through the gloom."

Another curious thing about this northern-looking forest of ocote pine and liquidambar is that it occurs at lower elevation than a forest that appears more tropical—the cloud forest that grows from about 2,000 to 3,000 meters. While the pine and liquidambar forest tends to have limited shrubs, vines, or epiphytes, the cloud forest is lush with tree ferns, begonias, vines, and such a profusion of orchids, bromeliads, and other epiphytes that it's often hard to tell what kinds of trees the epiphytes are growing on. Even some trees, such as rubbery-leaved *Clusia*, grow as epiphytes. Yet despite its hothouse look, the cloud forest is not warmer than the ocote pine one; in fact, it is much colder because the sun rarely shines. The lushness results from the perpetual fog and drizzle at its elevation. Most of the cloud forest trees on which the "tropical" epiphytes riot are temperate zone genera.

Above 3,000 meters grows a forest that does have far northern affinities, and that remained almost as legendary as the quetzal until fairly recently because it is so remote. In the 1950s, botanist Paul H. Allen knew that the summit of Cerro Santa Barbara above northern Hondu-ras's Lake Yojoa was covered with "shadowy groves of giant conifers" because they were "silhouetted against the sky, clearly visible in good weather from the highway," but he had to climb for two days up sheer limestone cliffs to learn what the species were. On the top, he found giant firs, cypresses, and pines growing with yew, blueberry, lobelia, barberry, creambush, and other plants typical of Oregon. Such places are scattered over the heights from Chiapas to central Honduras. A few places in Guatemala even have sugar maples.

Celaque, the extinct volcano that overlooks Gracias, has an unusually accessible highland vegetation transect on a trail to its summit, which I climbed during my 1992 visit. The peak's old-growth firs and pines had looked invitingly cool from the blazing valley, but it took a day of walking to reach them. I set out from Gracias in the dark, on a dirt road through the dry forest remnants of the valley floor, and it was just light when I reached the ocote and oak zone at the peak's foot. A big black bird perched in a roadside pine, and I recognized a raven from its hoarse croak. Like pines, ravens live as far south as the Nicaragua highlands now. In the Pleistocene, they must have been megafauna scav-engers, cleaning up saber-tooth and dire wolf kills along with condors and vultures. Their apparent failure to spread into South America is a mystery.

Another raven came flying along, and the two went off northward, their Roman nose beaks silhouetted against the dawn. The trail entered a steep ravine, and the woods took on the feel and smell of temperate forest, with fewer strange undertones than tropical (which can smell like a florist's one moment and a butcher's the next); temperate forest generally just smells leafy and loamy. Evergreen, flaky-barked straw-berry trees and silvery deciduous hornbeams grew under the oaks and pines. A tan *Sceloporus* lizard like the U.S. fence lizard perched on a clump of whitish volcanic rock. Banana, coffee, and manioc patches on the slopes were the only tropical notes.

Halfway up the ravine, the columnar trunks and bright green, pal-mate leaves of liquidambars appeared, and a bigger, darker pine, another of Celaque's six species, replaced the spindly ocote. A swift stream boomed over boulders. When the trail crossed it, I half expected to see trout in the pools, but there were only big tadpoles and small, whitish crabs, which are among the commonest animals in Central American mountain streams, perhaps occupying them because of a scarcity of coldwater fish. Their presence still is surprising to temperate zone pre-conceptions, although other usually marine creatures frequent Central American fresh waters. I was once startled, looking into a Honduran stream, to see a small branch come to life and snatch at passing fish. It was the claws of a lobsterlike creature hiding under a rock.

The trail switchbacked through more liquidambars, and a flock of blue birds swooped downslope among the trunks—Steller's jays, an-other species that extends south to Nicaragua in the conifer zone. Their cries seemed subdued compared to their California cousins', but a lemon yellow, black-scalped Wilson's warbler sang exactly like its north-ern counterparts. A flock of bush tanagers and a scattering of bromeliads and dumb canes growing on the ground were the only reminders that I wasn't a thousand miles north of the Tropic of Cancer. As the switch-backs continued, however, the soil got darker and wetter, and cloud forest plants appeared. Tree ferns and pink begonias with foot-wide leaves grew in moist ravines. Tall miconia and solanum bushes crowded the understory, and bromeliads, philodendrons, and monsteras grew on tree trunks, first near the ground, then in the branches. I started hearing nightingale thrushes, which sound like hermit thrushes.

The trail emerged into a large clearing with two tumbledown log cabins, relics of squatters who had tried to exploit the cloud forest's rich soil. The clearing's slopes were impossibly steep, however. Blackberries, nettles, and fuschias overgrew the cabins, and young alders covered the former fields, as though on an Oregon clearcut. A band-tailed pigeon perched on a branch, another California species, and a little viper crawled across the trail. Tan-reddish in color with a faint diamond pat-tern on its back, it looked like the copperheads I'd known in the 1950s Connecticut woods. Above the clearing, the slopes got even steeper, and the trees were huge, with trunks a meter or more in diameter and bromeliad-hidden tops. Some looked like lowland rain forest trees, with root buttresses and thick, cinnamon colored bark. Others were huge, bluish-needled pines with long pendant cones, their purplish bark fili-greed with chartreuse wolf lichen. Clusias, palmettos, cactus vines, and bromeliads with bright red and yellow flowers grew on trunks, branches, and the ground.

The slopes became almost perpendicular, so that I was pulling myself upward on trailside rocks, and the hardwoods and epiphytes disappeared, replaced by pure conifer forest growing over deep needle-duff. Scattered large agaves like those of the Mexican plateau were the only understory plants. The summit trees flung out their branches in the extravagant gestures of ancient conifers, and I thought of John Muir when he found a giant sequoia in the Sierra Nevada forest—at an altitude similar to the Gracias firs'—"looking as strange in aspect and behavior among its neighbor trees as would the mastodon among the honey bears and deer." Pine needles hissed and sparkled in the wind, and the air smelled of resin, duff, and, despite the late afternoon heat, a hint of frost. Gracias had faded into the dry forest below. The only clear features on the valley floor were whitish river bluffs that might have been giant femurs and tibias scattered in brush.

Costa Rican and Panamanian highland forests differ dramatically from conifer-rich Celaque's. Although oaks, magnolias, alders, and walnuts prevail, they grow in less easily recognizable altitudinal bands, and they tend to be so moss- and epiphyte-covered, and so mixed with South American species, that they lose all resemblance to the tidier Honduran woods. I find the South American trees in Central American highlands harder to recognize than North American ones. A common one, podcarpus, is a gymnosperm, like pine, but doesn't bear cones or needles. It has broad evergreen leaves and plumlike fruits that make it hard to pick out from the laurels in the crowded canopy. Another temperate South American tree, *Drimys*, or winterbark, is considered the most primitive living angiosperm because of its wood structure, but its white flowers and evergreen leaves also resemble laurel or magnolia.

There's something unreal about the southern highlands. In their deep forests, which Oviedo likened so aptly to an ocean, various species do grow at different elevations, but the apparent uniformity of evergreen lushness makes botanizing hard. A 1990 climb up extinct Barva Volcano in Costa Rica's Cordillera Central was typical. Dry forest species on the floor of the Valle Central shifted almost imperceptibly to a wetter, more diverse forest, then to the dank luxuriance of cloud forest. I was literally in the clouds as I trudged up a series of muddy switchbacks past alder thickets and *Drimys* saplings, and the landscape was eerily silent in the drizzle. The slope leveled out, and I found myself surrounded by huge evergreen oaks of several species, one with the most remarkable bark I've seen, massive gray plates that clothed the trunk like armor. The trees were so weighted by epiphytes that the tops of many had broken off, littering the ground with gigantic branches smothered in bromeliads, orchids, cactuses, ferns, philodendrons, and monsteras, all still living and flowering.

The mist turned to windy rain as the slope steepened again, and the huge oaks faded from sight, replaced by a tangle of *Clusia*, bayberry, *Didymopanax*, *Oreopanax*, and other "elfin forest" species. Spiky stemmed, huge-leaved *Gunnera* plants, another South American highland species, grew beside the path like giant rhubarbs. *Gunnera* is called "poor man's umbrella" because of its leaves, and because it grows where it's always raining. Reaching the summit was like arriving somewhere in a dream. There was no view, and it would have been hidden in mist if there had been. I crested a knoll covered with gnarled little trees and found a black lake in an ancient crater. Silvery pebbles floored the dim but transparent water as far as I could see, and mist hung over the surface, drifting in patterns that would have had a hypnotic attraction if the place hadn't been so cold and wet. It seemed enchanted, but not in a comfortable, storybook way. The year before, some German tourists had tried to walk around the little lake and had disappeared for eleven days, wandering in the forest until they'd stumbled on a road.

Much of southern Central America's highland forest is remote and almost unknown, particularly in the Talamancas. A vast expanse of primary forest remains in Costa Rica's and Panama's La Amistad national parks on their border. The cloud forest at a place called Cerro Punta at the south end of Panama's La Amistad was the most effulgent I've seen, although the approach to it wasn't sylvan: a volcanic gorge that was being farmed with almost vertical potato and cabbage plots. Stucco houses at the gorge's bottom devolved into board shacks at the top, where a solid new bridge and roadway marked the La Amistad border, looking strangely affluent for a Central American park. Even more strangely, three-meter-tall alder saplings crowded the new road, their fallen leaves thickly littering the asphalt.

When we got to the park station, a comfortable stucco building, park service employee Eneida Palma explained that General Manuel Noriega had given this part of the park to "one of his colonels," and the man had built the house and roads, cleared pastures, and started a dairy farm. Noriega's 1990 overthrow had intervened, however, and the colonel had fled "to Miami." The people of the gorge had come and taken everything movable from the estate, including the roofs, and the alders had overgrown everything. Later the park service had regained possession and restored the house, the living room of which was occupied by one of the largest banquet tables I've seen, a slab of polished, reddish wood.

"The colonel had that made out of a single magnolia log," explained Palma, a grave, pretty woman. "When *la gente* came after he ran away, it was too heavy to carry off."

The colonel hadn't had time to cut the forest on the slopes above, at about 2,000 meters, and it made the primary cloud forest on Celaque seem sparse. Most of the trees could have made banquet tables, and understory vegetation was thicker than any lowland tropical rain forests I've seen. It was literally impossible to step more than a few feet into it, because one sank immediately into a tangle of ferns, horsetails, club mosses and shrubs so thick and wet that all momentum was lost. Some of the trees had the massive slabs of bark I'd seen on oaks at Volcán Barva, but foliage was too far up and epiphyte-covered to identify them. The biggest *Gunnera* plants I've seen grew at Cerro Punta, more like oriental potentates' parasols than poor man's umbrellas.

Vegetable luxuriance seemed to have crowded out animal life. Eneida Palma said there were rabbits, opossums, white-tailed deer, coatis, and a few pumas and tapirs in the area, but it was too high for jaguars and monkeys. The only animal I saw except for songbirds and skinny, pale gray toads was a white and black hawk that sat in a treetop just beyond binocular range, so that there was no way of identifying it, or of even being sure it was a bird. This was typical of today's highlands, which are like the valley savannas in seeming bereft of fauna compared to coastal plain forests. All the large animals that occur in the highlands —white-tailed deer, peccaries, pumas, tapirs—occur in lowland forest too, but many tropical forest animals don't live above 2,000 meters. Except for shrews, weasels, and some tree squirrel, pocket gopher, and cricetid rodent species, there are no endemic highland mammals. The only trace of a mammal I saw while climbing Celaque was an opossum's jawbone. On Volcán Barva, I saw a few scats on the trail and glimpsed a squirrel.

"I am convinced," wrote Archie Carr, who lived for many years on the Honduran plateau, "that the faunal poverty of the cloud forests is no illusion. It is a curious, at times bewildering, but very real condition." The relatively small size of Central American highlands, and their shrinkage since the last glaciation, are logical causes of this scarcity. It still seems strange to walk through landscapes like the Rockies or Andes and not see the furry things—marmots, pikas, vizcachas—that flit around every rock on the continents.

Lost Worlds Apart

Central America's glaciated areas—the Altos Cuchumatanes and Chirripó—epitomize the strange mixture of discontinuity and affinity between the northern and southern highlands. I visited both within two weeks in the summer of 1995, and was struck by their differences. About the same distance apart as San Francisco and Seattle, they almost might have been on separate continents. Subtler similarities lurked under the differences, however.

A scrubby grassland called *zacatal* that is typical of Guatemala's and Mexico's highest peaks covered the Cuchumatanes' valley floors and drier slopes. Bright with yellow composites, red paintbrush, and blue wild geraniums in rainy July, the boggy Llanos de San Miguel reminded me of meadows which wind below the peaks in California's Klamath Mountains. Flowers also dotted slopes and ridgetops, despite nightly frosts and a chilly mist that sometimes hid the landscape as Guzmán and I walked above the glacial cirque. They were low-growing, like arctic flowers. Little lavender violets and white sorrels grew in sheltered spots. A daisylike composite brandished white ray petals above a sprawling, succulent leaf rosette, and the paintbrush had no leaves at all, just two or three blossoms on a wiry stem.

Yet, despite the 4,000-meter altitude, pine and juniper woodland covered much of the Cuchumatanes' summits right to the top. Dr. Guzmán told me there are three pine species on the plateau, although *Pinus tristis* was the only one I saw. It looked like a miniature ponderosa to me, with yellow bark and light green needles in bundles of five. "It's called *tristis* because its needles are thinner and sparser than pino macho," Guzmán said. "There used to be more pino macho (*P. Moctezumae*) here, but a borer beetle wiped them out." He also showed me a lush Guatemalan fir forest on a steep slope north of the Llanos de San Miguel. The firs were slender, but he said he'd seen huge ones in other stands. Alders, strawberry trees, and tall currant bushes grew under them.

Cuchumatanes animals were as North American as the plants. A large bumblebee buzzed over a patch of red *Amanita* mushrooms in the fir forest, where a minute of turning over mossy logs located a diminutive brown salamander. A brown *Sceloporus* lizard that shot out from under a *zacatal* rock might have been in California, although its iridescent blue-green mate looked more exotic. Some were species common to the U.S., like the flying squirrels Guzmán had seen in the fir forest. Flocks of eastern meadowlarks rocketed out of the *zacatal*, Steller's jays squawked in the pines, and a rufous-sided towhee skulked above the cirque.

Most of the birds I saw at Chirripó, on the other hand, were species endemic to the southern Central American highlands—slaty flower-piercers, flame-throated warblers, and long-tailed silky flycatchers foraging at treeline; sooty robins and volcano juncos picking crumbs from the park shelters in the glaciated zone. Silvery-throated jays haunted the cloud forest understory, making oddly sotto voce calls, like Steller's jays heard from far away. Chirripó's plants also had a southern orientation. Yellow composites and red paintbrush flowered in the valleys, but its vegetation otherwise looked quite different from the Cuchumatanes'. Above about 3,000 meters, it consisted of a grassy scrub of dwarf bamboo and other shrubs; this scrub is called *paramo* because of its similarity to northern Andean vegetation, with which it shares many species.

The most striking difference between the two landscapes was that the Costa Rican peaks were unforested except for a few strawberry trees in protected ravines. I knew fire was a cause of this, as black snags along the *paramo*'s lower edge showed. Ecologist Sally P. Horn has sampled Chirripó lake sediments and found charcoal and pollen suggesting that repeated fires have prevented forest from invading the peaks since

the last glacier melted. Yet it still seemed strange that such a wet, relatively mild climate did not produce denser vegetation, particularly in
light of the lush forest I'd passed through on the hike up. Cuchumatanes
pines and junipers thrive at the same elevation as the Chirripó *paramo*,
and this made me wonder if the northern conifers somehow are more
fitted than southern trees to the lightning fires and other stresses of
alpine life. Three years after its most recent fire, few of the dead trees
in Chirripó's recently burned areas were sprouting from the base or
otherwise regenerating. It reminded me of the Peruvian peaks around
Machu Picchu, where trees were almost as sparse at a similar elevation.
I didn't know what the forest fire situation was in the Cuchumatanes—
I didn't see evidence of recent fire there—but Cuchumatanes conifers
have to contend with livestock and logging as well as the probability
of fires set by lightning or humans, while uninhabited Chirripó has not
even been grazed since the park was established in 1975.

Yet the more I looked, the more similarities I found between the
Guatemalan and Costa Rican peaks. Chirripó didn't lack North American plants, not only the oaks and magnolias of the cloud forest but the
manzanita, ceanothus, barberry, heather, and blueberry I saw in the
paramo zone. The commonest Cuchumatanes birds, rufous-necked robins, and yellow-eyed juncos were very like Chirripó's sooty robins and
volcano juncos. Tan and green *Sceloporus* lizards hid under both Cuchumatanes limestone and Chirripó granite. In fact, the animals that live
in Central American *paramo* today are different enough from South
American alpine fauna to suggest that there was never a "*paramo* corridor" between the Andes and Talamancas. Andean plant pollinators, for
example, are very diverse and specialized, while more common and
widespread insects such as bumblebees pollinate Talamancan plants.
Andean mammals like vizcachas and spectacled bears don't occur in
the Talamancas, while North American coyotes and rabbits do. I saw
a cottontail at Chirripó, although the vizcachas I'd seen in Peru, rodents
vaguely similar to rabbits, with squirrel-like tails and hind legs like
kangaroos', would have seemed less exotic among the dwarf bamboos
and *pinuelas*.

Chirripó's strikingly Andean vegetation may have arrived by air.
Spores and small seeds can travel far on the wind, and songbirds and
shorebirds can transport larger ones in their guts or on their feet.

Darwin showed that even hawks can carry seeds when he fed oats to sparrows, fed the sparrows to hawks, then germinated the oats from the hawks' castings (regurgitated undigestible pellets). I didn't see any shorebirds or hawks at Chirripó, and not much that seemed likely to attract them. Its lakes are low in nutrients and so deficient in aquatic life that I saw not even a dragonfly, only tiny mites and bugs. Still, food scarcity wouldn't necessarily prevent the odd Swainson's hawk or spotted sandpiper from stopping to rest during its intercontinental migration.

Of course, wind and birds would have carried Mexican plants to Chirripó as well as Andean ones. North American organisms have prevailed in the land bridge highlands, following a largely unbroken series of plateaus and sierras south from Mexico. Yet they've prevailed in a puzzlingly incomplete way. If northern conifers are as fitted to alpine conditions as the contrast between the wooded Cuchumatanes and treeless Chirripó suggests, why haven't pines, junipers, cedars, and firs spread south of Nicaragua? The Nicaraguan Depression is obviously a barrier to cool climate genera, yet northern broadleaf trees have passed it—alders were among the most common trees I saw in the Peruvian Andes. Even *lowland* conifers like Caribbean pines haven't spread south of Nicaragua naturally. Concepts like fitness can be hard to apply to the Central American highlands.

Impressive as the temperate zones' invasion of Central America was, it is largely a thing of the past (or will be until glaciation returns). Its most striking manifestation, the migration of cool-climate megafauna between the continents, has stopped, and its surviving plants and animals tend to be isolated highland relics. For the present, its effects are overshadowed by the major evolutionary spectacle of the land bridge today: a postglacial flood of South American tropical forest that has surged through the lowlands as far as Central Mexico. Fitness seems to apply handily to a forest that has occupied nearly all Central America's Caribbean slope, and invaded other areas as well, since the land bridge opened.

13

The Emerald Tide

N EAR THE END of my 1987 gaudy bird–watching trip to Costa Rica, I took a boat to Tortuguero through the inland waterways of the northeast coast. This is as close as anything on the land bridge to an Amazon River trip, and as frustrating for anybody who thinks it will provide a close look at jungle creatures. Like the Amazon's, Tortuguero's riverbanks presented an intricately woven curtain of leaves in which the gaudiest birds were about as conspicuous as the flecks of scarlet and purple in Harris tweed. Once in a while, the boat would pass groups of water birds on mudflats or snags outside the leaf curtain—herons, egrets, anhingas. These were interesting, but familiar, and hardly gaudy. One such group did contain a bird I hadn't seen before, a long-necked, long-legged, egret-sized creature with a brown body and a black-and-white-striped head. I regarded it as I'd regarded the agouti at Tikal in 1971—it was strange, but too unfamiliar to be impressively exotic.

As the bird passed into my peripheral vision, however, something impressively exotic happened. Where it had been, two red, yellow, and black sunbursts flashed. I realized I had just seen one of the gaudiest things I remembered from *Life* magazine's *The World Around Us*, the book that formed my early notions of neotropical rain forest. The bird was a sunbittern, a species that lives only along neotropical rivers, and whose only relatives live in South America and the southern Pacific. Sunbitterns are survivors of an ancient bird group which existed before Gondwana drifted completely apart. Little is known about them, but the sunburst effect I saw, which they make as they suddenly spread their wings to reveal bright-colored feathers on the backs, is thought to be an aggressive display.

The sunbittern seemed emblematic of the time I'd spent in the Tortuguero rain forest—a nondescript bird suddenly, like a butterfly, flashing the sun from its wings. There was a kind of unfathomable deviousness to the forest, a capacity for endless surprise hidden in a veil of leaves so similar in shape and size, and a maze of tree trunks so relentlessly *not* the same in shape, color, and texture, as to defeat comprehension. On a trail outside the town of Tortuguero, I thought I heard someone loudly breaking sticks, then saw what appeared to be giant popcorn kernels flying about the forest floor. It turned out to be a pair of tiny birds, white-collared manakins, hopping and snapping their wings in the underbrush. They were simply males trying to attract females, but their activities seemed more biotic prank than reproductive behavior.

Thomas Belt spent most of his four and a half years in Nicaragua in what he called "the great Atlantic forest ... the dark, nearly black-looking forest," and never lost this sense of the unfathomably devious. Regarding it from the savannas to the west, he confessed a confusion and pessimism unusual for the confident nineteenth century. "Though I have dived into the recesses of these mountains again and again, and knew that they were covered with beautiful vegetation and full of animal life, yet the sight of that leaden-colored barrier of cloud resting on the forest tops, whilst the savannas were bathed in sunshine, ever raised in my mind vague sensations of the unknown and unfathomable. . . . Man's intellect strives to grapple with the great mysteries of his existence, and like a fluttering bird that beats itself against the bars of its cage, falls back baffled and bruised."

Belt sent the Atlantic forest birds he collected to English ornithologist Osbert Salvin, who found that species with Costa Rican, and ultimately South American, affinities predominated over those with Mexican or North American ones. H. E. Bates drew similar conclusions about Belt's insect collections, and Belt concluded that this South American affinity prevailed in the Caribbean lowland forest at least to northern Honduras. Given the low regard for the south expressed in his political commentaries, perhaps some of the disquiet he felt about the "Atlantic forest" arose from this predominantly southern nature. His description of the birds' and insects' South American affinities comes in the same chapter of *A Naturalist in Nicaragua* as his commentary on the United States' manifest destiny to colonize Latin America. It was as though Belt perceived in "that leaden-colored barrier of cloud resting on the forest tops" a tide that ran against "a healthful and continuous intercourse with the enterprising north." Although he recognized the Caribbean forest's antiquity, Belt didn't speculate about its prehistoric past as he did with more "northern" things like glaciation. Science knew virtually nothing about tropical forest evolution then, so he had little to speculate on, but it seems significant that such a perceptive observer should have lacked curiosity about the evolution of the most compelling, if least reassuring, natural phenomenon he encountered in Nicaragua.

We still don't know much about the evolution of Central America's rain forest. The elusive Gracias and Panama Canal plant fossils suggest that some tropical rain forest tree species lived there during the Miocene epoch, but this doesn't necessarily mean tropical rain forest as we know it today. Among the few other known rain forest fossils are plant materials from late Ice Age lake and bog cores. Analyzed by Paul Colinvaux and his coworkers at the Smithsonian Tropical Research Institute, 10,000-year-old pollen from Central Panamanian lake sediments suggest a different forest than today's.

The pollen, from sites at La Yeguada and El Valle, belongs both to lowland tropical forest plants like those in the area now, and to temperate climate plants such as oaks which presently grow at higher elevations. It's not clear if the highland plants actually lived in the lowlands with the tropical ones, or if their pollen merely blew in from the mountains. Other plant fossils found in the lakes called phytoliths suggest the former, however. Phytoliths are cellular silica structures which can indicate the genus of a plant after it decays. They are less likely than pollen to be carried long distances on the wind, so oak and magnolia phytoliths from the Panamanian lakes suggest the trees grew nearby. Yet phytoliths can be water-transported, so it's also possible that streams carried them into the lakes from higher elevations. Rainforest plant fossils from other Central American sites are similarly ambiguous. Fossil leaves found in the late Pliocene El Sisimico lake deposits of El Salvador also represent temperate trees like oaks as well as tropical ones like ceibas. They also could show either that the oaks and ceibas were living together, or at separate elevations.

Today's lowland Central American rain forest has little of this apparent temperate admixture. Belt's conclusion was right. Botanists such as Ghillean Prance have shown that Caribbean slope rain forest from southern Mexico to Panama is largely identical to Amazonian in its dominant trees. The same genera—*Brosimum, Vochysia, Anacardium, Dipteryx, Swietenia, Tabebuia, Caryocar*—and often the same species form the forest canopy in Central American lowland rain forest as in Brazilian. Central American canopy vines and lianas are Amazonian as well. The Caribbean rain forest's understory shrubs, palms, and small trees largely belong to different genera than Amazonian ones, but they are very similar to the understory plants of South America's Andean slope rain forests. Central and South American rain forests also share the world's greatest diversity of arboreal mammals; not only monkeys, but porcupines, anteaters, opossums, sloths, and kinkajous—all but kinkajous originally South American—and of forest birds, including the originally South American manakins, parrots, potoos, toucans, antbirds, puffbirds, woodcreepers, hummingbirds, and cotingas. It is only among "lower" vertebrates that the similarity between Central and South American rain forest fauna decreases. Green iguanas live in Central and South American rain forests, but in most of the South American, teiid lizards such as tegus replace "iguanids" such as basilisks and ctenosaurs.

The strong similarities of living Central American rain forest organisms to South American ones suggest that today's rain forest has spread north relatively recently, and evolutionists tend to agree that it probably did not cover the Caribbean lowlands until after the last ice age ended. Then what did cover the lowlands during the three million years since the land bridge's formation? During glaciated periods it evidently was a mixture of tropical and temperate species and/or a drier vegetation of savanna and thorn scrub. Yet during warmer and wetter interglacial periods, an absence of rain forest from an isthmus that probably wasn't very different from today's seems unlikely. A possibility that occurs to me is that South American rain forest may have flowed north a number of times since the land bridge opened, receding during glaciations. If it first flowed north when the land bridge formed, that might help explain why it seemed to take so long for temperate zone animals to start crossing between continents.

Given this possibility, rain forest organism distribution on the land bridge might be compared to that of marine organisms on a rocky tidal flat. When the "tide" was in, Amazonian rain forest would inundate most of Central America's Caribbean slope, as it does now. When it was out, rain forest fragments might survive in tidepool-like refugia, while some adaptable rain forest organisms might survive in other habitats, but most of each successive tide would be obliterated by the glacial cooling and drying that followed it, and then swamped by the next tide that swept north during the succeeding interglacial. There might be relics of past tides, however—endemic species that evolved in rain forest refugia, then survived the arrival of more widespread, related species when rain forest became continuous again. In the 1980s, biologist Robert Horwich discovered that howler monkeys in the lowland forests of Belize and the Petén are genetically different enough from the rest of Central America's golden-mantled howlers (*Alouatta palliata*) to be classed as a separate species. They're now called black howlers (*Alouatta pigra*). Since Belize and the Petén may have contained a rain forest refugium during the last or earlier glaciations, perhaps black howlers evolved then.

The tidal metaphor doubtless oversimplifies the rain forest's past. Comprehending its present is hard enough. Sometimes I think human language, or simply human mentality, hasn't evolved yet to the point where tropical rain forest *is* comprehensible or describable. There's simply too much going on for grammar to handle. I'll start to describe something and find my attention diverted by something else which probably has some connection to the original subject, but none that I can comprehend. Central American rain forests' very complexity can make them seem "one monotonous whole," as Belt wrote. I saw continual changes during visits from Darién to Chiapas, but they often weren't easy to perceive, much less understand. Yet there is one clear pattern. Although South American affinities are marked in rain forests throughout, to move northward from Darién is to move from a rain forest that essentially *is* South American to forests where South American elements progressively dwindle.

The Darién Forest

The tidal simile seems very apt to Darién. A sense of depth in the forest there was greater than I experienced elsewhere in Central America, as though I were in a bay of the rain forest ocean to the south. As I flew into El Real on my 1993 visit, huge pale-barked trees exploded above the multicolored canopy, their branches bare except for the cottony white flowers of the dry season. They were the "emergents" that characterize classic five-tiered neotropical rain forest. The most famous is ceiba (*Ceiba pentandra*) which reaches a height of fifty meters and circumference of over seven meters. In Darién two equally huge members of the same family, the Bombacaceae, also occur as emergents—barrigon (which means "bigbelly" in Spanish and refers to the species' flask-shaped trunk) and cuipo. Both species and ceiba live throughout South American rain forest, but barrigon ranges north only to Nicaragua, and cuipo to central Panama.

On a Cerro Pirre trail one late afternoon, I heard peevish squeaks in the understory. When I squeaked back, a troop of tiny Queen Victoria impersonators crept down the trunks to regard me haughtily. They were tamarins, typical small monkeys of South American forest which, like cuipo trees, extend north only to Panama. I'd seen similar creatures on the Peruvian Amazon, but the white, V-shaped crests above the plump, jowly faces of the Panamanian species (*Sanguinus oedipus geoffreyi*) made them look uncannily like lace-capped dowager empresses stuffed into monkey suits, or squirrel suits. Tamarins scamper through the branches on all fours, have nonprehensile tails, and are about the same size as small squirrels, although they have clever monkey hands and eat mainly insects, tree sap, and fruit. They scolded me a while—not at all amused—then departed with the jerky speed of an ancient silent film.

Other understory creatures enhanced an impression of palatial Victorian obscurity. Fireflies lit pale lamps before the sunlight had left the treetops, and chestnut-backed antbirds whistled like chamberlains announcing my intrusive presence as I passed. Tinamous, rotund and small-headed South American birds, skulked silently except at dawn and dusk, when their melodious, mournful calls evoked the weeds and veils of widowed aunts. Like governesses, blackish brown wood quails shepherded files of chicks so tiny and dark they were quite invisible unless they moved. Everything seemed blackish brown—leaf litter, bark, frogs, lizards—except the purple-throated fruitcrows (not real crows, but a kind of cotinga) that peered and shuffled like chaplains in the subcanopy trees. Even the ecclesiastical color at the birds' throats was barely visible against their rusty black plumage.

Only in the canopy were there rumors of riot. Deep, echoing squawks would approach, and a flight of great green or red-and-green macaws would flash past a gap in the leaves. Once there was an unseemly crash in a cecropia tree, and an immature king vulture was revealed, perched on the top like a burglar up a drainpipe. Troops of spider monkeys swarmed through the trees, the coal black Colombian species, *Ateles beelzebuth*, instead of the red Central American *A. geoffreyi*. At night I heard rakish whistles, perhaps night monkeys—little, owl-eyed creatures that inhabit rain forests as far north as western Panama, the world's only nocturnal monkeys.

I'd hoped to see capybaras in Darién, the only part of Central America where South America's giant aquatic rodents live today. Reaching five feet in length and weights of over one hundred pounds, the species is like a combination of beaver and hippopotamus, and lives in small herds beside rivers, grazing on riparian plants and fleeing from predators in the water. Fossils like those at Estanzuela show it once occurred much farther north, and its subsequent disappearance from the rest of Central America is mysterious, since it still inhabits South American waterways south to Argentina. Its absence might seem evidence of rain forest's disappearance from Central America during the last glaciation, except that the Estanzuela fossils show that capybaras *lived* in Guatemala then.

The Cerro Pirre streams were too small and rocky for capybaras, unfortunately, but I did see plenty of South American fish. Suckermouth catfish perched like giant tadpoles on rocks, and there were many characids, the South American group that includes piranhas. Silvery little tetras were trying to evolve into piranhas, nipping my skin so energetically that bathing was uncomfortable. Even the cichlids were South American. Blue-spangled acaras (*Aequidens*) guarded schools of fry in riffles, a genus that lives throughout tropical South America, and may be very close to ancestral Gondwanan cichlilds, since it is almost identical to an African cichlid genus. Tan-colored eartheaters (*Geophagus*) hovered over the sand in quiet pools, sorting through the substrate with underslung mouths. Eartheaters are also mouthbreeders, which means that instead of depositing their eggs on rocks or leaves as do most cichlids, one of the parents shelters them in its mouth until they hatch, and sometimes afterward. Mouthbreeding occurs in African as well as South American cichlids, but never has evolved in Central American ones, perhaps because fewer egg and fry predators inhabit its less diverse waters.

The Pacific Rain Forest

Darién's diversity and fecundity manifest an explosive quality of rain forest evolution, which seems to fly off in all directions, scattering organisms in patterns too complicated for comprehension. That evolution seems particularly explosive in western Panama and southern Costa Rica. Tall rain forest there doesn't hug the Caribbean as it does farther north, but spills over into the Pacific lowlands where the central cordilleras are high enough to stop the trade winds from causing too intense a dry season. These Pacific rain forests do have more of a dry season than the Caribbean ones, but it actually may enhance their size. "The abundant rainfall coupled with a short, three-month dry season seems ideal for tree growth," wrote botanist Gary Hartshorn about Costa Rica's Osa Peninsula, "for these forests are by far the most exuberant in Central America. In fact, the Corcovado forests are just as impressive in height as the best forests I have seen in the Amazon basin or the dipterocarp forests of Malaysia and Indonesia."

Corcovado National Park on the Osa has over 500 tree species, mostly South American rain forest genera, although other species more typical of the drier Pacific forests also occur. When I was there in 1987, it seemed a peculiarly vibrant place even by rainforest standards, with a brilliance of color that set it apart from the steamy Caribbean's green, as though Amazonian lushness had been imposed on a desert's hot reds and yellows. Scarlet macaws thronged red-leaved almendro trees on beaches, and reddish iguanas and basilisks reclined on tree limbs or crouched haughtily beside the trail. They were the biggest of their kind I'd seen, and they seemed impressed with their magnitude, too. The terrier-sized basilisks refused to get up on their hind legs and flee from

my approach, and the iguanas fled only from one another, diving spec-
tacularly into the creeks when challenged by bigger individuals. Even
the cichlids were unusually large and red.

Corcovado is not as diverse as Darién, or even as Costa Rica's Caribbean forest. Despite its apparent suitability, tamarins and night monkeys
don't live there, although another typical South American monkey
does—the slightly larger squirrel monkey. Its Central American presence is puzzling, however. In the Amazon, squirrel monkeys are so
common that they form troops of dozens or even hundreds. I saw tree-
fulls of them in Peru, like bushes swarming with anthropomorphic ants.
It was hard to make out the tiny individuals, but their high-pitched
chattering was unmistakable. One might expect such a common species
to be widespread in Central America too, yet they seem to occur only
in the Pacific forests of western Panama and southwest Costa Rica. Like
black howlers, they may be a relic of a previous rain forest tide, although
French biogeographer Robert Hoffstetter thought Indians brought them
from South America as pets.

I didn't see squirrel monkeys in Corcovado, but I did see them in
Manuel Antonio, about a hundred kilometers north, as little groups
searched cecropia trees for big, greenish-white grubs which they ate
like sausages. They are surprisingly colorful mammals, with bright orange fur on their backs, greenish sides, and black-and-white faces. They
ran through the trees like squirrels, making breathtaking leaps that
sometimes landed them almost on top of three-toed sloths, which resembled mops hung out to dry.

Surrounded by banana and oil palm plantations, Manuel Antonio's
rain forest remnant still seemed explosive when I was there in April,
the early rainy season. The canopy rang with birdcalls, and I saw three
flycatcher species nesting in a single small palm. Lizards were everywhere, grayish garobos, green ameivas, yellow-and-maroon basilisks,
striped brown skinks. Some that were bright green in the early morning
apparently turned yellow-brown in the afternoon, but perhaps they
were a different species. Towering, cascading thunderstorms struck
every afternoon, and in the twilight afterward basilisks stalked about
on their hind legs as though inspired to dinosaurian warmbloodedness,
and gray-necked wood rails shouted back and forth in *"cookit, cookit"*
duets.

After dark, an atrocious guttural roar filled the air, a sound unlike any I'd ever heard. I investigated with a flashlight and found a seasonal swamp packed with goggle-eyed, long-legged frogs, each as large as my hand. They evidently were tree-dwellers—they had long, suction-tipped fingers, and were colored like camouflaged airplanes, gray mottled with olive. I have no idea of their species. Central America has hundreds of frog species, and, like Oviedo when faced with lizards, I throw up my hands. The frogs made the roar by inflating and vibrating two sacs on the sides of their heads, and it increased as more kept arriving, speeding toward their communal bath with great leaps. Somehow, I could discern another sound under the roar, a soft moaning that added a plaintiveness to the brusque pandemonium. Little warty toads crouched here and there, and may have been doing the moaning, although I wasn't sure. My ears pulsed and rang. I took a step and almost fell into a hole, at the bottom of which a small turtle blinked, like a chthonic spirit emerging from the underworld. I guessed that the turtle had stumbled into the hole, too, and lifted it out. It trundled purposefully toward the swamp, and perhaps a feast of frog eggs.

The frogs had disappeared next morning when I walked past the swamp. Even the carcasses of those that had been run over on the road were gone, leaving not a smear of blood. While I breakfasted at a nearby restaurant, however, a live one crouched in a heliconia hedge beside my table. I lifted the leaf above it and found a little bat asleep, clinging to the midrib. It was half the frog's size, and the tiny snout poking out of its folded wings seemed more on an insect's scale than a mammal's.

Rain Forest Pioneers

Manuel Antonio is near the northern extremity of the Pacific rain forest, yet many Amazonian organisms have spread not only to the Pacific coast, but to just about every kind of forest in Central America below two thousand meters, and sometimes above that. These include the animals commonly seen on rain forest resort verandas—keel-billed toucans, scarlet macaws—as well as lesser-known creatures like anteaters, agoutis, pacas, and tropical porcupines. The remnant dry deciduous forests actually are better for seeing them than rain forest, because the trees are smaller and the animals concentrate around water in the leafless dry season.

Organisms continually migrate between rain forest and other habi-

tats. Many insects, birds, and bats fly between wet and dry forests following the complex tropical patterns of plant flowering and fruiting.
Daniel Janzen has observed that more than a hundred moth and butterfly species arrive to breed in northwest Costa Rican deciduous forests
when the yearly rains begin, after they have spent the dry season in
the wet forests to the east. Many of their predators and parasites migrate
with them. Big, wide-ranging animals such as tapirs, jaguars, and white-
lipped peccaries may include both dry and wet forest in their territories,
and many animals also migrate between highland and lowland forests
following reproductive or feeding cycles. One of the reasons birds like
the quetzal are disappearing is that they need to disperse from high
ridges to increasingly deforested foothills for part of the year.

Among the most conspicuously successful mammals in most kinds
of reasonably tropical forest are Central America's common monkey
species—white-faced capuchins, golden-mantled howlers, and red spiders. They belong to the commonest South American genera, and aren't
much different than their southern cousins, but have adapted to most
lowland Central American habitats, and some highland ones. The first
howlers I saw were in Costa Rican farmland where almost the only
large trees were nonnative mangoes along a stream. The first capuchins
were in cloud forest along a misty, windswept ridgetop in the Cordillera
de Tilaran at about 1,500 meters. Central American capuchins have
black-and-white fur and pink, grannylike faces, and it was bizarre to
see them matter-of-factly yanking apart huge epiphytes in the gloomy
highland forest. When I was on Volcán Cacao at a similar elevation, all
three species seemed comfortable in a climate wherein I was glad to
have a down sleeping bag. Monkeys occur in northern Central American
pine forests, as long as there are tropical hardwoods nearby, and I saw
capuchins and howlers ensconced in mangroves at Cuero y Salado Wildlife Refuge in Honduras.

I find Central American monkeys mysterious because their anthropoid nature is uncannily readable, although they stem from thirty million years of evolution quite separate from our Old World primate
ancestors. One can sit near a waterhole in leafless dry forest, with capuchins, howlers, and spiders only a few meters up in jobo trees, and
watch the same expressions of boredom, peevishness, or curiosity
cross their faces as in any group of humans on a city street. It's as

though there is a fundamental primate nature to which thirty million years of isolation is irrelevant. Some diseases and parasites don't discriminate between New World monkeys and humans. Night monkeys can get human malaria, and howlers and spiders disappeared from much of Belize in the 1960s because of yellow fever epidemics.

I experienced a man–monkey parasite link in Belize. On the plane returning from a trip in 1994, I felt a burning pain on my left shoulder blade, and in the next week two pimple-like swellings developed there, like smaller versions of swellings I'd seen on black howlers. The burning got worse if I ingested caffeine or alcohol, suggesting I had guests who objected to toxins in my bloodstream. I'd fallen victim to *Dermatobia hominis,* a botfly, which looks like a housefly but has a typically devious rain forest life history. *D. hominis* females lurk beside waters where mosquitoes are emerging from pupae. They catch female ones and attach their eggs to them, then when the mosquitoes bite monkeys or people, the eggs get on the prospective hosts. The larvae hatch, burrow in, and live on the host's body tissues until they pupate. They're easy to kill by covering their breathing holes with Vaseline, but then must be squeezed out. It took me two weeks to eject two white, black-bristled, vaguely spark plug–shaped grubs from my shoulder blade.

The three common Central American monkeys even seem to embody different anthropoid tendencies. Spider monkeys have an elfin aspect, and seem remote and solitary as they brachiate through the canopy, like orangutans. Howler monkeys are gorillalike with their calm eyes, sedentary vegetarian habits, and tendency to glumness. Capuchins seem disturbingly like chimpanzees with their manipulative cleverness (they have opposable thumbs and use rocks to break nuts), highly motivated group dynamics, and tendencies toward fierce, devious aggression. Capuchin intelligence impresses everyone. Francisco Ximénez wrote that they "tame easily and learn many things," and Marston Bates thought them as smart as chimpanzees. Thomas Belt had a pet capuchin called Mickey who couldn't be tied because he would pull apart chain links and "loosen any knot in a few minutes." Mickey used bread to lure baby ducks into his clutches, and pulled objects toward him with sticks. "When any one came near to fondle him, he never neglected the opportunity of pocket picking," Belt wrote, with amused disapproval.

I discovered capuchin tendencies the hard way. I was watching all three species at a Santa Rosa water hole, and had become engrossed in a baby spider monkey that was being teased by a juvenile. The baby screeched, its mother rushed to its rescue, and at the climax of this fracas, a black, strange-smelling fluid splattered my notebook and hat. It was the dung of a capuchin who had sneaked up on me so subtly that I never saw it, only heard it fleeing, although I knew it was a capuchin from the rapt looks of others who'd gathered to watch. Whenever I encountered the local troop after that, two individuals would threaten me. One would climb on the other's back, and both would grimace hideously, a piggyback gargoyle of ill will.

Volcán Cacao's smaller capuchin troops didn't bother with gargoyle displays, but leaders never failed to stamp threateningly if I presumed to look at them. Howlers and spiders there were less touchy. Howlers didn't make direct threats, although males might stamp and roar in an absentminded way. Spider monkey threats were usually made from very safe distances, and consisted of shrieking and flinging about that was remarkably unintimidating. One juvenile so bored other troop members with its tantrums directed at me—across a deep ravine—that they tried to calm it with hugs, then abandoned it, whereupon it forgot me and rushed anxiously after them. Monkeys also are like humans in their unpredictability, however. When biologist Alvaro Wille was at Corcovado, howlers threw dung at him, spiders were friendly, and capuchins ignored him.

Less conspicuous than monkeys, but even more successful in pervading Central American forests, are South American rodents, particularly the ubiquitous agouti which troubled my tropical daydreams in Tikal. With glossy chestnut fur and big, liquid eyes, agoutis seem like midget deer as they lope through the woods, but they dispel the impression by sitting on their haunches to eat nuts with their forepaws. They survive in many places from which monkeys have been extirpated—I saw one foraging on the lawn below the Canal Administration Building in Panama City—as do the larger, spotted pacas, their close relatives. The nocturnal pacas are as difficult to see as agoutis are easy, but also may persist in peopled areas even though hunters kill many for their prized meat.

Biologist Winnie Hallwachs's studies of agoutis in Costa Rican dry forest have shown their vital role in dispersing tree seeds. Agoutis relish the fruit and seeds of guapinol, and carry fruits as far as several hundred yards from parent trees to bury and hoard them. This saves the seeds from being destroyed by collared peccaries, spiny pocket mice, and insects, which can congregate under the parent trees and consume most of them. Agoutis are less efficient about eating the seeds than the other creatures, so many of the seeds they hoard germinate and a few grow to be mature trees. If agoutis have assumed an important role in spreading Central American dry forest seeds in the past three million years, their dispersal role in South American rain forest must be greater, since they and their ancestors have been evolving in it for thirty million years. Agoutis carrying and hoarding seeds of South American trees must have been a factor in spreading the forest north through Central America. In fact, rain forest has spread just about as far north as agoutis.

Of course, the diverse rain forest flora has many more ways of spreading its seeds than agoutis. Many other rodents disperse seeds, and rodents are less important dispersers in tropical forests than temperate ones because most tropical vertebrates eat fruit, not only ungulates, monkeys, and birds, but bats, lizards, and even carnivores. According to Daniel Janzen and D. E. Wilson, the only carnivores in Costa Rica that *don't* eat fruit are otters and pumas. Since carnivore stomachs aren't adapted to digest seeds, they defecate more viable ones than do herbivores such as peccaries. Bat digestion is similar, and thick deposits of various tree and shrub seeds cover the forest floor under Central American fruit-eating bat roosts. Bats are by far the most abundant and diverse neotropical mammals, with over a hundred species in Honduras alone, so their seed dispersal importance is incalculable.

The San Juan Basin Forest

The Caribbean rain forest from Costa Rica to Nicaragua, the forest that perplexed Thomas Belt in the late 1860s, is another regional unity. It lacks the South American specialties of the Panamanian or Pacific rain forests—tamarins, squirrel monkeys—and has a kind of dark-green consistency. Golden mantled howlers, white-faced capuchins, and red spider monkeys live throughout it, as do tree sloths, giant anteaters, great potoos, sunbitterns, and other South American immigrants. It is the heart of Central American rain forest.

La Selva Biological Station in northeast Costa Rica is a "slice of life" of this rain forest. The station has protected 1,500 hectares since the 1950s, so wildlife is confiding and the forest is accessible over a fifty-kilometer trail system. Even more important, La Selva is connected to Braulio Carrillo National Park, a roughly 50,000-hectare primary forest that extends to the top of the volcanic cordillera, so migratory species and large animals can still move in and out. A walk in La Selva is a kind of Caribbean rain forest hologram—one encounters a diversity of animals that might be shyer and more dispersed in a larger natural area, and therefore harder to see, or extirpated from a smaller one.

As I set out one morning in 1990, a tamandua or lesser anteater was crossing a suspension bridge across the Puerto Viejo River on the hand-rail. Reaching the foliage on the far side, it grasped a branch with its hooklike front claws, walked down it to the tree trunk, and descended like a pigeon-toed telephone lineman. The bridge was always a good place to spot arboreal mammals. I stopped in the middle and looked down into the water, seeking an unfortunate side effect of mammal-spotting the previous night. I'd come to La Selva with herpetologist Harry Greene, who was conducting a long-term study of predatory vertebrates there. The station has one of the greatest recorded predator diversities in the world, including at least fifty-six species of snakes, Greene's specialty, and he'd seen forty-six to forty-eight of those at the time. I've never seen as many snakes as I did with Harry Greene. They seemed to materialize around him, even to multiply, as when we went looking for a female fer-de-lance he'd fitted with a radio transmitter, and found the eight-foot snake curled up with a smaller male. A genial personality, Greene also attracted other herpetologists, including a young German who was visiting Central America before going to study Asian cobras. The German was wise to ease into cobra study via the more sluggish Central American vipers, but I wondered how wise he was to study venomous snakes at all. He was large, and, judging from a trail walk with him, not too nimble.

The night before, I'd been on the bridge while Greene described how a pair of male three-toed sloths had fought for possession of a cecropia tree, a rare show of sloth territoriality. Then a kinkajou had climbed into the same cecropia, its eyes glowing pink. Although related to raccoons, kinkajous have prehensile tails and other primatelike features. They may be relics of the North American tropics' mysterious arboreal fauna, and their similarity to primitive primates like lemurs and lorises makes it seem as though humanity's remote ancestors are evolving a second time. I hadn't seen a kinkajou in the wild, and wanted a good look. Since Greene was spotlighting it, I put down the other expensive flashlight he'd lent me so I could look with my binoculars. It was then that the German came striding across the bridge and kicked the flashlight into the river. We'd seen it down there, still shining.

As I looked down the next morning, the underwater flashlight probably was still shining, but the sunlight was already too bright for me to see it. I put off trying to recover it until the evening (though I never did recover it) and continued across the bridge. White-fronted and yellow-fronted parrots squawked in palms, collared aracaris, small toucans, ate fruit from a red-flowered *Hamelia* tree, and two agoutis foraged on opposite sides of a clearing. I saw a swift movement as a beagle-sized black animal with a cream-colored chest and bushy tail raised its head to look at me. It was a tayra, a large weasel-family species which lives throughout the neotropics. As I followed the trail in its direction, it drifted out of sight behind some banana plants, but soon reappeared with a yellow fruit in its mouth, demonstrating Janzen's point about fruit-eating carnivores. Then it ran into the forest, and another tayra emerged from the banana plants and ran after it.

I followed the trail into a swamp where huge powder blue damselflies (*Megalopteris*, the world's biggest) flew around the cream-and-tan mottled trunks of sura trees (*Terminalia oblonga*) so big that the spaces between their root buttresses were like rooms. Howler monkeys called, not full-pitched, lionlike roars, but half-hearted coughs that meant they were only mildly upset about something. Suddenly, thumps and crashes came from the underbrush, heading straight for me, then the commotion veered aside and one of the tayras shot past. Whatever it was doing, stealth was not required. The trail ran up a creek where buff-rumped warblers caroled and flicked their tails, and I glimpsed the howler troop, so high in the huge suras that there was none of the sense of anthropoid identification I'd felt in dry forest. They seemed far away up their other branch of primate history. When a breeze shook the treetops, winged objects spun down, sura seeds, among the few wind-dispersed rain forest seeds. More typical were round objects beside the trail, fruits of the monkey pot tree (*Lecythis ampla*). These contain seeds attached by white, fatty bodies, or arils, which bats relish. The bats light on the hanging pots, break off the seeds, and fly to their roosts, where they eat the arils and drop the seeds to soil fertilized with their feces.

The trail rose toward the slopes of Braulio Carrillo, where Harry Greene had been on a 1980s collecting expedition that had found twenty-eight new plant species in a week. I didn't need to go on an expedition to find something unknown, however. Right beside the trail were several of the largest mushrooms I'd ever seen, large enough to sit on, like kitschy lawn furniture. They were growing on a bare mound that had been a leafcutter ant nest, and when I later asked a mycologist why, she said the mushrooms might be parasitic on the leafcutter ants' fungus, but were so rare they hadn't been studied.

I spent the rest of the morning walking to the station's south border, seeing no animals larger than tinamous, which were unusually lively, perhaps because it was nesting season. Related to ostriches and rheas, tinamous don't usually fly when approached, just skulk off into the underbrush, yet the first one I saw scurried before me trailing a wing, then flew off with a grouselike whir. Butterflies, mostly blue morphos and orange heliconians, hovered everywhere that sunlight penetrated the canopy. A large gray one had bright red marks on its underwings, a device for provoking predators to strike at the least vulnerable part, and indeed something had bitten one mark. In the canopy, a white-fronted nunbird shook a plain yellow one into shreds in its beak and swallowed it.

I passed the noon heat beside one of the clear streams that meandered between the foothills. It was as shady and cool as a West Virginia hollow, although instead of sycamores the water reflected lacy-foliaged gavilans (*Pentaclethra macroloba*), which, like guapinols, are South American trees with African counterparts. As I sat on a log bridge, a sample of riparian life passed by. A sparrow-sized pygmy kingfisher dive-bombed the stream, its green and tan plumage camouflaging it so perfectly that I could only see it in motion. A brownish anole materialized on a stick protruding from the water, flourished its bright yellow dewlap, then surprised me by pattering away across the surface on its hind legs. I'd thought only basilisks ran on water. A moss-backed black river turtle didn't notice me as it walked sedately under the bridge, but an otter that swam under a moment later caught my scent and panicked, diving and fleeing back upstream, where it craned its neck and barked at me. It shot downstream again, underwater this time, surfaced well below the bridge, and continued on its way like a pedestrian distancing himself from a potential mugger.

I might have seen any of these animals or plants in Darién, but the fish in the small stream were distinctive. If I'd been helicoptered to La Selva blindfolded with only Bussing's *Pesces de las Aguas Continentales de Costa Rica*, I'd have been able to tell pretty much where I was. There were silvery, aggressive tetras, as in Panama, but suckermouth catfish were absent, as were acara and eartheater cichlids. The cichlids were exclusively Central American: big, basslike guapotes (*Nandopsis dovii*) which cruised obliviously past cookie crumbs that had driven the tetras into a feeding frenzy, and sunfishlike mojaras (*Archocentrus septemfasciatum*) that squabbled for the crumbs.

That night I walked part of the same trail with Harry Greene. (The German had left. "He did some really nice stuff on Asian cobras," Greene told me in 1996.) We encountered two snakes before we even reached the trailhead: a little white-headed one (*Enulius sclateri*) and a little pepper-and-salt one (*Sibon nubulata*) that Greene said ate mainly slugs. It had rained, and the forest was very dark and still except for water dripping from the branches. Something called "*bu-bu-bu-bu*" and something else made a growling sound, possibly a potoo, Greene thought. Potoos are tropical relatives of whippoorwills which, instead of whistling, are said to have the strangest call in the forest. Archie Carr described a call that probably came from a potoo as "the most stirring animal voice I had ever heard . . . combining a disturbingly human quality with the reedy suggestion of some little-used stop of a pipe organ." But this potoo, if it was one, only growled.

In the swamp of sura trees, a translucent, jade green frog with huge golden eyes sat on a leaf. I could see its bones in the flashlight beam, which its eyes followed as though in fascination at this unexpected sunrise. Greene said it was a young *Hyla rufitila*, which would be three times larger when full grown. Nearby, he pointed to a slender, pop-eyed snake crawling along a limb called a cat-eyed snake (*Leptodeira septentrionalis*). Cat-eyed snakes are venomous, but never bite humans. They hunt masses of eggs laid on leaves by frogs; they hang from limbs and weave their heads in the darkness to sense the eggs with their chins or tongues.

I shined my flashlight into a hollow trunk and caught the pale orange eyeshine of a large rat with a white belly and a furry tail. It might have been a wood rat or other North American cricetid rodent, but Greene pointed to its back. Spines stuck up among the hairs. It was a spiny rat (*Proechimys semispinosus*), a South American rodent more closely related to porcupines or even agoutis than to wood rats. Like the giant mushrooms on the leafcutter ant nest, spiny rats are seldom seen, and less studied. As though secure in its obscurity, the rat just blinked at the flashlight a moment, then resumed gnawing a green-husked fruit.

The Petén Forest

In northeastern Nicaragua and Honduras, rain forest changes again. Sloths and strawberry frogs disappear, and forest itself is absent from vast areas of Caribbean pine savanna. Geographer Bernard Nietschmann has described the "almost surreal" experience of being in "an area that receives 100 to 150 inches of precipitation yearly" and emerging suddenly "onto a vast savanna that looked and felt like a huge golf course: rolling grass-covered terrain, stands of pine on ridges, and clumps of papta palms in the humid depressions." When I asked people on Nicaragua's Mosquito Coast why there was savanna instead of forest, they said it was because of fire. This certainly was true around the town of Puerto Cabezas, where the ground everywhere I walked was black. Yet fire alone seems insufficient to explain the huge uninhabited savannas. Lightning starts fires, but heavy rain usually accompanies it. The Mosquitia's sandy soils are infertile, but rain forest grows in many infertile places.

Whatever the reasons, Mosquitia rain forest occurs mainly along rivers and on inland mountains. When Archie Carr visited it in the 1950s, he found climax groves of almendro, cedro macho, and monkey pot that had "the primeval and somewhat Gothic look of true selva." "Game is more plentiful than we have seen it anywhere," he wrote. "The booming call of the curassow can be heard on every side, and each ravine or blowdown tangle has its flock of pavas." Civil wars have isolated this forest for most of the time since Carr's visit. (Outside Puerto Cabezas in 1993, I climbed on a bank after taking a swim in a forest-lined creek and found I was standing on a corroded but live pile of machine gun bullets.) It thus has remained little studied.

North of Honduras, in the lowlands of Belize, the Petén, and eastern Chiapas, the forest undergoes another shift, its greatest after Darién. Although South American plants still overwhelmingly predominate, it is not quite rain forest as farther south. Because of reduced rainfall and quickly draining limestone bedrock, the understory is sparser, and the canopy less festooned with epiphytes. The highly adaptable capuchin monkeys make a puzzling disappearance, as do rarer South American creatures such as giant anteaters and spiny rats. A number of endemic species appear, including the small, freshwater Morelet's crocodiles I saw at Crooked Tree Lagoon, and a primitive river turtle, the hickatee, as well as ocellated turkeys, and black howler monkeys. French explorer Arthur Morelet noted the Petén forest's distinctness in 1847, and was the first to describe the ocellated turkey and his namesake, Morelet's crocodile. He described the crocodile from a still-living individual "three yards in length" which some Lake Petén Itzá fishermen brought him for sale when he happened to be prostrate with malaria. Although he tried to kill it by feeding it a lot of "arsenical soap," it lived another twenty-four hours, breaking its tether and wandering under his hammock in the small hours like a fever dream.

The crocodile's name, Morelet wrote "was about the only reward that I received from carrying out an enterprise in which I largely exhausted my health, energy, and means." Less chauvinistic than Thomas Belt about Central American culture, Morelet sounded exactly like the English naturalist when he wrote about its forest: "Here, man is only an accident; the part he is required to play is so insignificant that he hardly seems requisite to the general harmony of the world. I was greatly impressed by this idea, in pursuing my way through these old forests, where we struggled like so many pygmies against constantly recurring obstacles."

Flying in to a place called Gallon Jug in northwest Belize was like approaching a northern version of Darién's Cerro Pirre. Both are protected, although Gallon Jug isn't a park but the property of Belizean entrepreneur-conservationist Barry Bowen. Both lie below stream-laced escarpments within the largest remaining forests at their respective ends of the land bridge. Gallon Jug is situated where the Petén karst plateau drops to the Belize River system, part of a forest that extends north almost unbroken to the Gulf of Mexico. From the air, its canopy was as dense and green as Cerro Pirre's, dotted with yellow tabebuias and orange *Vochysias,* although there were fewer of the soaring emergents that had impressed me in Darién. Parallels with Cerro Pirre even included a border kidnapping near both places, although the Gallon Jug kidnapping had happened months before my visit in March 1994. Timber poachers had grabbed a Belizean official who'd stumbled on their activities.

Wildlife Conservation Society biologist Bruce Miller took me up the escarpment to see huge mahogany logs the poachers had taken from the Maya Biosphere Reserve in the northern Petén. They were about two meters in diameter at the base. "You don't see mahoganies this big in Belize anymore," said Miller, who'd been surveying Belizean forests for various conservation projects. "They were all cut out during the British colonial days. The northern Petén is the last place north of Honduras that has mahoganies like this."

While we were looking at the logs, some Guatemalans appeared, a crew from CONAP, Guatemala's protected areas agency, who had been sent to deal with the logs. They said it had taken them days to get there from Flores on Lake Petén Itzá. All but one of their vehicles were broken, and they were stuck at an army post that Guatemala had established after the kidnapping. I didn't envy them. The few dozen kilometers of road from Gallon Jug to the border had been bad enough—much of it underwater even though this was the dry season. Miller said he'd raced formula cars once, and I could believe it from the way he drove. "The trick to these roads," he said, "is to *never* stop moving forward."

Miller and his wife Carolyn had been working with endangered species preservation in U.S. zoos, and had decided to do it *in situ* instead. They'd been in Belize since the mid-1980s, long enough to both have had malaria. They told me they'd gotten so tired of taking chloroquine, which made their ears ring, that the disease had seemed preferable, even though the cure is taking big doses of chloroquine. Things like malaria seemed anachronistic in the Miller's pleasant new house atop a limestone knoll. At the bottom of the knoll, however, by the driveway, was a stone tomb from when Gallon Jug had been a nineteenth-century logging station. The station had lain abandoned for decades before Barry Bowen recleared the site, and the tomb was empty, its limestone already too eroded to read the epitaph. It reminded me of the old graveyards in Belize City, also with empty tombs, their occupants swept away in the hurricanes that periodically level the town.

The Gallon Jug forest seemed more austere than Darién's, but more confiding. Vines and epiphytes were abundant, huge floppy monsteras and wild grapevines as thick as my leg, but the trees weren't completely covered as in Darién. Relatively clean-limbed Mexican cedars, chicles, and mahoganies seemed the most common trees rather than the extravagantly decorated almendros and espavels at Cerro Pirre. Date palm–like cohune palms (*Orbygnya*) covered moist level areas in relatively open groves. The forest floor was well shaded, but there was not Darién's dreamlike sense of being sequestered in a Victorian palace. Wildlife was boisterous compared to Cerro Pirre's, although macaws were absent. A black howler troop wheezed and mumbled all night outside my window, and in the morning, the "*Pia! Pia!*" squawks of brown jays drowned out even the parrots' screams. Agoutis, ocellated turkeys, tinamous, collared peccaries, coatis, and white-tailed deer trundled back and forth across paths like busy commuters in the morning and evening. The agoutis were particularly bold, often not fleeing when I approached, but erecting their back hairs in an aggressive display. A tapir's horsey smell often hung over a swampy oxbow by Chan Chich Creek. The Millers had installed automatic cameras along the paths, and had found that jaguars, pumas, and ocelots regularly used them at night. I missed a jaguar sighting by a minute or so.

Once a gray fox stopped a few meters in front of me, cocking its head curiously. It fled into the trees as I passed, and I thought I'd seen the last of it, but when I glanced back it was following me. I stopped, and the fox hesitated, then lifted a dead leaf from the ground with its nose, reared back on its hind legs, and flipped the leaf in the air, like a dog inviting me to play. It kicked up its heels and frisked away, then returned and repeated the leaf toss before finally drifting out of sight.

The only fish Gallon Jug had in common with Darién's or La Selva's were the sardinelike *Astyanax* tetras that live from Argentina to New Mexico, and little barbeled *Rhamdia* catfish that nosed about the bottom, tickling my toes. The cichlids were northern species like blue-eyed cichlids (*Archocentrus spilurum*) and gold cichlids (*Thorichthys aureum*). Big, green-spangled sailfin mollies hung at the surface of sunlit pools, feeding on floating algae and small invertebrates, and a few times I saw schools of pike livebearers (*Belonesox belizanus*), mollie relatives that occur only in northeast Central America. Unusual among poecilliids, pike livebearers have evolved into eight-inch predators that cruise stream pools like diminutive pickerels.

As I walked with the Millers beside a small lake, red-winged blackbirds sang and Morelet's crocodiles glided among sungrebes and least grebes. Whitish objects lay about the bank—slider turtle eggshells which had hatched or been dug up by raccoons and coatis. The path turned into the forest, and when Bruce imitated an owl, a gang of small understory birds came to scold—a stub-tailed spadebill, a black-headed shrike tanager, a tawny-crowned greenlet, a red-throated ant tanager, a wedge-billed woodcreeper, and a white-throated robin. The Millers reeled off the names as though at a suburban backyard feeder. The owl call also disturbed a spider monkey troop. A big male growled and shook branches at us with great cracking and crashing. Females clutched their babies, and monkeys of all sizes fanned out and swept away through the treetops.

I thought of John Lloyd Stephens's description of his first sight of the Copan ruins. "The only sounds that disturbed the quiet of this buried city were the noise of monkeys moving among the tops of the trees, and the cracking of dry branches broken by their weight. They moved over our heads in long and swift processions . . . and with a noise like a current of wind, passed on into the depths of the forest. It was the first time we had seen these mockeries of humanity, and, with the strange monuments around us, they seemed like wandering spirits of the departed race guarding the ruins of their former habitations." In fact, the little hills from which the Gallon Jug monkeys' trees grew were the unexcavated ruins of Maya pyramids surrounding a plaza. I could see this when Carolyn Miller pointed it out, although I probably wouldn't have noticed it otherwise. In the dappled shade of the ramons, ceibas, and cohune palms, the conical shapes looked natural.

14

The Bridge of Manioc and Maize

I T WAS STRIKING HOW much of the forest at Gallon Jug grew on Maya ruins. No landform there seemed to lack some ancient urban function, as when the Millers showed me a limestone fissure beside a pond. It was the entrance to a storage vault, although I'd have thought it was just a hole in the ground. The pond had been a reservoir. Everywhere, clumps of steep, tree-covered hills marked former buildings. The unexcavated and unrestored state of the Gallon Jug ruins actually increased an impression of human pervasiveness. Since leaf mold and trees uniformly covered the hillocks and pits, it was easy to feel that the entire area had once been "developed" as uninterruptedly as today's most paved-over mall and housing tract.

Tikal in 1971 had given me a different impression. With its elegantly restored plazas and temples, it had seemed much more the mystic "city in the forest" sought by early archaeologists like Stephens. The contrast between the carefully restored structures and the ancient forest had made the ruins seem almost supernatural, more like a city from outer space than a civic center and shopping district serving vast suburbs. This had reflected the prevailing romanticism about Classic Maya civilization before the late 1960s—the idea that the cities were the ceremonial centers of stargazing priests who ruled benignly over peaceful villages, that the Maya somehow had been exempt from the despotisms and greeds of other civilizations. Maya archaeology since 1971 largely has been concerned with the erasure of this attractive but slightly antlike picture. Decipherment of glyphs at Tikal, Copan, and other ruins has shown a society as ridden by wealth, power, and warfare as others, and analysis of late Classic burials and farmlands has revealed a decadence of eroding soils and declining health as squalid as Rome's or Babylon's. The moldy rubble at Gallon Jug, where the main "excavation" I saw was the robber-emptied plaster tomb of some forgotten oligarch, seemed exemplary of the newly mundane archaeology.

It isn't surprising that the ancient Maya were like the ancient Old World—human. It is a bit surprising, though, that Western science took until the 1970s to realize it. The absence of a historical record was the delay's main cause, yet it perhaps also stemmed partly from the mixture of admiration and guilt that New World civilization and its destruction evoked in Europeans, and from the disdain that early scientists like Buffon felt toward inherently inferior and/or degenerated America. Admiration and disdain lingered in later scientists like Thomas Belt, whose attitude toward New World humanity was complicated.

Belt regarded the old Nahuatl civilization of Nicaragua as superior to the shaky 1860s republic, yet he also seemed to feel that Old World ideals such as democracy and civil liberty were not for Native Americans. He thought Spanish rule had ruined native cultures by stopping intertribal warfare, thus ending natural selection and vitiating the population with "selfish and sensual instincts." "It was this constant struggle between the different tribes," he wrote, "that weeded out the weak and indolent and preserved the strong and enterprising; just as among the lower animals the stronger kill off the weaker, and the result is the improvement of the race." If the Spanish Conquest had never occurred, he concluded, "that ancient civilization . . . might have been Christianized and purified without being destroyed, and today have stood one of the wonders and delights of the world." This seems to conflict with his belief that the United States was destined to colonize Latin America, but perhaps Belt thought colonization would not have been called for if "that ancient civilization had been saved."

Another complication of Belt's attitude toward New World civilizations was that he didn't consider them indigenous. He thought Polynesians or Asians had colonized Central America's Pacific side via a glaciation-exposed land connection, and that Europeans or Africans had reached the Caribbean by a corresponding lost Atlantis. "All over the world," he wrote, "curious questions concerning the distribution of races of mankind, of animals, and of plants were rendered more easy of solution on the theory that land was more continuous once than now." Belt was not original in this. Most archaeologists and ethnologists before him had sought the origins of New World civilization in the Old. When British diplomat John Crawford found maize growing in Java in 1808, he assumed that it had been cultivated there before European discovery of the Americas, and was thus an Old World invention.

Such beliefs had logic. It does seem improbable that agriculture and cities should have been invented quite separately on opposite sides of the world. Some almost miraculous intervention seems called for, a mythic culture-giver from China or Egypt, or even from outer space. The known evidence supports the seemingly improbable, however—that the people who developed New World civilization had already been there a long time, having arrived as hunter-gatherers over the Bering land bridge, and that they developed it by themselves.

Humans Cross the Bridge

Native mythologies may contain information about Central America's human past. The Quiché Maya creation story, the *Popul Vuh*, says the first people originated somewhere to the east and crossed mountains, forests, and even oceans to reach Guatemala. A Kuna told anthropologist Clyde Keeler of a creature named Achusimmutupalits, which was like a tapir but much larger, with tusks and a long snout. Native American myths are more concerned with affirming present occupation of home-lands than past wanderings, however. Jesuit José de Acosta wrote in 1588 that the Indians "believe confidently that they were created at the first beginning of this New World, where they now dwell." The Kuna know that they moved to the San Blas archipelago from farther east in the last two centuries, but what is important to them is that they origi-nated from Cerro Tacarcuna, the mountain at the center of their cosmos. This geocentrism is perhaps why the Lacandon *bruja* Kaa objected to Barnum Brown's bone digging. The notion that the Lacondones were latecomers in a land that monsters had trampled over for millions of years might have seemed to undermine Lacandone occupation, and Lilian Brown *was* trying, in her well-meaning way, to displace Kaa as her village's cultural mentor.

Acosta, who thought it "a matter of no importance to know what the Indians themselves report of their beginnings, being more like dreams than histories," probably was the first to suggest they had crossed from Eurasia as early hunters. "I believe it is not many thousand years since men first inhabited the New World," he wrote, "and that the first men that entered were rather savages and hunters than bred up in a civil commonweal." The idea didn't attract much attention, however, until the growth of evolutionary thinking three centuries later. More common was the notion, which Francisco Ximénez mentioned in his writing about the Mayas, that the Indians were descended from the lost tribes of Israel. Ximénez didn't speculate as to how the lost tribes might have reached Central America, and didn't seem very interested, although he noted supposed parallels between Maya religion and Judeo-Christianity. Having discovered and translated the *Popol Vuh*, he was aware of the superficiality of such parallels, and thought Quiché religion closer to Satanism than Judaism.

In 1876, Alfred Russell Wallace's *The Geographical Distribution of Animals* narrowed the scope for solving "curious questions concerning the distribution of races of mankind" through land bridges. Wallace saw evidence for only two western hemisphere land bridges during the past few million years, the Bering and the Central American. Human migration presumably had been confined to them, as had animal and plant migrations. That same year, discovery of crude stone tools in Trenton, New Jersey, seemed evidence that humans had occupied the New World long enough to evolve indigenous civilization. The tools at first were thought contemporary with Paleolithic European ones, but paleontologist Ales Hrdlicka proved that they were actually half-finished tools discarded by historic Indians, and interest in North American human origins underwent a four-decade lull. Apparent early artifacts which turned up in South America also were disregarded, and humans figured hardly at all in the land bridge theories that evolved during the fin de siècle.

Like Belt's ethnology, this neglect of possible human actors in the land bridge epic was complicated. Triumph-and-tragedy doyen Henry Fairfield Osborn regarded man as the culmination of the northern hemisphere mammalian evolution that had spread to conquer the southern continents. He and many other paleontologists thought Central Asia was the likely site of human divergence from the apes, a belief that remained prevalent until the African fossil discoveries of the 1950s. Evolutionists with such ideas might have seen the spread of Paleo-Indians from Alaska to Tierra del Fuego, accompanied by the extinction of archaic southern ground sloths and glyptodonts, as another triumph of progressive evolution. Yet the Indians' spread through the Americas was contemporaneous with extinction not only of southern mammals but of many of the big northern ones—horses, mastodons, camels, saber-tooths—that had "triumphed" over the archaic southerners when the land bridge opened.

Evolutionists never have welcomed the idea that early humans could have driven such magnificent, highly evolved faunas to extinction. Osborn apparently never seriously considered it, although he described a number of North American sites where human remains had been found with extinct animal bones in his book *The Age of Mammals* (1910). He mentioned weather, deforestation, and disease as possible extinction causes, but not human hunting. In another book, he quoted early naturalist George Turner's speculation that humans had exterminated the mammoth, but dismissively called it a "unique theory." Indeed, Osborn seemed to associate New World humans as much with backward South American mammals as with advanced North American ones. In *Man Rises to Parnassus* (1918), Osborn wrote of Tierra del Fuegians: "The primitive races of man, like the primitive races of mammals, are constantly being thrust out from the center of dispersal into the most remote terminal regions."

In 1927, a Stone Age human presence in North America became undeniable with the discovery of beautifully made "fluted" projectile points with extinct bison skeletons in Folsom, New Mexico. The discovery pushed human arrival in the New World back to at least 10,000 years ago, when the last glaciation ended. The 1930s discovery of a Patagonian cave, Fell's Cave, which contained fluted projectile points along with ground sloth and horse bones, proved an early human presence there too. Stone Age people definitely had crossed the Central American land bridge.

The exact time and manner of their crossing were unclear, however, and have remained so despite growing paleontological evidence. Fossil dates have fluctuated bewilderingly as different dating methods were used, and theories have changed accordingly. Available evidence doesn't even prove that people reached North America before South America, although common sense says they must have. In the mid-1990s, a possible oldest New World archaeological site was at Monte Verde in south central Chile, where twelve wooden structures, wooden mortars, grinding stones, wild potatoes, mastodon and guanaco bones, and stone choppers and projectile points have been found under a layer of peat. Monte Verde could be as much as 14,000 years old, although it also could be less than 11,000 years old. A North American site, the Meadowcroft Rock Shelter in Pennsylvania, may be older, but the stone tools and flakes found there are even less conclusive as to date than Monte Verde's artifacts.

Given such confusions, we may never know when or how the first people crossed Darién. That crossing is important to ideas about the Americas' first humans, however, so theories about it have evolved along with more general ones about the hemisphere's colonization. There basically are two theories, with a lot of confusing variations. One is that humans occupied the Americas rapidly, crossing the Bering Strait at most 12,000 years ago and reaching Tierra del Fuego in as little as 500 years. The other is that humans occupied the Americas relatively slowly, crossing the Bering Strait over 20,000 years ago and reaching Tierra del Fuego after several thousand years.

According to the first theory, articulated by ecologist Paul S. Martin in the early 1970s, the first Americans were specialized big game hunters who used fluted projectile points so efficiently to kill large mammals, and whose populations thus grew so rapidly, that they advanced in a kind of inexorable wave through any land where megafauna lived. (Presumably, New World big game was more vulnerable than Old World, which had coevolved with humans.) Since megafauna lived in Central America, the wave spread through it regardless of rain forests or other tropical habitats which might seem to present adaptation problems for people whose recent ancestors had been Siberians. This theory's adherents use the paleontological record as its main support, and in fact, most of the verified evidence of the earliest humans in the Americas is of people who used fluted points to kill big game from roughly 12,000 to 8,000 years ago. As I've said, they seem to have arrived in North and South America almost simultaneously.

There's even circumstantial evidence that such people may have crossed Panama quickly. Fluted points have been found at Lake Alajuela near Panama City. Also near Panama City is a large deposit of yellow chert, an excellent material for making projectile points, yet none of the fluted points at Lake Alajuela are made of the yellow chert, suggesting that fluted point makers may have passed through the area too quickly to find the chert. There's extensive evidence that the people who lived in central Panama about 7,000 years ago quarried the chert to make tools, but they didn't make fluted points for killing big game, which had died out there by that time.

There may be an archaeological problem with fluted points. North American points tend to differ from South American ones. Folsom points are lanceolate, shaped rather like willow leaves, while Fell's Cave points are oblanceolate and flared at the base like fishtails. In Central America, both kinds of points have been found, with the Fishtail type predominating in Panama and Costa Rica, and the Folsom type predominating to the north. This pattern suggests that Fishtail points originated in South America and Folsom points originated in North America, which may not fit the "inexorable wave" theory, unless the inexorable wave suddenly changed its fluted point style when it got to South America. The difference between the two kinds of points may not be that significant, however. There is a lot of variation in both continents' projectile points, and Folsomlike points have been found in South America.

The other theory, articulated by anthropologist Gordon Willey in the early 1970s, is that the first Americans were relatively unspecialized hunter-gatherers who didn't make fluted points, but used diverse stone, bone, and wood tools to get a variety of foods. They crossed the Bering Strait about twenty or even thirty thousand years ago, and spread gradually southward, adapting to local ecosystems as they went. When they reached the tropics, some groups occupied rain forest, retaining an unspecialized hunting-gathering way of life, while others spread down the

Andes to temperate South America. Specialized big game hunting with fluted points evolved later in areas where megafauna was abundant, with centers in the temperate grasslands of both North and South America.

The difference between Folsom and Fishtail points may support the second theory, but otherwise there is less archaeological evidence for it than for the first. Unspecialized stone, bone, and wood artifacts are not as common in early sites as fluted points, although they do exist in sites like the Chilean Monte Verde. In 1975, anthropologist Alan Bryan and his associates excavated a site called El Bosque near Estelí in northeast Nicaragua, which yielded a few possible stone tools—"crudely flaked pieces of jasper"—and campfire remains. These were associated with ground sloth, mastodon, and horse bones that could be over 18,000 years old. Such artifacts have yet to be proved conclusively older than fluted points, however. Another problem with the second theory is that glaciers covered most of northwestern North America before about 12,000 years ago, and may have hindered overland migration from the Bering Strait. Coastal migration still might have been possible, however. People reached Australia in boats 50,000 years ago. The Monte Verde site is near the coast, suggesting that the first Americans may have been oriented to coasts.

Now almost thirty years old, the controversy continues. In 1996, I heard a white-haired Paul S. Martin propound the doctrine of the inexorable wave with unabated vigor at a U. C. Berkeley Museum of Vertebrate Zoology seminar. He had been studying Grand Canyon caves where Shasta ground sloths, giant mountain goats, and condors left their remains, and he passed around a softball-sized piece of sloth dung which, although dry and odorless, looked as if it had been deposited yesterday instead of 11,000 years ago. It contained mainly globemallow, a common, pink-flowered shrub of today's Southwest. He also showed a slide of an extinct mountain goat skull with bits of flesh and skin on it. Martin said the last remains of these creatures correlate with the age of fluted points, and that the last fossil dates of many other large animals such as saber-tooths do also.

"I can't invest much faith in the idea that our species could come into a Garden of Eden and not proliferate," he replied to questions about the possibility of earlier, slower migrations. "America was a real opportunity ecologically to the first people who got here, so if they did and they were scarce, I wonder what's going on. The only way this model will work is fast." Martin acknowledged that much is unexplained by the inexorable wave, such as the *non*extinction of many large animals. He speculated that caribou and bighorn sheep may have escaped the big game hunters because they lived in inaccessible terrain, but couldn't explain why bison survived in such abundance. "Maybe the hunters lived on the bison while they were exterminating the mammoths and ground sloths," he joked.

Neither of the two theories seems likely to prevail until the evidence improves. Neither may be altogether right. In a way, they are an extension of the hoary oppositions between Old and New World, North and South. The "inexorable wave" is on the Old World–North side in positing a conquest of both the Americas by a few generations of Siberian big game hunters. The "slow trickle" is on the New World–South side in positing evolution of specialized big game hunters from many generations of indigenous Americans. The truth may be somewhere between the two, or somewhere else.

Farming Peoples

There is not much question about what happened in the Americas immediately after the fluted point cultures disappeared. Fossil sites show that the descendants of big game specialists had to adapt to a life farther down the food chain after mastodons and other megafauna vanished by around 7,000 years ago. They probably were unhappy campers as population grew and game declined. Richard MacNeish's exhaustive excavations of the archaeological pasts of valleys in Mexico and Peru—the Tehuacan and Ayacucho—showed that foods such as cactus, tree roots, and grass seeds predominated. In the Tehuacan Valley, hunters depended on deer and rabbits after horses and pronghorns disappeared about 8,000 years ago. They also seem to have eaten skunks, and investigators found human coprolites containing the remains of mice which apparently had been charred with the fur on, then swallowed whole.

Megafauna extinction probably affected vegetation. Disappearance of grazers may have converted grasslands to brush or forest in some areas. Daniel Janzen has speculated that tree species adapted to large mammal seed dispersal may have started disappearing. Winnie Hallwachs's agouti studies suggest the rodents have assumed the seed dispersal role of mastodons and other big mammals, which probably chewed up guapinol, almendro, palm, and other fruits and defecated many live seeds in places far distant from parent trees. Agoutis don't broadcast the seeds as effectively as the megafauna did, however, because they don't transport as many seeds as far. The fallen fruits of species like guapinol often collect uneaten under the parent trees and become infested with seed-eating insects such as bruchid beetle or weevil grubs, which can kill most of a tree's yearly seed production. Disappearance of such trees could have had further ramifications. Since smaller game like peccaries also eat the fruits, their increasing scarcity could have made hunting even harder for post-megafauna humans.

A roughly 6,000-year-old site I saw in Nicaragua seemed to reflect a hard life. The site, Las Huellas de Acahualinca on Lake Managua, consists of a volcanic ashfall deposit with footprints. Discovered during construction in the 1940s, it's about four meters below the surface. Most of the footprints are human, arranged in a straggling file that suggests they were walking fast, as though to get away from an eruption. Some are punched deep into the ash, perhaps because their makers were carrying burdens. I got the impression they'd been made by small, determined people with the bandy physiques that come from strenuous activity and sparse diets. The few other tracks at the site, of a couple of small deer and a wading bird, did not suggest a landscape of abundance. Other descriptions of Lake Managua deposits mention bison hoofprints and mastodon bones, but I didn't see any.

I visited the footprints with an anthropologist, Tony Stocks, who had never heard of them, although he'd spent a lot of time in Nicaragua. I knew about them from a tourist guidebook, which mistakenly said they were 10,000 years old instead of 6,000. "If they were really 10,000 years old, they'd be truly significant," Stocks said, and went back to his job studying indigenous land claims for the Nature Conservancy. Leaving only footprints, the determined waders in volcanic mud seemed losers in the human evolution lottery, falling on thin times between paleolithic meat windfalls and neolithic grain bonanzas.

Increasing dependence on plant foods led to domestication of a variety of plants at about that time. Lake bottom pollen and phytoliths at

La Yeguada in central Panama suggest large-scale cutting and burning of vegetation after around 7,000 years ago, with an increase in semiwild human food plants such as palms and arrowroot. White-tailed deer and armadillos seem to have been the main game species. Maize pollen appeared in lake sediments there about 5,000 years ago, and farming became so intense that resource depletion apparently forced partial abandonment of the area by 4,000 years ago.

The farming cultures that developed in Central America distributed themselves rather as had wild animals and plants before them. Archaeology and historical factors like languages suggest that North and South American contingents met and interacted on the isthmus. The northerners based their culture on maize, domesticated in the Mexican highlands where its wild relative *teosinte* still grows. The southerners also used maize, but depended on root crops such as manioc and sweet potatoes, which almost certainly originated in South American rain forest, although we don't know how or when. (Also called cassava or, in Spanish, *yuca*, manioc is a shrub with large starchy tubers.) With the rise of the Mexican highlands' first great cities about 3,000 years ago, maize-based urbanism spread south through the seasonally dry lands of the Pacific coast. Jade from Mexican and Guatemalan mines has been found in archaeological sites throughout this area, and apparently was a universal ceremonial artifact. At the same time, a culture similar to that of Colombia prevailed on the Caribbean side from Honduras south. Less urbanized than the Mexican-oriented cultures, and therefore less known archaeologically, it probably was based on shifting cultivation of manioc and other rain forest crops.

This was a relatively stable period which lasted 2,000 years. The Maya expanded from the Guatemalan highlands into the Petén during it, and built their Classic cities. About 1,100 years ago, however, urban centers throughout Central America shifted away from lowland river sites which were best for farming and trade to a more random arrangement, with new sites in easily defended locations such as hilltops. Population pressure and political conflict seems to have caused partial collapse of the Mexican-oriented trade network that had prevailed for two millennia. Abandonment of the Classic Maya cities was the most dramatic symptom of this overall instability.

South American artifacts increasingly appeared in southern Central

America about this time—gold worked with Colombian metallurgy, lime flasks for coca-leaf chewing, llamalike figurines. Towns like Guayabo near Turrialba in eastern Costa Rica had largely southern affinities. On a slope high above the Reventazon River Valley, Guayabo's terraced stone structures reminded me more of Machu Picchu than Tikal. A sense of "stepped" orientation toward the river valley, and many channels and pools for distributing water through the site, seemed typically South American. According to archaeologist Richard Cooke, Guayabo has "a striking resemblance to Tairona villages in the Sierra Nevada de Santa Marta, Colombia." Yet the northern influence remained strong. The cities on Honduras's Plátano River may have been part of the Mexican trade network, perhaps as a cacao growing center. "The habits of these people are nearly all like those of the Mexicans," wrote Benzoni of the Nicaraguans. "They eat human flesh, and they wear cloaks, and waistcoats without sleeves." Even in central Panama, a practice described by the Spanish chronicler Andagoya of erecting pyramids of heads as battle monuments suggests Aztec influence.

A partially restored site I visited in northeast El Salvador demonstrates pre-Columbian cosmopolitanism. Occupied for at least 3,000 years, it is called El Tazumal, and sits beside the cemetery of the contemporary town of Ahuachapan. The earliest artifacts found there, chubby statuettes of women, are said to show Olmec influence, but they also reminded me of statuettes in Costa Rica and Peru. Burials from the mid to late Classic period about 1,500 to 1,000 years ago contained Panamanian-style gold jewelry as well as Maya and Toltec artifacts, such as a red-painted stone skull with iron ore eyes. Other pottery of that period may have been made by the Lenca, ancestors of the people with whom I shared a bus ride to the Honduran town of La Esperanza. Its decoration reminded me of Navajo art—slender, stylized figures adorned with feathers. About 800 years ago, the volcanic explosion that formed Lake Ilopango depopulated the site for many years. After that, the Nahuatl-speaking Pipils occupied it until the Spanish Conquest, leaving more Mexican-looking artifacts than pre-explosion ones.

While sitting on El Tazumal's main structure in late afternoon, I noticed that a hedge separating it from the street was filling up with North American migrant warblers. I walked over for a closer look, and found that it was also full of foot-long lizards I'd never seen before. Some were bright green with blue tails, and very aggressive, doing "pushup" displays and chasing each other up and down tree trunks. Others were gray brown and quieter, evidently the females. I'd seen similar lizards in the Amazon, and it seemed likely that these Salvadoran ones were teiids, members of the originally North American family which migrated into South America, died out in North America, then eventually spread back north. El Tazumal seemed an appropriate place for them.

Historical Central American languages followed geographical patterns similar to, if even more complicated than, crops and archaeological artifacts. Columbus found the diversity of tongues on the Caribbean coast bewildering. "The villages have each a different language," he wrote, "and it is so much so that they do not understand one another any more than we understand the Arabs." Such diversity still prevails in some places. When Dr. Pedro Guzmán showed me around the Altos Cuchumatanes, he spoke feelingly of the difficulties of coordinating the six or seven ethnic groups which inhabit the plateau into his rural development project. They include not only the Mam Mayas, but other Maya groups, and others related to non-Maya Mexican tribes. Dr. Guzmán echoed Columbus's very words.

"You can go from one little *municipio* to the next," he said, "and find not just a completely different language, but a completely different way of looking at the world."

Ladinos like Dr. Guzmán aren't the only ones who have difficulties. I heard a leader of the Tawahkas, a tribe in the Honduran Mosquitia, complain about the impossibility of learning to speak Pech, his neighbors' language. He just couldn't make those weird, nasal sounds. You had to be born Pech to make them.

Linguists have sorted out the confusion to some degree. They class Nahuatl languages such as Chorotega and Pipil in a group called Uto-Aztecan which occurs north to the Rockies and Great Basin, and includes Paiute and Hopi. Maya languages are classed as Penutian, a large North American group which includes California Miwok as well as New Mexico Zuni and Mississippi Natchez. Most other Central American languages such as Miskito, Tawahka, and Kuna are classed as Macro-Chibchan, a group which occurs south into Colombia. So a North American contingent of Uto-Aztecan and Penutian speakers inhabited the highlands and seasonally dry Pacific lowlands from Tehuantepec to the Nicaraguan Depression, as far south as North American oak-pine forest, and a South American contingent of Macro-Chibchan speakers inhabited the wet Caribbean slope from Darién to the Gulf of Honduras, almost as far north as South American rain forest.

It wasn't quite that tidy, of course. Penutian-speaking Mayas occupied the Caribbean lowlands of the Petén and Belize, while Chibchan-speaking Lencas settled the pine-forested highlands of Honduras and Nicaragua. The South American origin of Macro-Chibchan also may be in doubt. Anthropologist Tony Stocks thought it as likely that the Macro-Chibchan languages had evolved in Central America as South America.

There is one definitely South American language in Central America, but it is a recent arrival. A people who call themselves Garifuna and occupy the Caribbean coast from northern Honduras to southern Belize speak a language belonging to the Carib group, which extends from Venezuela to the southern Amazon. Of mixed Carib and African descent, they lived in the southern Caribbean around the island of St. Vincent during the seventeenth century. A Garifuna I talked to, a guide at the Cuero y Salado Wildlife Refuge, thought they had originated as the warlike Caribs raided slave ships and plantations, taking women as captives. In any case, they proved troublesome enough to colonial authority that in 1797 the British deported hundreds to the Honduran Bay Island of Roatan. Most then moved to the mainland, where they took up a fishing and farming life like that of the Afro-English Creoles north of them and the Afro-Chibchan Miskitos to the south.

Central American cultural *ambientes* still reflect aboriginal geography, despite the loss of many native groups and languages. When I stayed at the town of Altagracia on Isla Omotepe in Lake Nicaragua, its stucco buildings and central plaza reminded me strongly of another town I'd stayed at years before, Ajijic on Lake Chapala in the Mexican state of Jalisco. The people in both had a quiet urbanity that runs right down through the old Nahuatl world where modern cosmopolitanism hasn't overlain it, and that perhaps hasn't changed since the Cacique Nicarao greeted Dávila in 1524. Although I wasn't in either town very long, I saw solemn, businesslike parades in both.

When I visited the Miskito town of Barra del Plátano in the Honduran Mosquitia, its muddy lanes and lack of plan reminded me of river towns in Darién or the Amazon. The people had an independent-minded informality that seems typical of neotropical rain forest cultures, and that hasn't changed since Columbus ran afoul of the Chiriquís in 1503. The only evidence of formal planning at Barra del Plátano was a very solid steel and concrete latrine that some development agency had built on the dune between the town from the Caribbean. The latrine was a good demonstration of planning's limitations, because a recent hurricane and flood had left it a couple of meters above the present dune level, quite unusable without a stairway or ladder, neither of which was in evidence. It towered emptily between town and sea, a monument to man's search for order in a particularly disorderly place.

Of course, land bridge linguistic links have their limits. Despite their common Penutian languages, similarities between the Maya and, say, the California Miwoks are not obvious. Yet that doesn't mean there aren't any. When I was in the remotest part of the Altos Cuchumatanes, where the Mam houses are made of hand-split planks, I noticed that each homestead had a little earth-roofed structure beside the house. I asked Dr. Guzmán what they were.

"What do you think?" I said they looked like pottery kilns. "They're steam baths," he replied. In fact, the structures resembled miniature versions of the men's sweat lodge in the reconstructed Coast Miwok village of Kule Loklo at Point Reyes National Seashore in California. The Miwoks' smaller family sweat lodges probably looked just like the Mam Mayas'.

Utatlán

For some reason, I felt my land bridge explorations wouldn't be complete until I'd been to Utatlán, the Quiché Maya capital that Hubert Bancroft described in such glowing terms. Perhaps it was because of another legend told by John Lloyd Stephens. When he was there in 1840, Stephens related that "under one of the buildings is an opening which the Indians called a cave, and by which they said one could reach Mexico in an hour. I crawled under and found a pointed arch roof formed by stones lapping over each, but was prevented from exploring it by want of light." Such stories of caves leading magically to other places are common. Stephens mentioned several others, and Francisco

Ximénez wrote of caves "to which a bottom cannot be found" in "the old buildings of Santa Cruz del Quiché." In Honduras, I heard of a house in the village of Los Andes which was supposed to be connected by a cave to the local graveyard. The stories seem suggestive of evolutionary as well as legendary translocations, of the way life descends into the obscurity so typical of Central American prehistory, then emerges again in new shapes and places.

When I went to Utatlán in 1995, it was another place I had to walk to. The nearby market town of Chichicastenango had crawled with tourists, but the dirt road from Santa Cruz del Quiché to the ruin was empty except for a few children, one of whom ran screaming into a house as I approached. I passed through cornfields and scattered groves of oak, pine, and black cherry to where the road forked below the cypress-covered hill that had been the city. The *dueño* was just opening the little museum at the site, and I was the only visitor. He made me clean my muddy boots before I entered. The sun was still low, and it was dark inside the low building. He said the electricity had been cut off three years before.

"You can go to the cave," he said, evidently anticipating what most visitors came for. "It's down at the end of the path." I followed his direction past humus-covered mounds of masonry, which looked gloomy under the cypresses, to where the path dropped into a wooded ravine. Halfway down was a low opening, its sides overgrown with small plants but its floor slick and bare, obviously much visited, although nobody was there. A crude, angry face was carved into the soft volcanic stone beside the entrance, and three walking sticks leaned against it. I took one and went inside. It was as Stephens described, a narrow shaft with a pointed arch roof. Having a flashlight, I was not "prevented from exploring it," but it extended only a few hundred feet. Rubbish strewed the floor, mostly the remains of votive candles which had been burned along the walls. Side galleries led off at right angles to the shaft, smelling of the chickens which Quiché prayermen sacrifice.

It was not a spectacular space, yet the walls were curiously firm and intact compared to the rubble aboveground. Like Herman's Cave in Belize, it felt like an entrance to Xibalba, the Mayan underworld. The darkness and silence where the shaft dead-ended corroded everyday notions of time and space, as they had in the Masaya lava tube (below

Santiago Crater), and reduced my comfortable expectation that I would emerge from the cave in the same place I'd entered. Ideas of underworlds and prehistory are perhaps not so different. Both are the land of dead forebears, and both can be entered by caves. The same Santa Cruz del Quiché padre who told Stephens of seeing a living Maya city from a mountaintop also told him "that in a cave near a neighboring village were sculls [sic] much larger than the natural size, and regarded with superstitious reverence by the Indians. He had seen them, and vouched for their giant dimensions."

Aboveground again, I gravitated to a sunny place before a steep pyramid, the only partly intact building in the site. Two vases of pearly everlasting flowers stood in a niche at its base, and some men were clearing grass around it. Much of the nearby ground was bare plaster pavement, now puddled from heavy rain the night before. The place looked bulldozed, and I thought of yet another tale the Santa Cruz del Quiché padre had told Stephens. "The padre told us that thirty years before, when he first saw it, the palace was entire to the garden. He was fresh from the palaces of Spain, and it seemed as if he were again among them." The padre evidently had enjoyed a vivid imagination.

A middle-aged Quiché man came up wheeling a bicycle, and we started talking. His name was Don Paolo. "This place is as important as Tikal or any other ruins," he said. "All they know about them is from carvings, but this place has a living *historia*." He told me a brief version of it. The Quiché were descended from the Toltecs, who had migrated to Mexico and Guatemala via Alaska, and also from the successive men of mud, wood, and maize in the *Popul Vuh*. An extraordinary personage, a Quiché version of the Mexican Quetzalcoatl, had given them their arts and sciences. I told Don Paolo about Bancroft's description of the unruined city, and he agreed that it had been like that, covered with semiprecious stones, gold, and silver. When I mentioned Stephens's story about the site having been "entire to the garden" in the early nineteenth century, he said that also was true. The mayor of Santa Cruz del Quiché had caused a lot of the ruins to be hauled away to build the municipal building there in 1910.

I asked why the site was paved with plaster, and he said that was the Quiché way of establishing political authority. "The Quiché name of the city is 'K'umarkaj,'" he said, "which means the place of pavements.

They burned river stones and mixed the lime with *pavo* eggs, and made plaster terraces at different levels, and that was their place of power. There were two leaders who built a lot of it, Nine Coyotes and Three Deer. Each of them had the strength and cunning of that number of animals each.

"There's a lot more to the story," Don Paolo said. "I have tapes in Quiché that tell it. Quiché is Guatemala's second language—people speak it everywhere because of all the emigration. But our young men aren't interested in listening. All they care about is nice clothes and motorbikes."

The day was advanced enough that I thought the light in the museum would be better. I walked to it past a tin-roofed pit which, the *dueño* told me, had been the site of a burial exhibited there. The skeleton of a big-boned man with the flattened skull of the Maya nobility lay in a glass case surrounded by pots. A smaller, nondeformed skull sat on his rib cage. It wasn't mentioned in the display label, and I asked the *dueño* about it. He said it was a younger male's, perhaps a funeral sacrifice to the big man. It had a hole about the size of an axe blade at its top. The big man clearly had been important. We marveled at the size and condition of his teeth, a complete set, without a cavity.

"Strong," said the *dueño*. "Not like today."

15

The Bridge of Cattle and Coffee

HISTORY CAME TO Central America with Columbus, changing land bridge evolution as an influx of Old World organisms interfered with the New World's natural experiment in intercontinental migration. Modern civilization has diminished native plants and animals, and has threatened some with extinction. Yet history doesn't supersede evolution, it merely complicates it. The land bridge experiment hasn't ended. Species continue to migrate between the continents, and their persistence in doing so has brought new twists to the vortex.

The Spanish Conquest's effects on native ecosystems were ambiguous. The collapse of native human populations caused forest to return to many places, so that nineteenth-century observers like John Lloyd Stephens regarded Central America as almost primeval. Yet the conquistadors were quick to introduce livestock, crops, and industries where they could, and some areas remained populated and prosperous at least until Spain's imperial decline in the eighteenth century. Stephens was almost as impressed by Spanish ruins he saw in 1839 as by Maya ruins. "Their colossal grandeur and costliness were startling," he wrote after passing seven "gigantic" churches "in a region of desolation, and by mountain paths which human hands have never attempted to improve."

Thomas Gage, the Englishman who described Guatemala as "seated

in the midst of a paradise on one side and a hell on the other," saw
Central America during the empire's height. Leaving home to join the
Dominicans, Gage served as a priest in Chiapas and Guatemala from
1626 to 1637. He turned against Catholicism, however, and after
amassing a small fortune by pocketing parishioners' donations and selling church property, fled south through Nicaragua and Costa Rica to
Panama to escape the authorities. He eventually returned to England
and became a puritan preacher. Gage's *New Survey of the West Indias*,
published in 1648, made Central America seem almost as settled as
Europe, and more pleasant. The book was loaded with descriptions of
"the greatness and beauty of fair towns," "very great and spacious estan-
cias," and "abundance of cattle."

Gage's descriptions were astute, but one-sided. He had an ulterior
motive, for one thing. He wanted to convince Oliver Cromwell to conquer the Caribbean, and succeeded in promoting an expedition which
led to his own death in 1655. Gage also was oblivious to just about
everything except religion and riches, and seldom described anything
not related to them, although a few glimpses of native Central America
crept into his narrative when they piqued his piety, avarice, or anxiety.
He wrote that the Pokoman Maya near Antigua used toads to spike
their beerlike *chicha* and worshiped idols in mountain caves, one of
which he discovered and burned, provoking an assault by its enraged
devotees. Iguanas and porcupines as well as deer were important foods
for both Indians and Spaniards, and Gage was "much affrighted" when
"a huge and monstrous cayman or crocodile" chased him at Lake Nicaragua. But he usually dismissed natural phenomena with stock phrases,
seeing "nothing worth committing to posterity, but only mighty woods
and trees," on the journey from Lake Nicaragua to Cartago in Costa
Rica. Of crossing Panama by the Chagres River, he wrote nothing at all.

Yet for all Gage's attempts to make the Spanish empire seem settled
and prosperous, one senses how much it was restricted to the old Maya
and Nahuatl heartlands. Outside those, he found largely hardship, hunger, and disease. When he went on an expedition against the uncon-
verted Petén Maya, they found no lost cities (although Tayasal still
existed), and fled after skirmishing with "about a thousand Indians . . .
which uproar and affrightment added sweat and fear to my fever." Pirates relieved him of his ill-gotten gains when he tried to take ship out

of Costa Rica on the Caribbean. To reach Panama and the Spain-bound galleons, he had to sail from Costa Rica on the Pacific, and almost got marooned on a desert island. There may have been less cultural contact between northern and southern Central America in Gage's time than before the conquest. The aboriginal division into a north-oriented urban society on the Pacific and a south-oriented forest one on the Caribbean continued, reinforced by the Caribbean resistance to Spain that had begun in sixteenth-century Veragua.

The Miskitos became the main resisters, stemming from a coastal branch of the Chibchan-speaking Sumu in northeast Nicaragua. William Dampier described them in the 1680s as "a small nation of not more than one hundred men, long-visaged, with lank black hair and copper complexions." Pirates hired Miskitos to provision their ships by "striking" green turtles and manatees, and Dampier wrote that they were "ready to imitate us in whatsoever they saw us do at any time." Seafaring transformed them rather as horses transformed the Plains tribes. When I was in Miskito towns, the people reminded me more of the Cheyenne than the linguistically-related Sumu or Guaymi. Although their diverse genetic background produces many physical types, they tend to be tall, robust, and aggressive compared to other Chibchan-speakers. As their numbers grew, partly by recruitment of runaway slaves, they joined the buccaneers in raiding Spanish cities and other tribes. Their last raid on the Guaymis in Panama took place in 1805.

Other Caribbean groups resisted Hispanic hegemony during and after the empire. The Yucatec Maya fought for independence in the 1850s Caste War, and the Darién Kuna rebelled successfully in the 1920s, gaining semiautonomy from Panama. This resistance combined with the Old World diseases of malaria and yellow fever to hinder colonization of Central America with Old World plants and animals. Blocked from turning the Caribbean into plantations and ranches, the Spanish had to concentrate on the highlands and Pacific coastal plain—and even the Pacific lowlands had malaria and other scourges which limited population.

Restricted colonization had an odd effect on land bridge ecology. Instead of simply obliterating native ecosystems, it rearranged them in ways that can make it hard to tell what is really aboriginal. The savannas that now extend along most of the Pacific coast are an example. As I've said, there probably were savanna corridors during the Pleistocene, and large pre-Columbian human populations created savannas by burning. It's hard to say whether today's savannas have much relation to prehistoric ones, however. When I was in the Santa Elena Peninsula savanna, endemic species such as little agaves that were blooming suggested it was an old habitat. A savannalike vegetation typically grows on peridotite bedrock throughout the world, and Santa Elena's bunch grasses and wildflowers reminded me of similar plants in northern California's peridotite areas, although the genera were quite different. Yet Daniel Janzen, who has studied Guanacaste for so many years, thinks its savanna is a historical phenomenon. He told me in 1989 that he believed Santa Elena was covered with dry forest before the conquest, and has been turned into savanna by repeated fires. He pointed out dry forest stumps that persist on parts of the peninsula.

Janzen thinks that some of the typical savanna plants that grow throughout Central America's Pacific coast today may have been absent in pre-Columbian times. An example is guanacaste (*Enterolobium cyclocarpum*), the leguminous tree for which the province is named. Its large fruits, shaped oddly like human ears, are sweet-tasting and relished by livestock. Although famous, guanacaste is a relatively uncommon species in Costa Rica, growing mainly as spreading old individuals in pastures and other nonforest sites. "Ironically," Janzen wrote in 1983, "this tree probably did not occur naturally in Costa Rica in the period from 10,000 years ago to when the Spaniards arrived, but was probably a more northern Mesoamerican tree that came to Costa Rica as seeds riding in the guts of the first Spanish horses and cattle. For the next 400 years, it was distributed throughout Guanacaste through seed dispersal by the horse and cow (just as it probably was dispersed by the prehistoric giant mammals, including horses, that ranged through Mesoamerica until 10,000 years ago)."

The empire's collapse in the 1820s was the beginning of a renewed onslaught of Old World organisms even more exotic and complex than Spanish ranches and plantations. Its impetus came from the expanding industrial powers of the north, chiefly England and the United States, but the transplanted organisms came from the Old World tropics. Coffee was the first and probably the most important, because it produced the wealth that allowed colonial enclaves to become nation-states. The main coffee countries—El Salvador, Costa Rica, and Guatemala—developed effective nationhood earlier than the others. In his *Travels*, John Lloyd Stephens rapturously and perceptively described a newly coffee-domesticated Costa Rican Valle Central, an account in stark contrast to his pained, ignorant description of the wilderness around his Nicaraguan canal route. "The deep green of the coffee plantations, the sward of the roads, and the vistas through the trees at all the crossroads were lovely," he wrote. "It was not, like the rest of Central America, retrograding and going to ruin, but smiling as the reward of industry. Seven years before the whole plain was an open waste."

Coffee didn't have as destructive an effect on native habitats as some crops, although its effects on indigenous land rights were another matter. It is an Arabian woodland shrub with many American relatives, and the varieties grown in the nineteenth and early twentieth centuries required shade, so even the most intensive plantations had to retain trees. Some wildlife thus survived. I've seen motmots, trogons, and various lizards near the apartment buildings that are replacing the Costa Rican plantations Stephens described. In hilly or rocky areas, coffee simply was planted in the uncleared forest understory. Both of El Salvador's least disturbed natural areas, Montecristo and El Imposible, were planted to coffee in the nineteenth century. People told me that El Imposible, which has fertile volcanic soil but impossibly steep terrain, was covered with it, although it's not grown commercially there now. At Montecristo, coffee is still grown in the pine and liquidambar forest of the lower slopes. Workers were harvesting it when I was there.

The nineteenth century's other main export crop was the banana, also an Old World tropical shrub with Central American relatives—the red and yellow flowered heliconians. Native Americans began growing bananas and plantains as soon as they were imported in the sixteenth century, and they have joined manioc and maize so completely as staples that the Darién National Park rangers were surprised and skeptical when I said their fried plantains were originally Asian. Every rural community has banana and plantain bushes mixed with other crops, sometimes fed upon as much by wildlife as by people. Bananas couldn't be grown thus for export, however, and they couldn't be grown economically in the traditional farming areas of the Pacific coast and interior valleys. From the 1880s to the 1920s, banana plantations thus became the first partly successful assault on rain forests.

North American entrepreneurs—Minor Keith in Costa Rica, the Vaccaro brothers in Honduras—built railroads into the lowlands and sent immigrant laborers, mostly West Indians, to raze the forest at a cost to life equivalent to the Panama Canal's. "Here is an industrial army engaged in constant battle with the forces of tropical nature," wrote inventor Frederick Upham Adams in 1914, echoing the canal builders. "To me this mastery of time and space and flood and sea has all the spell of the romantic." The rain forest resisted with a sustained assault on the banana plants, however. Thomas Belt had complained of the obstacles to maintaining even a small garden: "Caterpillars, plant lice, bugs, and insect pests of all kinds were numerous and did much harm . . . and I had to wage a continual warfare against them." Obstacles multiplied geometrically in plantations, where over 200 insect species attacked bananas, and Panama fungus and Sigakota disease were even more destructive. The banana industry's history has been one of boom, bust, and continual movement to keep ahead of ever-spreading rot. A lot of second growth and pasture I traveled through had been bananas.

Export and subsistence agriculture had occupied most of Central America's interior valleys and Pacific coast by the mid–twentieth century, an occupation that was near total in heavily populated areas such as El Salvador. When biologist William Beebe visited it in the late 1930s, he found a landscape where "for many miles every speck of level or reasonably oblique ground was covered with coffee or maize." Almost the only birds he saw on a trip from the coast to San Salvador were in the Natural History Museum, where "several hundred abominably made bird skins hung by their feet. Some, beneath the dust, were recognizable as caciques and others as tanagers and herons; many were literally skins, with all the feathers in piles on the floor of the case."

Despite the banana industry, lowland rain forests remained predominant until World War II, when bulldozers and chainsaws arrived during Pan-American Highway construction. Technology then combined with population growth to turn huge expanses of rain forest to scrubby pasture in about three decades—about the time it had taken the conquistadors to destroy native civilizations. Loggers built roads into the Caribbean coastal plain, and farmers from the impoverished interior followed them and burned cutover forest for crops. Most rain forest soils become infertile after a few years of cropping, however, so the farmers then moved to newly cut forest and sold or abandoned their land. Ranchers acquired much of it, and used it to produce low-grade beef. Variations of this colonization process operated on other habitats. Clearings rose higher on highland slopes, and eroded soil choked rivers and reefs. Intensive cotton plantations replaced dry forests and savannas. Mangrove forests were cut for charcoal and converted to shrimp farms. Trawlers and lobster boats denuded the sea bottom.

Cerro Santa Barbara

It's hard to miss the colonization process in Central America today. The forest of Cerro Santa Barbara, where botanist Paul Allen discovered giant firs and yews in the 1950s, was on the frontier when I was there in 1992. It might have made a significant site for evolutionary studies if it had been preserved. In the hills below the fir-crowned summit, Allen found lowland South American tree species growing alongside highland North American ones, as if this were a relic of the Ice Age forests that left oddly mixed pollen in Panamanian lakes. He described big rain forest trees like mahogany, sura, and *Vochysia* a few yards from oaks, ocote pines, and liquidambars, and likened the forest to "a giant projection both in size and relief of the Florida Everglades, with each hill and depression a kind of gargantuan 'hammock' which may support basically North American or South American flora, the margins of which may be separated from one another by only a few yards."

A few patches of this "giant projection" remained when I visited. On a wildlife reserve owned by the Lago Azul fishing resort, acorn woodpeckers frequented pines and oaks on grassy hillocks above Lake Yojoa, while parrots and toucans flew among tabebuias and suras on the shore. The chachalaca population on an adjacent wooded peninsula was large, and at sunrise the pheasantlike birds all started screaming "*chachalaca!*" so loudly and suddenly that it seemed unnatural at first, more like the random mechanical clatters to which city dwellers become inured than the cries of exotic birds.

The big trees that had covered the foothills when Allen climbed the

Cerro were largely gone, however, and the cloud forest on the plateau slopes was getting ragged, although the upper part is a national park. Only the summit forest remained untouched, because there was still no trail to it. Reaching the lower plateau's dwindling cloud forest by the warren of paths that ran from the village of Los Andes was hard enough, and I wouldn't have been able to do it without the guidance of Pat Niemeyer, the local Peace Corps volunteer. A young Midwesterner, Pat was assigned to teach sustainable farming, but found it slow going because people preferred the traditional slash-and-burn shifting cultivation. He told me he'd once spent a day explaining composting, terracing, and other techniques to a man who'd seemed interested. When he'd asked the man if he wanted to try them, he'd said, no, he'd just liked listening to Pat talk. His wife had added that what they wanted to do was emigrate to the U.S.

Los Andes was a typical frontier community, a steep straggle of huts on a dirt road, with a little *tienda* selling soft drinks and a few dry goods. There was no electricity, and little plumbing, although a water supply was piped in from springs on still-forested slopes above. Children thronged the street in the daytime, but older people were not much in evidence until nightfall, when they returned by trails from often distant workplaces. After dark, Los Andes grew quiet with a quickness strange to anyone used to electricity's artificial daylight. Only faint glows distinguished it from the brushy slopes. Pat lived in a house built by the previous Peace Corps volunteer, Vince Murphy, at the lower edge of town, and I spent the night there before we hiked up the mountain. It overlooked a vast eastern expanse of blue mountains and Lake Yojoa, polluted with mine tailings and farm runoff but still beautiful, ringed with green marshes and hills.

One of Pat's Honduran friends visited, a wry, cordial man who reminded me of Don Antonio Miranda, the fossil-collecting Gracias schoolteacher. We didn't talk about fossils, but about American music, which Los Andes could get on its transistor radios. The Honduran said he preferred country music to rock and roll. I asked him if it was because country music had more *corazón*, and he thought about it for a minute and then said, yes, in a qualified sort of way, as though he'd have had trouble explaining his feelings exactly.

Pat and I started up the mountain at dawn. The local *guardabosque* was to have come with us, but he was bedridden with a foot fungus endemic to the area. The street was already full of people, and we stopped a moment to talk to a man who seemed very cheerful and excited for such an early hour. He wanted to tell Pat about a new vegetable patch he had started in the cloud forest. Continuing to the upper edge of town, we turned off the road onto a trail that led into a gully, then up a succession of precipitous slopes improbably patchworked with cabbage, sugar cane, and maize as well as forest remnants. Pat said he'd seen a man hanging on one slope by a rope in one hand as he hoed his bean plot with the other.

The trail wound around an open ridgeline studded with cypresses, and I got a closer look at Allen's "shadowy groves of conifers" above the limestone cliffs. It was about as close a look as I'd get, because the trail then dropped into a ravine, and the cloud forest began, first as second growth on a long slope even steeper than those below, then suddenly as huge primary trees on the strange limestone terrain of the plateau. The forest floor was dense with myconia, tree ferns, and bromeliads, and the trees that shot up from it were too tall to identify, although I saw the hen's egg–sized acorns of one oak species on the ground. Here and there were glades where the bedrock had collapsed, but a pink-flowered vine overgrew the ground so thickly that it hid the sinkholes. The soft rock was eroding rapidly. In 1955, Paul Allen wrote: "Some of the largest trees were found to be perched on limestone blocks 5 [to] 8 feet in height, which would seem to indicate that the apparently solid stone is actually almost as soluble as rock salt, and that the trees . . . may have begun life when the tops of these pedestals were at the level of, or below, the soil."

We came to a cliff overhang that had been part of a cave before the strata above it dissolved. Shrunken stalactites hung from the top. More forest grew above it, and I glimpsed distant conifers again, but we had entered fog as soon as we'd reached the primary forest. Visibility was intermittent, sometimes dazzling sunlight, sometimes near twilight. Wind tossed the treetops, although it was quiet at ground level except for the lilting songs of nightingale thrushes. We heard a "*cuk-cuk*" sound in the fog, and I glimpsed a short-tailed bird that might have been a female quetzal. Pat said he also saw a long-tailed one fly over. Quetzals were supposed to live on the plateau, although these were the first he'd seen during his year there—if indeed that's what we had seen.

I'd told Pat about my interest in Central American salamanders, and we looked for them all day, without success. We glimpsed a frog, which Pat said was the first he'd seen on the mountain. He was disappointed at the scarcity of wildlife in this remote place where he'd spent a year of his life. There were supposed to be deer and peccaries, but he'd never seen any. There'd been monkeys until fairly recently. A man who'd shot some of the last ones had told him he'd seen them hold leaves over the bullet holes in their sides, as though trying to stanch the flow. "Aw, that's *cuuute*," Pat had said.

On our way back down the mountain, we encountered two men who were cultivating a bean plot that was just inside the park boundary on Pat's map. They seemed startled and apprehensive, but were reassured when Pat disclaimed any authority and started talking about the importance of forests for water supply. They knew about that, and were contemptuous of the farmers in the Comayagua Valley when Pat mentioned it as an example of a watershed destroyed by forest-clearing. They said they planned to grow tree crops on the plot eventually, limes and avocadoes. Then they knocked off work for the day and started the four-hour climb back to their homes in El Mochito down near Lake Yojoa. One was carrying a log as well as his farming tools. They'd told us they'd bought the plot from someone in town.

"Who knows?" Pat said.

Islands on a Bridge

Today, like Cerro Santa Barbara, natural habitats that once extended throughout Central America are islands in largely man-made landscapes. The islands didn't just happen, but were the result of arduous, sometimes dangerous, work by Central American conservationists, and otherwise would be much smaller and fewer. In the 1960s and 1970s, naturalists such as Costa Rica's Olof Wessberg, Nicaragua's Jaime Incer, Honduras's Gustavo Cruz, and Guatemala's Mario Dary began pushing their governments to protect wild remnants. (Wessberg and Dary were murdered, perhaps because their efforts threatened economic interests.)

"First World" naturalists like Archie Carr and Leslie Holdridge also supported habitat protection. These efforts eventually led to conservation infrastructures in the land bridge countries.

Costa Rica was the leader, putting over ten percent of its land in a park system by 1990, and Panama and Belize established effective protected area systems. Honduras, Guatemala, and Mexico put large areas in protected categories in the late 1980s, although they lacked funds to administer them. Civil wars retarded protection efforts in Nicaragua and El Salvador until the 1990s, but both have growing national park and reserve systems. Indigenous peoples have been active in forest conservation too, particularly in Darién, where the Kuna and Embera-Wounnan have resisted the colonization process, and in the Mosquitia, where Miskitos and Tawahkas allied with urban conservationists in 1993 to thwart Stone Container Corporation's proposal to clear-cut Caribbean pines for pulp.

Economic benefits from protecting habitat islands have been substantial. Income from tourism to Costa Rica's parks surpassed coffee and bananas in the early 1990s, and Belize's annual tourist visitation exceeded its population. Nature tourism revenues became significant in Guatemala, Honduras, and Panama. As Mario Boza, the farsighted director of Costa Rican national parks from 1968 to 1974, said: "Promoting this kind of tourism can demonstrate how, through conservation, we can put food in our mouths and make conservation a more attractive idea to politicians and people alike." Central Americans have not seen conservation only in market terms, of course. "Yes, parks are for people," Boza told me in 1990. "But the principal reason for parks is the need to protect nature. The real reason for parks is to protect species." Alvaro Ugalde, another Costa Rican parks director, has written: "What I want is for every citizen in this country to see parks on the same level as health, education, and defense."

Yet it is doubtful that isolated protected areas alone can save all of Central America's flora and fauna. The effect of habitat isolation is predictable according to "island ecology" theories developed by evolutionary biologists. In the 1950s, Edward O. Wilson and Robert MacArthur noticed that "the faunas and floras of islands around the world show a consistent relation between the area of the islands and the number of species living on them. The larger the area, the more the species."

Other studies showed this to be true not only of actual islands, but of other isolated habitats, such as forest groves in grassland regions. When biologists began applying island theory to natural areas isolated by human activity, they found that species numbers also declined in proportion to protected area size. In an extensive study begun in the 1970s, Thomas Lovejoy showed that isolated Brazilian Amazon rain forest patches lost species at predictable rates. The smaller the patch, the more the loss, although species might take years or decades to disappear.

A classic Central American example of species loss is Barro Colorado Island, isolated in 1914 by the rise of the Panama Canal's Gatun Lake. Protected since 1923, the 1,564-hectare island is far from depauperate—its diversity dazed me when I was there in 1993. Scientists spend lifetimes studying its 1,360 vascular plant species, 30 frog species, 22 lizard species, 56 bat species, or 200 ant species. A new tree was discovered there in 1981. Yet Barro Colorado has been losing species since its isolation. When ornithologist Frank M. Chapman lived on the island in the 1920s, he photographed pumas and white-lipped peccaries, and over 200 bird species were known to breed there. Those spectacular mammals are not seen now, and the breeding bird list has declined by about sixty species, while thirteen bird species have disappeared from the island altogether.

Species extinction is another predictable result of habitat "islanding," as large, widespread populations become small, fragmented ones, each vulnerable to extirpation by disaster or disease. Extinctions are occurring in Central America, although not always according to theory. I happened to make "before and after" visits to the sites of the two best known ones. Neither of the vanished species seems to have been a once common and widespread one whose habitat was reduced to an island by human activities. Both always seem to have been rare and isolated, but their fates still show fragmentation's dangers.

When I was at Guatemala's Lake Atitlán in 1971, I had no idea an endangered bird, the Atitlán giant grebe, or "poc," lived there. Pocs were giant, flightless relatives of the common pied-billed grebe, and evolved only on Lake Atitlán, presumably because there was enough small fish and crustacean food and lakeshore nesting marsh that they didn't need to fly elsewhere. About 200 pocs existed in the 1950s, when the tourist industry introduced largemouth bass into the lake and increased resort construction on its shores. Bass ate poc food and baby pocs, and construction destroyed breeding habitat, so poc numbers had dropped in half by the early 1960s. Biologist Anne LaBastille discovered the poc's decline in 1965, however, and convinced the government to take conservation measures, including a habitat preserve. Pocs regained their previous population in the next decade, but then came the double disaster of the 1976 earthquake and the 1980s guerrilla war. The earthquake lowered Lake Atitlán's water level by rearranging its underground drainage patterns, which destroyed much of the poc's breeding habitat. The war caused the death of the poc reserve's warden, and an end to conservation measures.

Poc numbers dropped so low by the mid-1980s that the species was declared extinct, although some individuals were said to survive, possibly interbreeding with pied-billed grebes. When I visited Lake Atitlán again in 1995, I saw no pocs. In fact, I saw no water birds of any kind. I didn't even see any fish under the boat docks, just garbage and algae. The lakeside town of Panajachel, vaguely recalled as a sleepy village, had become a crowded tourist metropolis. When I asked a local tourism official about pocs, mentioning that someone at the national museum in Guatemala City had told me they might not be extinct, he said they were "in the process of extinction," a nice open-ended way to put it. (The museum still had LaBastille's yellowing photo display about the 1960s conservation campaign on its wall.) When I asked young U.S. tourists on a boat trip if they'd heard of flightless giant grebes called pocs, they laughed at me.

I was well aware of Central America's other famous yet doomed organism when I first visited its habitat during my 1987 gaudy bird trip. Costa Rica's Monteverde Cloud Forest Preserve was created in part to protect the golden toad, discovered there in 1967 by herpetologist Jay M. Savage. Like the poc, the golden toad lived only in one place—the mist-bathed ridges of Monteverde. The species spent most of its time underground, emerging en masse only for a few days during their late rainy season mating time, when the brilliantly orange-colored males congregated at breeding pools. "I must confess," Savage wrote, "that my initial response when I saw them was one of disbelief and suspicion that someone had dipped the examples in enamel paint." I saw living toads during my April 1987 visit because they had bred recently, and a terrarium at preserve headquarters displayed a male and a slightly larger, reddish-brown female.

Although the golden toad was better protected than the poc, 1987 seems to have been its last year as a reproducing species. Biologist Martha Crump had become interested in studying the toads when local naturalist Wildford Guindon showed her that year's breeding. When she returned to start her study in spring 1988, however, she couldn't find any breeding, although she found ten individuals. Guindon said it was the first year he knew of that the toads hadn't bred. When she returned in 1989, breeding failed again, and she found only one toad. By my next visit to Monteverde, in April 1990, the toads' disappearance was well established, and they had not reappeared as of 1996. The reasons for their disappearance are as mysterious as those for the poc's are clear. One theory is that ocean warming related to the 1980s' El Niño events reduced precipitation on the Cordillera so much that not enough water for breeding has been available. In the absence of the toads, however, this will be difficult to confirm.

Although the poc and golden toad apparently weren't victims of man-made "islanding," there is plenty of evidence that it is threatening more widespread species. Harpy eagles, the largest New World eagles, occurred throughout the rain forest in the 1950s, but now live only in Darién, Talamanca, the Mosquitia, and possibly the Petén. When I was in Darién, Park Service Research Director Indra Candañedo told me there were four known harpy eagle nests in the entire park. Scarlet macaws occurred throughout the lowlands as late as the 1930s, but now survive only in the Mosquitia and scattered "islands" of the Pacific lowlands and Belize. Sergio Volio, a former ranger at Costa Rica's Santa Rosa National Park, described the species' final disappearance there in the 1970s. "I'd see a pair flying down the Cañon de Tigre to roost in the mangroves near the shore. Or hear them: 'Scraaa! Scraaa!' Then, a little later, there was one. Then there were none."

Bruce and Carolyn Miller, the biologists I met at Gallon Jug, had been studying a likely candidate for "islanding" extinction: the keel-billed motmot, one of the colorful group that evolved in the Oligocene North American tropics. The species is about blue jay size and has mostly green and turquoise plumage and a broad bill with a keel like a boat hull's along the top. It once occurred in Caribbean slope forest from southern Mexico to northern Costa Rica, but has disappeared with the forest from most of its former range. A breeding population the Millers found in southwestern Belize was the only significant one known in the early 1990s, although Carolyn told me in 1996 that they'd discovered a few more isolated populations in the same general region. Belize has established a new protected area, Chiquibul National Park, in the area partly to protect the motmot (it also contains Caracol, the country's most significant Maya site). As the golden toad's fate shows, however, a single park or preserve is no guarantee that isolated populations will survive to perpetuate a species.

Natural habitat fragmentation is particularly threatening in Central America, because it is so small, and because its unique natural history has arisen from its land bridge identity, from organisms migrating through it. Even before humans arrived, many of its native species had small and isolated populations compared to those on the continents. As Daniel Janzen told me, a country like Costa Rica's forest is tiny compared to a continental one like Venezuela's.

Yet land bridge geography has been an asset to conservationists as well as a liability. In the 1970s, Mario Boza and Alvaro Ugalde used Costa Rica's fame as a biological and cultural crossroads to convince President Daniel Oduber to become, as Ugalde told me, "the greatest friend the national parks ever had." Oduber was a Guanacaste rancher who had been hostile to parks, and had tried to get Santa Rosa National Park disestablished. Once Boza and Ugalde changed his mind, the park system quickly doubled in size, and the Park Service budget tripled. "The ultimate goal is to maintain Central America as an ecological bridge," Ugalde told me. "That of course is a very difficult dream because it doesn't depend on us, it depends on every little country in this region. But yes, on a national basis, that is the ultimate dream. How do you keep genes flowing north and south, and evolving?"

In 1990, Archie Carr's conservationist sons, Archie III and David, conceived an international initiative that uses the land bridge as a central theme in trying to minimize fragmentation. "We can defeat the island effect by enlarging protected areas, which is often unrealistic," Archie Carr III said in a 1992 *Audubon* magazine article interview with Elizabeth Royte, "or by linking them, which makes better political, economic, and environmental sense." Called Paseo Pantera ("the path of the panther" in reference to the big cats' migrations across the land bridge), the project works with local conservationists and agencies from Mexico to Colombia to encourage a linked system of protected areas throughout the region, particularly on the Caribbean side where forest remains less fragmented, but also with "branches" into highland and dry forest remnants of the interior and Pacific coast.

Paseo Pantera's goal is maintenance of enough linked natural habitat to permit native flora and fauna to keep flowing naturally along the land bridge. To some, this may seem grandiose, but as David Carr has said, "In a world where so few act and so much is at stake, it's not possible to set one's sights too high." In fact, large protected areas already exist on the Caribbean slope borders of every country that has a Caribbean coast. Even the one that doesn't, El Salvador, has Montecristo Cloud Forest, which is linked with Guatemalan and Honduran parks. Paseo Pantera has gotten a lot of support, and there's a chance that protected areas, combined with the inherent difficulties of exploiting the rugged or swampy terrain, will allow the land bridge's natural habitats and migrations to continue.

Cattle Egrets and Killer Bees

Protecting a land bridge has some unique practical and philosophical problems, however. It's not quite like protecting a forest or a coral reef. There are things about a land bridge per se that don't quite fit into our present models for nature conservation, useful as they are. As I have tried to convey, a land bridge is a somewhat amorphous, ambiguous natural phenomenon. Instead of simply being destroyed by logging, soil erosion, and pollution as forests and reefs are, a land bridge can, in a way, "turn bad." It can turn into a different land bridge, a vortex that reflects and perhaps magnifies destructive energies, like a waterspout racheted into a hurricane.

Central America has remained a biotic link between North and South America despite civilization's dismantling of its ecosystems. One native mammal, the vesper rat (*Nyctomys sumichrasti*), spread from western Panama's Chiriquí Province to the Colombian border from 1920 to 1964. It became abundant "possibly throughout the Republic, at all elevations and in both wet and dry situations," according to biologist

Charles L. Handley, Jr. A member of the explosively diversifying cricetid family, the vesper rat evidently didn't care whether it migrated into pristine rain forest or scrubby ranchland, and the reasons for its migration are unknown. It is by no means the only recent native traveler. Coyotes have spread east along the deforested Panamanian Pacific coast, and other savanna organisms are spreading into deforested Darién.

It's possible that the dismantling of native habitats is *increasing* land bridge migrations. Archie Carr III points out that the largely forested Central America that existed at least from the end of the last glaciation until a few years ago has been a "filter bridge," which nonforest organisms found more of a barrier than a passageway. As Pleistocene fossils amply show, nonforest organism migrations were much more frequent when there was less forest during past glaciations. "First it was an open bridge, now it's a filter bridge," Carr says. "If we reopen it again through forest destruction, not only are local extinctions implied, but all hell breaks for the hemisphere according to theory—not to mention the fossil record." Since both North and South America are already in a degree of ecological chaos from native extinctions and exotic introductions, a more open bridge at this point could multiply chaos. In fact, exotic organisms already have taken advantage of forest destruction to make two of this century's most spectacular intercontinental migrations.

The cattle egret's migration has been uniquely spectacular, since it crossed the Atlantic without human help before it crossed the land bridge, and is the only wild vertebrate known to have accomplished this. The small white egret is native to Asia and Africa, where it lives with wild or domestic cattle, feeding on insects the animals disturb. Somehow, possibly blown across the Atlantic in storms, cattle egrets began turning up in northern South American pastures in the 1870s. Their numbers stayed small at first, but they'd begun breeding by the turn of the century, and after World War II, as agricultural colonization got into high gear, they spread explosively. Their first appearance north of South America was around Florida's Lake Okechobee in the early 1940s, coincident with the intensive ranching that later spread through the Caribbean rain forest region. They must have come directly from South America since there were no breeding egrets on Caribbean islands until the 1950s.

Central America also had to wait until the 1950s for cattle egrets, but once they'd reached the Canal Zone, in 1954, they crossed the land bridge in an evolutionary microsecond, appearing in Guatemala and Yucatán in 1958. Today, they are the most abundant wading birds, and their tree roosts are beautiful sights, sometimes almost the only beautiful sights in landscapes from which colonization has stripped most native flora and fauna. I remember one in an isolated ceiba on the largely deforested San Juan River between Lake Nicaragua and El Castillo. It was like a tree with giant, pure white leaves, all quivering and drifting in some zoomorphic breeze, and it compensated a little for the absence of the macaw flocks I might have seen in Thomas Belt's time. Yet cattle egrets also have their ugly side. They've been seen stalking and killing exhausted migratory songbirds on Belizean cays, and their sheer numbers may crowd native wading birds out of rookeries.

Another spectacular exotic migrant seems almost a retribution for the dismantling of native ecosystems, like a Biblical plague. The African honeybee was introduced to Brazil in 1957, when a captive hive that was being used for strain improvement experiments accidentally escaped. Although of the same species (*Apies mellifera*) as European ones, African honeybees are untameable because they attack any perceived threat to their hives or swarms with a vengeance for which the hyperboles of nuclear warfare seem oddly just. "Overkill" and "massive retaliation" are not exaggerations for attacks like an episode in 1986 in Guanacaste Province, where a single victim was stung an estimated *eight thousand* times. Migrating swarms even *sound* like incoming missiles as they approach. The first one I heard, on the Santa Elena Peninsula savanna, made me want to flee even though I wasn't sure what it was, as though I were getting a genetic warning from australopithecine ancestors.

African honeybees are well adapted to highly competitive, predator-rich tropical ecosystems. The Brazilian escapees thrived, killing and replacing European bee colonies, and crowding out the native, stingless bees that indigenous cultures had used for honey. They spread north through Amazonia at a rate of 200 miles a year, and sped up when they reached Venezuelan rangelands. They got to Darién in 1982 and Costa Rica a year later despite attempts by the Smithsonian Tropical Research Institute and the U.S. Army to stop them at the Canal Zone. Each Central American country underwent a number of human deaths as the bees swarmed in, and a forty- to sixty-percent drop in honey production. Despite more attempts to stop them at Tehuantepec, they reached Mexican North America in 1987 and the southwestern U.S. in 1991, crossing the land bridge in the same time as the cattle egret. If they also match the egret's feat of colonizing most of the continental U.S., it will be hard on the honey industry and farming in general, since tame honeybees pollinate many crops. It is hoped that climate will prevent them from invading much farther north, but they occupied 8,523 square miles of southern California alone in 1995.

African bees were the scariest natural phenomenon I met in the neo-tropics. When I was at Masaya's Santiago Crater, looking at the molten lava, I heard a buzzing under the volcano's huffs and puffs. The sound rose and fell ominously, but I couldn't see its source, and there was something so lulling about the rhythmic volcano sounds that I very unwisely disregarded it. Seconds later, when I glanced down the crater wall, an orange cloud of bees was surging toward me. I ran, and luckily the bees perceived my former silhouette at the brink as the extent of the threat. They zipped viciously around it for a while, then sank out of sight again, back into the vapors and brimstone. I don't know if they were merely swarming in the crater or actually living there (parakeets somehow nest on Santiago's walls despite the toxic fumes), but they seemed at home in the conquistador Pedrarias's "mouth of fire that never ceases to rage."

Epilogue
The Future of a Vortex

At Gallon Jug in 1994, I felt I'd come full circle in the—whatever it was . . . exploration? . . . education? . . . I'd started at Tikal in 1971. With its ocellated turkeys and toucans, gray foxes and agoutis, the Belizean forest was the same as the Guatemalan forest, and yet not the same. I knew more about it in 1994. When I saw the spherical orange fruits I'd watched monkeys eating in 1971, I knew they came from the ramon tree, *Brosimum alicastrum*, a member of the fig family also called "*palo de leche*" because its white sap is edible too. When I heard haunting Rima-like calls in the twilight, I knew one of the drab, plump tinamous common in every neotropical forest was making them.

A busy crowd of gray-headed tanagers, tree creepers, and barred antshrikes in a logwood bajada alerted me to an army ant column that was frightening insects into the birds' beaks. In 1971, I had heard of army ants, but most of my information about them had come from a 1958 Charlton Heston movie, *The Naked Jungle*, wherein the ants ate everything in their path, including people and trees. My 1971 self might not have noticed the trickle of blackish ants in the underbrush, and I'd probably have been unimpressed if I *had* noticed them. Similarly, when I saw little bare dirt trails meandering everywhere through the Gallon Jug forest, I knew they were the foraging routes of leafcutter ants, which had one of their enormous nests in the vicinity. Long files of the red ants carrying leaf or flower fragments often can be seen on such trails, but they sometimes are unused because the ants have changed their foraging sites. Seeing unused trails at Tikal in 1971, I'd thought small mammals like agoutis had made them. If I had seen the ants on the trails, I probably wouldn't have connected the two. I hadn't known that ants are the most important tropical forest animals.

In a way, the stimulating puzzlement I'd felt at Tikal in 1971, the sense of confronting phenomena unexplained by authority, had been an illusion arising from my ignorance. Despite its incongruities with the romantic notions of "jungle," the Tikal forest had been much more of an Amazonian forest than I had imagined. I simply had not recognized the classic ecological relationships—among plants and insects for the most part on which the rain forest's imposing edifice is built. Science had known about those basic relationships in 1971, although impressively less than it did by 1994.

Yet my increased acquaintance with rain forest ecology in 1994 didn't really exclude me from the stimulations of puzzlement. If I understood something of a basic consistency between the Darién and Petén rain forests, this was only one of the easier things to understand about the Central American land bridge, because the Caribbean rain forest is the most recent ecosystem to cross the bridge. It is harder to see consistencies between, say, the savannas of western Panama and eastern Honduras, or the forests of Altos Cuchumatanes and Talamanca. Even Caribbean rain forest retains many more puzzles than solutions.

Early one morning at Gallon Jug, as I walked through a swampy area near a stream, I heard rustling in a thicket and glimpsed the flank and hind leg of a deer. I was about to move on, having seen plenty of Central American white-tailed deer, when something about the flank made me look twice. Although the light was dim, it was a subdued but rich red, different from the dun-colored fur of the whitetails. I looked closer with my binoculars, and saw that the deer had a narrow tail unlike the whitetail's powder puff, and that its snout was shaped differently. It was a brocket deer, the small genus that inhabits lowland forest from southern Mexico to Argentina. The geologist who'd been in parts of the Mosquitia where even his Tawahka Indian guides became lost had seen many brocket deer, but he was the only person I'd met in Central America who had.

"Because of their predilection for impenetrable thickets, brocket deer are not easily studied," wrote ecologist A. Starker Leopold, who could learn little about the species' food preferences or social habits, and was unsure about its classification and distribution. "In fact, they are not even easy to see. Near El Real, Chiapas, where we camped for ten days in the great mahogany forest, a brocket lived in a patch of *monte* seventy-five yards from our tent and was seen only once. We tried repeatedly to collect the animal, but it always dodged out by some new route, and no ambush that we could contrive was successful."

If brocket deer are seldom seen alive, they are even scarcer dead. Like so many other rain forest organisms, they have virtually no paleontological record. It's possible that the genus, *Mazama*, evolved in Central America from ancestors that originated in Eurasia or North America during the mid-Pliocene. It later may have crossed Darién and spread throughout the tropical South American forests. If so, it is yet another relic of the North American tropics, unlike other South American deer genera, which probably evolved after their ancestors had crossed the land bridge. But so far there's no way of proving these things because there are no fossils. Knowing more about brocket deer might increase knowledge of neotropical rain forest evolution as a whole. If they did evolve in Central America between five and three million years ago, this would suggest that there was rain forest then, since contemporary Central American brocket deer live mainly in rain forest. But nothing is known about how brocket deer ancestors adapted to the tropics.

The Gallon Jug brocket deer was the only one I'd seen in all my trips to neotropical rain forest. I didn't see it for long. It was gone as soon as I'd identified it, fading into the undergrowth without the thumps and crashes that a fleeing whitetail would have made. The forest resumed its leafy unfathomability. Motmots and trogons hooted, parrots squawked, tinamous quavered. A female cardinal glided out of sight, strangely shy for its suburban species. Something whistled in the trees, a loud, deep sound I hadn't heard before, and haven't heard since.

Although I know more about the land bridge now than I did in 1971, I still don't understand it as one can understand, say, a coral reef or a rain forest. Much remains mysterious about coral reefs and rain forests, but we have a fairly clear idea of how those sublime natural phenomena fit into the story of evolution, and even into a kind of human value system. Reefs and rain forests are the result of 500 million years of life's diversification and adaptation to environment, and it is these qualities that we try to protect with national parks and projects like Paseo Pantera. Seeing values in diversity and adaptation is not hard, once we look a bit past immediate self-interest, because there is great beauty and fascination in them and because they work for our benefit. According to evolutionary theory, they made us.

A land bridge is a sublime evolutionary spectacle, but not in the way that a coral reef or a rain forest is. For all its geological complexity, it is crude and mechanical compared to the marvelous stability of the coral polyp and the tree, which have kept their essential forms and functions while the Central American land bridge has heaved up and down on its random, catastrophic career. Unlike reef and rain forest, the land bridge has been an agent of evolutionary destruction as much as creation. The ease with which highly aggressive creatures like Africanized bees have exploited it is not untypical. Imagine if big game hunters had not crossed it from North America. We might be able to see not only living ground sloths, glyptodonts, and toxodonts, but gomphotheres and saber-tooths. If North American mammals had never crossed, we might be able to see even older South American oddities— marsupial carnivores, liptoterns, astrapotheres, and pyrotheres. If South American rainforest had not surged north across the isthmus, the North American tropics might still exist, perhaps with lemurs, tarsiers, tree shrews, or animals completely unknown to us.

Where are the human values, or even the ecological values, in a tectonic accident randomly spilling one continent's laboriously diversified and adapted organisms into another's? The idea of preserving and protecting such a phenomenon per se seems tantamount to preserving volcanoes or seafloor spreading zones. On a planet where diversity and adaptation were truly valued, wouldn't continents stay reliably in place, allowing their organisms to evolve their full potentials without random invasions from colliding landmasses?

Of course, such a planet is not within our power to design. If the land bridge per se seems outside our values, it may be the values' fault. There might be values to learn in the land bridge's random connecting of continents. One aspect of the land bridge that keeps recurring to me is that it is a particular feature of a *spherical* world. If the earth were flat, wandering continents might still collide, but they'd be less likely to because they would have the option of wandering off indefinitely in straight lines. Flatness implies infinite extension, or at least a limitedness less inherent than that of the spherical, where every movement forward leads one step closer to the starting point.

Perhaps human values have yet to assimilate the earth's shape. Although every physical evidence suggests that endless forward movement, endless growth, is impossible on a sphere, civilization is trying to grow endlessly. Our economics and politics are based on endlessness, and even our ideas of organic evolution, which of all things should have transcended flat-earth thinking, have an essential two-dimensionality. Cladistics, the latest form of mapping evolutionary lineages, still sees them as flattened bushes, continuously expanding in the uncurved space of the diagram and computer screen. Yet if there is one thing the land bridge demonstrates, it is that evolutionary lineages do not continuously expand in flat space. They continuously cycle on the planet's curved space, which occasionally brings them into terminal contact with other lineages. And it is not only the *planet's* curved space that terminates lineages. The solar system's curved space may have terminated the dinosaurs', if an asteroid's collision with Earth's orbit was indeed the cause of their extinction. Physics seems to mandate universal if untidy sphericality—spherical planets, spherical solar systems, spherical galaxies, perhaps in some barely comprehensible way a spherical or at least curved universe, according to the relativity theory of which the land bridge's biological relativism seems a reflection.

Central America's highest value as a natural phenomenon may be not in its diversity and adaptations, priceless as those are, but in its powerful demonstration of life's sphericality. Life would have been fundamentally different if it had evolved on a limitless flat substrate instead of a limited, spherical one. It's hard to imagine what it would have been like, but one possibility is that it never would have evolved beyond the first unicellular organisms. If they had been able to expand their populations ad infinitum, they might never have undergone the competitive pressures that led to natural selection and increasingly complex organization. Civilization has come to see the sphere's limitations as an obstacle, but this is unimaginative, like being angry at the curved horizon because it hides objects more than a few dozen kilometers away. Imagine if the earth's surface was *not* curved, and extended to infinity.

There would *be* no horizon. The surface simply would stretch away until it filled the sky. It would be like living at the bottom of a pit.

It is the sphere's limitedness that has caused life to develop instead of simply to grow. Life grows by multiplying, but develops by dividing into new populations, species, genera, families. Land bridges are part of the division process, forcing multiplying populations into bottlenecks that reduce and change them. Land bridges are particularly dramatic demonstrations of this, but all growth eventually leads to reduction and change on a round planet. Civilization will be reduced and changed at the limits of its growth, just as mollusks and corals were reduced and changed by the dwindling of the former Panama seaway.

Human communities do differ from invertebrate ones in being able to shape themselves to the sphere's limitations as well as be shaped by them, and many have done so. The tendency of indigenous ones like the Kuna to define themselves by their place is an example. Such communities see the cosmos as spherical rather than planar, and aspire to stability. Genetic studies suggest the Kuna and their neighbors have been living in the Panama isthmus for at least 7,000 years. It's as though the Kuna decided, after getting about as far from the human starting point as any group, that wandering was finally pointless in a universe where "what goes around comes around." Their telling the U.S. Navy that God would kill them if they changed the land seems a corollary of this decision.

Civilization can't return to self-contained communities like the Kuna's. Not even the Kuna can do that. Tourism and remittances from emigrant workers keep their San Blas archipelago homeland going. Yet stability has a way of reasserting itself even in the disruptions of a land bridge. Although building the Panama Canal killed many people, as the Kuna predicted, it has become as much a factor of stability as of growth. Taking cargo through it uses less energy than other ways. The canal is also the reason why the rain forest of adjacent Soberania and Chagres national parks still exists. If the parks were colonized and deforested, erosion would silt up the canal and destroy Panama's main source of income. I was surprised at how natural the canal looks, with its low, forested banks. The boat ride from Gamboa to Barro Colorado Island might have been on an Amazon tributary. W. B. Scott even commented on this in 1911, when the work was just finished. "It . . . looked like a great canyon through the mountains," he wrote. "That it was a man-made valley seemed altogether impossible."

As Scott pointed out, this naturalness is illusory, "because so much of the vast work is hidden under the water that the visitor can form but a very imperfect conception of all that was accomplished." Scott mainly was impressed by the "colossal scale of the work, both in excavation and construction." The canal is still probably the greatest engineering feat of the twentieth century, except perhaps for space flight. Yet if the Panamanian isthmus was a symbolic locus for the growth era that the canal ushered in, it might also be a locus for an era of development, when global civilization could go beyond growth. (The term development is really more appropriate to *conservation* than to growth, because it refers to the self-limited maturation of organisms rather than to the environment-limited growth of populations.) The isthmus offers two splendid opportunities *not* to grow in the twenty-first century. Proposals for a sea-level canal across Panama or Nicaragua and for extending the Pan-American Highway through Darién to Colombia have existed for many years. Both would contribute significantly to growth— more and bigger ships roaring through a megaditch, more colonization and deforestation.

Megaprojects like the sea-level canal continue the project of "correcting" nature to desire that first brought Western civilization to Central America. Yet they also reflect a change. For most of history, civilization has viewed nature ambivalently: as a hostile entity from which desires must be forced, as with the canal builders, or as a friendly one that grants desires freely, like Columbus with his earthly paradise, or me with my tropical daydreams. Since 1750, science has gone a long way toward convincing civilization that nature is neither hostile nor friendly, but that it is something to be understood rather than fought or charmed. No sooner is this ancient ambivalence resolved, however, than another arises. A neutral nature can be seen as inconsequential, a marginal anachronism to be disregarded or "managed" with the small change of a fundamentally techno-financial world. As places like Central America lose forests and reefs, they can seem increasingly easy to disregard. On the other hand, a neutral nature can be seen as having an inherent structure to which desire must be accommodated. The land bridge and the cosmic sphericality behind it seem an example of such structure, and it is possible that the long-term effects of a sea-level canal or a Darién highway will not be inconsequential.

The present canal is still a barrier between the Caribbean and Pacific because it is a freshwater, lock and dam system. Even so, its ecology has become bizarre as exotic organisms have arrived on passing ships. At Barro Colorado in the middle of the canal, strange sounds in my room at night came from barking geckoes, a Pacific island species. Crabs from Iraq now live in the canal, and Caribbean brackish water oysters, gobies, and blennies have gotten almost to the Pacific. A sea-level canal would provide a saltwater link between the oceans, and there's no telling what might cross. *Acanthaster* starfish are voracious predators of Pacific corals. If they got into the Caribbean, they could decimate its huge reefs, just as Madison Grant imagined saber-tooths did the South American ungulates. The highly venomous sea snakes of Panama's Pacific have been seen swimming up rivers, so they might be among the first organisms to traverse a sea-level canal. "Because of tidal differences," wrote herpetologist Charles W. Myers, "a free-floating object would take only about two and a half days to transit an unobstructed canal from the Pacific side to the Atlantic, and if the object were a sea snake, it probably would find favorable habitats." Sea snakes are not supposed to bite people, but I've met a Costa Rican who was bitten by one.

Similarly, a road through Darién would cut the last rain forest "filter" between the continents, and begin a new episode of migration that could have dire effects for today's South American natives. Coyotes would almost certainly follow the road south, as they've followed roads east into North America's former forests. The spread of coyotes in my lifetime has been phenomenal, and mysterious, too, considering the lethal technology arrayed against them. When I lived in central Ohio in 1975, coyotes were unheard of. When I visited in 1995, they were heard on many nights, and use of 1,080 collars to protect sheep had just been approved. Coyotes contributed to the near-extinction of the North American red wolf by hybridizing with the species' last wild individuals. South America has more wild canid diversity than any other continent, and coyotes' effects on this could be catastrophic, as could their effects on South American wildlife and livestock generally.

I wouldn't want to be chauvinistic and slight the destructive potential of South America's native organisms. Who knows what biotic Dracula lurks in the Andes or Pampas, waiting to pounce on North American pastures and cornfields? Porcupines are good at damaging forest plantations and fruit trees, although, of course, they preceded civilization in North America. A more recently arrived South American rodent, the muskratlike nutria, or coypu, increased from a few hundred residents of a Louisiana fur farm in the 1930s to twenty million feral individuals in a dozen states by 1959.

Not building a sea-level canal and Darién highway would be a good project for the early twenty-first century's global development community, just as building the present canal was a good project for the twentieth century's growth community. Not building things might seem a negative way of heralding a new era, particularly compared to the promises of universal peace and plenty with which the growth era was heralded. But then, growth did not bring universal peace and plenty, and it brought a lot of conflict and poverty along with its benefits. *Not* building the canal and road would demonstrate civilization's realization that the only way to protect the bio*sphere* is to limit growth. This would not necessarily mean limiting development, which perhaps *can* be limitless because it works by change instead of proliferation.

So, protecting the brute geography of the land bridge as well as its flora and fauna could have some human value. Of course, the land bridge doesn't care if it's protected. Gomphotheres or megatheres, killer bees or coyotes—they're all the same to Darién. If they can pay the evolutionary ante, so to speak, they can play. The game runs on geological time, and human desires and values accelerate to squeaks, squeals, and finally to a dogwhistle whisper as the Cocos Plate grates and grumbles and roars its way under the Caribbean.

Maybe Darién will sink again in another three million years, and Central America will disintegrate into an island chain. Maybe it will keep piling up volcanic plateaus, exotic terranes and fault block sierras until it becomes the core of a new continent in some era as far from us as we are from the Cretaceous titanosaurs. Our descendants might survive to see this, although probability theory favors the descendants of plethodontid salamanders. If such a continent ever takes shape, one thing is certain. It sooner or later will bump into another continent, and another land bridge will be born.

A Land Bridge Bibliography

Abel, Suzanne, et al., *Between Continents, Between Seas: PreColumbian Art in Costa Rica.* New York: Harry N. Abrams, 1981.

Acosta, José de, *Historia Natural y Moral de Las Indias.* Sevilla: Juan de Leon, 1590.

Adams, Frederick Upham, *Conquest of the Tropics: The Story of the Creative Enterprises Conducted by the United Fruit Company.* New York: Doubleday, Page and Co., 1914.

Alameda, Frank, and Catherine Pringle, *Tropical Rainforest: Diversity and Conservation.* San Francisco: California Academy of Sciences, 1988.

Alee, W. C., and Karl P. Schmidt, *Ecological Animal Geography.* New York: John Wiley and Sons, 1951.

Allen, Paul H., "The Conquest of Cerro Santa Barbara, Honduras." *Ceiba: Scientific Journal of the Escuela Agricola Panamerica* 32, no. 5 (Sept. 5, 1955).

Axelrod, Daniel I., *Studies in Late Tertiary Paleobotany.* Carnegie Institution of Washington Publication 590, 1950.

Bancroft, Hubert Howe, *The History of Central America.* San Francisco: The History Company Publishers, 1886.

Bates, Marston, *The Land and Wildlife of South America.* New York: Time-Life Books, 1964.

Beebe, William, *Book of Bays.* New York: Harcourt Brace, 1942.

250 A Land Bridge Bibliography

Belt, Thomas, *A Naturalist in Nicaragua*. Chicago: University of Chicago Press, 1985.

Benzoni, Girolamo, *History of the New World*. London: The Hakluyt Society, 1857.

Berry, E. W., "Paleogeographic Significance of the Cenozoic Floras of Equatorial America and Adjacent Regions." *Bulletin of the Geological Society of America* 29 (1918): 631–36.

————, "Tertiary Plant Fossils from Costa Rica." Proceedings of the U.S. National Museum 59: 169–85.

Berta, Annalisa, *Quaternary Evolution and Biogeography of the Large South American Canidae*. University of California Publications in Geological Sciences 132. Berkeley: University of California Press, 1988.

Boorstin, Daniel J., *The Discoverers*. New York: Random House, 1983.

Boza, Mario A., *Costa Rica National Parks*. Costa Rica: Fundacion de Parques Nacionales, 1986.

Boza, Mario A., and Rolando Mendoza, *The National Parks of Costa Rica*. Translated by Susana Heringman. Madrid: INCAFO, 1981.

Brown, Lilian, *Bring 'em Back Petrified*. New York: Dodd Mead, 1956.

Browne, Janet, *The Secular Ark: Studies in the History of Biogeography*. New Haven: Yale University Press, 1983.

Buffon, Le Comte de, *Les Époques de la Nature*. Paris: L'Imprimerie Royale, 1780.

————, *Histoire Naturelle: Histoire des Quadrupeds*, Tome III. Paris: Chez Crapart, Caille et Ravier, 1804.

————, *Natural History: General and Particular*. Translated by William Smellie. London: A. Strahan and T. Cadell, 1791.

Bunkley-Williams, Lucy, and H. Ernest, "Global Assault on Coral Reefs." *Natural History* (April 1990): 47–54.

Bussing, William A., *Peces de Las Aguas Continentales de Costa Rica*. San José, Costa Rica: Editorial de la Universidad de Costa Rica, 1987.

Carr, Archie, *High Jungles and Low*. Gainesville: University of Florida Press, 1953.

————, *The Reptiles*. New York: Time-Life Books, 1963.

————, *The Windward Road: Adventures of a Naturalist on Remote Caribbean Shores*. New York: Alfred A. Knopf, 1965.

Chapman, Frank M. *My Tropical Air Castle: Nature Studies in Panama*. New York: D. Appleton, 1929.

————, *Life in an Air Castle*. New York: D. Appleton-Century, 1938.

Ciochon, R. L., and A. B. Chiarelli, eds., *Evolutionary Biology of the New World Monkeys and Continental Drift*. New York: Plenum Press, 1981.

Coates, Anthony G., ed., *The Paseo Pantera: A Natural and Cultural History of Central America*. New Haven: Yale University Press, 1996.

Colbert, Edwin H., *Wandering Lands and Animals*. New York: E. P. Dutton, 1973.

Cousteau, Jacques-Yves, and Phillipe Diole, *Three Adventures: Galápagos, Titicaca, the Blue Holes*. New York: A & W Visual Library, 1973.

Cruz, Gustavo Adolfo, *Areas Silvestres de Honduras*. Tegucigalpa: Asociación Hondureno de Ecologia, 1986.

Culbert, T. Patrick, "The Maya Enter History." *Natural History* (April 1985): 42–48.

Cuvier, Baron Georges, *Essay on the Theory of the Earth*. Edinburgh: William Blackwood, 1817.

Dampier, William, *Dampier's Voyages*. New York: E. P. Dutton, 1906.

D'Arcy, William G., and D. Mireya, and A. Correa, *The Botany and Natural History of Panama*. St. Louis: The Missouri Botanical Garden, 1985.

Darlington, Philip, *Zoogeography: The Geographical Distribution of Animals*. New York: John Wiley and Sons, 1957.

Darwin, Charles, *The Origin of Species*. New York: Modern Library, Random House, 1936.

———, *The Voyage of the Beagle*. New York: E. P. Dutton, 1950.

Darwin, Stephen P., and Arthur L. Welden, eds., *Biogeography of Mesoamerica: Proceedings of a Symposium*. New Orleans: Tulane University, 1992.

Davies, Nigel, *Voyagers to the New World*. New York: William Morrow, 1979.

De Candolle, Alphonse, *Géographie Botanique Raisonée*. Paris: Librarie de Victor Masson, 1855.

Dorst, Jean, *South America and Central America: A Natural History*. New York: Random House, 1967.

Ferrusquia-Villafranca, Ismael, "Biostratigraphy of the Mexican Continental Miocene." *Paleontologia Mexicana* 56 (1990).

———, "A Review of the Early and Middle Tertiary Faunas in Mexico." *Journal of Vertebrate Paleontology* 4, no. 2 (1984): 187–98.

Fiedel, Stuart J., *Prehistory of the Americas*, 2nd ed. New York: Cambridge University Press, 1992.

Finch, R. C., "Mesozoic Stratigraphy of Central Honduras." *American Association of Petroleum Geologists Bulletin* 65 (1981): 1320–333.

Flakus, Greg, *Living with Killer Bees: The Story of the African Bee Invasion*. San Francisco: Quick Trading Company, 1993.

Fleming, Theodore H., "A Day in the Life of a *Piper*-eating Bat." *Natural History* (June 1985): 52–60.

Forsyth, Adrian, and Ken Miyata, *Tropical Nature*. New York: Charles Scribner's Sons, 1984.

Fuente, Dr. Felix Rodriguez de la. *Animals of South America*. Translated by John Gilbert. London: Orbis Publishing, 1975.

Gage, Thomas, *Travels in the New World*, edited and with an introduction by J. Eric Thompson. Norman, OK: University of Oklahoma Press, 1958.

Gillete, David A., "A Marine Ichythofauna from the Miocene of Panama and the Tertiary Caribbean Fauna Province." *Journal of Vertebrate Zoology* 4, no. 2 (1984): 172–86.

Gomez, Luis P., "The Origin of the Pteridophyte Flora of Central America." *Annals of the Missouri Botanical Garden* 69 (1982): 548–56.

Gould, Stephen Jay, "Sticking Up for Marsupials." *The Panda's Thumb*. New York: W. W. Norton, 1980.

———, "O Grave, Where Is Thy Victory?" *Hen's Teeth and Horse's Toes*. New York: W. W. Norton, 1983.

———, "The Reversal of *Hallucigenia*." *Natural History* (Jan. 1992): 12–20.

———, "Can We Truly Know Sloth and Rapacity?" *Natural History* (April 1996): 18–23.

Graham, Alan, "Miocene Communities and Paleoenvironments of Southern Costa Rica." *American Journal of Botany* 74, no. 10 (1987): 1501–518.

Graham, Frank Jr., "Alexander Skutch and the Appreciative Mind." *Audubon* 81, no. 2 (March 1979): 83–117.

Grant, Madison, *The Origin and Relationship of the Large Mammals of North America*. New York: New York Zoological Society, 1904.

Greene, Harry, "Agonistic Behavior of Three-toed Sloths (*Bradypus variegatus*)." *Biotropica* 21 no. 4 (1989): 369–72.

———, "Species Richness in Tropical Predators." *Tropical Rainforest: Diversity and Conservation*, ed. Frank Alameda and Catherine Pringle, San Francisco: California Academy of Sciences, 1988. 259–80.

Guardia, Ricardo Fernandez, *History of the Discovery and Conquest of Costa Rica*. Translated by Harry Weston Van Dyke. New York: Thomas J. Crowell, 1913.

Hale, Sir Matthew, *The Primitive Origination of Mankind Considered and Examined According to the Light of Nature*. London: William Godbid, 1677.

Hallwachs, Winnie, "Agoutis (*Dasyprocta punctata*): The Inheritors of Guapinol (*Hymenaea courbaril*, Leguminosae)." *Frugivores and Seed Dispersal*, ed. A. Estrada and T. H. Fleming. Dordrecht: Dr. W. Junk Publishers, 1986.

Hanken, James, James F. Lynch, and David Wake, "Salamander Invasion of the Tropics." *Natural History* 89 no. 12 (1980): 46–53.

Hellmuth, Nicholas M., "Echoes of a Lost Colony." *Natural History* (March 1982): 18–25.

Horne, G. S., M. Genevieve Atwood, and Allan P. King, "Stratigraphy, Sedimentology, and Paleoenvironment of Esquias Formation, Honduras." *American Association of Petroleum Zoologists Bulletin* 58, no. 2 (Feb. 1974): 176–88.

Horne, Sally P., "Postglacial Vegetation and Fire History in the Chirripó Paramo of Costa Rica." *Quaternary Research* 40 (1993): 107–16.

Horne, Sally P., and Kurt A. Haberyan, "Costa Rican Lakes." *National Geographic Research and Exploration* 9, no. 1 (1993): 86–103.

Horwich, Robert H., and Jonathan Lyon, *A Belizean Rain Forest: The Community Baboon Sanctuary.* Gay Mills, WI: Orang-Utan Press, 1990.

Jackson, Jeremy B. C., with Peter Jung, Anthony G. Coates, Laurel S. Collins, "Diversity and Extinction of Tropical American Molluscs and Emergence of the Isthmus of Panama." Center for Tropical Paleoecology, Smithsonian Tropical Research Institute, 1993.

Janzen, Daniel H., "Caterpillar Seasonality in Costa Rican Dry Forest." *Caterpillars: Ecological and Evolutionary Constraints on Foraging.* New York: Chapman and Hall, 1993. 448–77.

———, ed., *Costa Rican Natural History.* Chicago: University of Chicago Press, 1983.

———, "The Deflowering of Central America." *Natural History* (April 1974): 48–53.

———, "*Spondias mombin* is Culturally Deprived in a Megafauna-free Forest." *Journal of Tropical Ecology* 1 (1985): 131–55.

———, *Swollen Thorn Acacias of Central America: Smithsonian Contributions to Botany* 13, Washington, D.C.: Smithsonian Institution Press, 1974.

———, and Paul S. Martin, "Neotropical Anachronisms: The Fruits the Gomphotheres Ate." *Science* 215 (Jan. 1982): 19–27.

Jennings, Jesse D., *Ancient Native Americans.* San Francisco: W. H. Freeman, 1978.

Keast, Allen, Frank C. Erk, and Bentley Glass, eds., *Evolution, Mammals, and Southern Continents.* Albany: State University of New York Press, 1972.

Keeler, Clyde E., *Secrets of the Cuna Earthmother.* New York: Exposition Press, 1960.

Knowlton, F. W., "Relations Between the Mesozoic Floras of North and South America." *Bulletin of the Geological Society of America* 29 (1918): 607–14.

Knowlton, Nancy, "A Tale of Two Seas." *Natural History* (June 1994): 66–68.

Koerdell, M. Maldonado, *Geological and Paleontological Bibliography of Cen-*

tral America. Pan American Institute of Geography and History Publication 204. Mexico, 1958.

Konings, Ad, Cichlids from Central America. Neptune, NJ: T. F. H. Publications, 1989.

Krauss, Clifford, Inside Central America. New York: Summit Books, 1991.

Kricher, John C., A Neotropical Companion. Princeton: Princeton University Press, 1989.

Kurten, Bjorn, The Age of Mammals. New York: Columbia University Press, 1971.

LaBastille, Anne, Assignment: Wildlife. New York: E. P. Dutton, 1980.

————, Mama Poc: An Ecologist's Account of the Extinction of a Species. New York: W. W. Norton, 1990.

Las Casas, Bartolomé de, History of the Indies. Translated and edited by Andree Collard. New York: Harper and Row, 1971.

Lee, Julian C., "Creatures of the Maya." Natural History (Jan. 1990): 46–50.

Leidy, Joseph, "Toxodon and Other Remains from Nicaragua, Central America." Proceedings: Academy of Natural Sciences. Philadelphia: Academy of Natural Sciences, 1887. 275–77.

Levine, Harold, Central America. New York: Time-Life Books, 1968.

Licari, Gerald Richard, "Geology and Amber Deposits of the Simojovel Area, Chiapas, Mexico." Master's thesis, University of California, Berkeley, 1960.

Lovell, W. George, Conquest and Survival in Colonial Guatemala. Kingston and Montreal: MacGill–Queen's University Press, 1985.

Lyell, Sir Charles, Manual of Elementary Geology. New York: Appleton and Company, 1960.

Macneish, Richard, The Prehistory of the Tehuacan Valley. Edited by Douglas S. Byers. Austin: University of Texas Press, 1967.

Marshall, Larry G., et al., "Mammalian Evolution and the Great American Interchange." Science 215, no. 4538 (1982): 1351–356.

Martin, Paul S., "The Discovery of America." Science 179 (1973): 969–74.

Maslow, Jonathan Evan, Bird of Life, Bird of Death. New York: Simon and Schuster, 1986.

Mayr, Ernst, "Inferences Concerning the Tertiary American Bird Fauna." Evolution and the Diversity of Life. Cambridge: Harvard University Press, 1976.

McClung, Robert M., Vanishing Wildlife of Latin America. New York: William Morrow, 1981.

McCullough, David, The Path Between the Seas: The Creation of the Panama Canal. New York: Simon and Schuster, 1977.

MacFadden, Bruce J., "Chronology of Cenozoic Primate Localities in South America." *Journal of Human Evolution* 19 (1990): 7–21.

McGrew, Paul O., "Special Correspondence" (on 1941–42 Honduras paleontological expedition). *Science* 96, no. 29 (1942): 85.

Morelet, Arthur, *Travels in Central America, including Accounts of Some Regions Unexplored Since the Conquest*. Translated by Mrs. M. F. Squier. New York: Leypoldt, Holt, and Williams, 1871.

Morison, Samuel Eliot, *Admiral of the Ocean Sea: A Life of Columbus*. Boston: Little, Brown, 1942.

Moser, Don, *Central American Jungles*. New York: Time-Life Books, 1975.

Moynihan, Martin. *The New World Primates*. Princeton: Princeton University Press, 1976.

Murray, John, *The Islands and the Sea: Five Centuries of Nature Writing from the Caribbean*. New York: Oxford University Press, 1991.

Myers, Charles, and John W. Daly, "Dart Poison Frogs." *Scientific American* 248, no. 2 (1983): 120–33.

Newberry, J. S., "Rhaetic Plants in Honduras." *American Journal of Science* 36, series 3 (1980): 342–51.

Nietschmann, Bernard, "Conservation by Conflict in Nicaragua." *Natural History* (Nov. 1990): 42–48.

———, *Caribbean Edge: The Coming of Modern Times to Isolated People and Wildlife*. Indianapolis: Bobbs-Merrill, 1979.

Olson, Everett C., and Paul O. McGrew, "Mammalian Fauna from the Pliocene of Honduras." *Bulletin of the Geological Society of America* 52 (1941): 1219–244.

Olson, Storrs L., "Oligocene Fossils Bearing on the Origins of the Todidae and Momotidae." *Smithsonian Contributions to Paleontology* 21 (1976): 111–19.

Osborn, Henry Fairfield, *The Age of Mammals*. New York: Macmillan, 1910.

———, *The Origin and Evolution of Life*. New York: Charles Scribner's Sons, 1917.

———, *Man Rises to Parnassus*. Princeton: Princeton University Press, 1918.

Oviedo, Captain Gonzalo Fernández de, *General and Natural History of the Indies*. Translated by Raymond Hewitt. Master's thesis, University of California, Berkeley, 1941.

Perry, Donald, *Life Above the Jungle Floor*. New York: Simon and Schuster, 1986.

Petit, Charles, "The War on Panama's Rain Forest." *San Francisco Chronicle*, 28 January 1990.

Petuch, Edward J., "Geographical Heterochrony." *Paleogeography Paleoclimatology Paleoecology* 37: 277–312.

———, *New Caribbean Molluscan Faunas.* Charlottesville, VA: Coastal Education and Research Foundation, 1987.

Poinar, George and Roberta, *The Quest for Life in Amber.* Reading, MA: Addison-Wesley, 1994.

Prance, Ghillean T., "A Review of the Phytogeographic Evidences for Pleistocene Climate Changes in the Neotropics." *Annals of the Missouri Botanical Garden* 69 (1982): 594–624.

Ralling, Christopher, *The Voyage of Charles Darwin: His Autobiographical Writings Selected and Arranged.* New York: Mayflower Books, 1979.

Raven, Peter H., and Daniel I. Axelrod, "Angiosperm Biogeography." *Annals of the Missouri Botanical Garden* 61 (1974): 540–673.

———, "History of the Flora and Fauna of Latin America." *American Scientist* 63 (1975): 420–29.

Ridgely, Robert S., *A Guide to the Birds of Panama,* 2nd ed. Princeton, NJ: Princeton University Press, 1989.

Royte, Elizabeth, "The Paseo Pantera." *Audubon.* (Nov.–Dec. 1992): 74–80.

Ruhlen, Merritt, *A Guide to the World's Languages. Vol. 1, Classification.* Stanford: Stanford University Press, 1987.

Salvin, Osbert, ed., *Biologia Centrali-Americana.* Vols. 1–63. London, 1879–1915.

Sanderson, Ivan, *Living Treasure.* New York: Viking, 1941.

Savage, J. M., "The Enigma of the Central American Herpetofauna: Dispersal or Vicariance?" *Annals of the Missouri Botanical Garden* 69: 46–547.

———, "The Isthmian Link in the Evolution of Neotropical Mammals." *Contributions in Science: Natural History Museum of Los Angeles* 260 (1974): 1–51.

Sawyer, John W. D., "University of Southhampton Research Project in the Sierra de las Cuchumatanes: November 1991–January 1992." 1993.

Schele, Linda, and Mary Ellen Miller, *The Blood of Kings: Dynasty and Ritual in Maya Art.* New York: Braziller, 1986.

———, and David Freidel. *A Forest of Kings: The Untold Story of the Ancient Mayas.* New York: William Morrow, 1990.

Scott, William Berryman, *A History of the Land Mammals of the Western Hemisphere.* Philadelphia: American Philosophical Society, 1937.

———, *Some Memories of a Palaeontologist.* Princeton, NJ: Princeton University Press, 1939.

Shutler, Richard, Jr., ed., *Early Man in the New World.* Beverly Hills: Sage Publications, 1983.

Sigurdsson, Haraldur, and David Gardella, "To El Chichon and Back." *Natural History* (July 1975): 46–54.

Silva-Barcenas, Angel, "Localidades de Vertebrados Fosiles en la Republica Mexicana." *Paleontologia Mexicana* 28 (1969).

Simpson, George Gaylord, *The Geography of Evolution*. Philadelphia: Chilton Books, 1965.

———, *Splendid Isolation: The Curious History of South American Mammals*. New Haven: Yale University Press, 1980.

———, *Discoverers of the Lost World*, New Haven: Yale University Press, 1980.

Slaughter, B. H., "A New Genus of Geomyoid Rodent from the Miocene of Texas and Panama." *Journal of Vertebrate Paleontology* 1 (1981): 111–15.

Smithe, Frank B., *The Birds of Tikal*. Garden City, NY: The Natural History Press, 1966.

Spalding, David A. E., *Dinosaur Hunters*. Rocklin, CA: Prima Publishing, 1993.

Squier, E. G., *Nicaragua: Its People, Scenery, Monuments and the Proposed Interoceanic Canal*. London: Longman, Brown, Green, and Longmans: 1852.

———, (Pseud. Samuel A. Bard), *Waikna: or Adventures on the Mosquito Shore*. New York: Harper Bros., 1855.

Stehli, F. G., and S. D. Webb, eds., *The Great American Biotic Exchange*. New York: Plenum Press, 1985.

Stephens, John Lloyd, *Incidents of Travel in Central America, Chiapas, and Yucatán*, 2 vols. New York: Dover, 1969.

Stiles, F. Gary, and Alexander Skutch, *A Guide to the Birds of Costa Rica*. Ithaca, NY: Cornell University Press, 1989.

Stuart, George E., "Maya Heartland Under Seige." *National Geographic* (Nov. 1992): 94–107.

Thompson, J. Eric, *The Rise and Fall of Maya Civilization*. Norman, OK: The University of Oklahoma Press, 1954.

Tomasini-Ortiz, Ana Cecilia, and Enrique Martinez-Hernandez, "Palinologica del Eocene-Oligoceno de Simojovel, Chiapas." *Paleontologica Mexicana* 50 (1984).

Trejos, Alvaro Wille, *Corcovado: Meditaciones de un Biologo*. San José, Costa Rica: Universidad Estatal a Distancia, 1983.

Voisin, Claire, *The Herons of Europe*. London: T & AD Poyser, 1991.

Vrba, Elisabeth, "Mammals as Keys to Evolutionary Theory." *Journal of Mammalogy* 73, no. 1 (1992): 1–28.

Wake, David, "Adaptive Radiation of Salamanders in Middle American

Cloud Forests." *Annals of the Missouri Botanical Garden* 74 (1987): 242–64.

Wallace, Alfred Russel, *The Geographical Distribution of Animals*. London: MacMillan, 1876.

———, *The Malay Archipelago*. New York: Dover, 1962.

Wallace, David R., *Adventuring in Central America*. San Francisco: Sierra Club Books, 1995.

———, "The Bones from Gracias." *Zyzzyva* 13, no. 4 (Winter 1992).

———, *The Quetzal and the Macaw: The Story of Costa Rica's National Parks*. San Francisco: Sierra Club Books, 1992.

———, "Tapir's Gourds and Smelly Toads: Life in a Little Known Rainforest." *The Nature of Nature*. New York: Harcourt Brace, 1995.

———, "Unfathomed Forests: Potential for Preservation in Honduras." *Pacific Discovery* 45 (Fall 1992): 30–35.

———, "A Walk in Guanacaste: Islands of Forest in a Sea of Grass." *Pacific Discovery* 42 (Fall 1989): 29–32.

Webb, S. David. "Ecogeography and the Great American Interchange." *Paleobiology* 17, no. 3 (1991): 266–80.

———, "Successful in Spite of Themselves." *Natural History* (April 1994): 50–53.

Webb, David, and Stephen C. Perrigo, "Late Cenozoic Vertebrates from Honduras and El Salvador," *Journal of Vertebrate Paleontology* 4, no. 2 (1984): 237–54.

———, and Francis G. Stehli, eds., *The Great American Biotic Interchange*. New York and London: Plenum Press, 1985.

Wells, William V., *Explorations and Adventures in Honduras*. New York: Harper and Brothers, 1857.

Weyl, Richard, *Geology of Central America*, Rev. ed. Berlin: Bebruder Borntraeger, 1980.

Whitmore, Frank C., Jr., and Robert H. Stewart, "Miocene Mammals and Central American Seaways." *Science* 148 (1965): 180–85.

Wille, Chris, "Peace Is Hell!" *Audubon* (1991): 62–70.

Wilson, Edward O., *The Diversity of Life*. Cambridge: Harvard University Press, 1992.

———, *Naturalist*. Washington, D.C.: Island Press, 1995.

Woodburne, Michael O., "A Late Pleistocene Occurrence of the Collared Peccary, *Dicotyles tajacu*, in Guatemala." *Journal of Mammalogy* 50 (1969): 121–25.

Ximénez, Francisco, *Escolios a las Historias del Origen de los Indios*. Guatemala City: Sociedad de Geographia y Historia del Guatemala, Publicacion Especial #13, 1967.

———, *Historia Natural del Reino de Guatemala*. Guatemala City: Sociedad de Geographia y Historia del Guatemala, Publicacion Especial #14, 1967.

Young, Allen M., *Sarapiqui Chronicle: A Naturalist in Costa Rica*. Washington, DC: Smithsonian Institution Press, 1991.

Index